THEATRE REVIEW '73

THEATRE REVIEW '73

edited by Eric Johns

W. H. ALLEN · London and New York
A division of Howard and Wyndham Ltd
1973

Printed by Fletcher & Son Ltd, Norwich
for the Publishers W. H. Allen & Co Ltd,
44 Hill Street, London W1X 8LB

Bound by Richard Clay (The Chaucer Press) Ltd,
Bungay, Suffolk

ISBN 0 491 01231 4

Designed by John Munday

CONTENTS

ACKNOWLEDGEMENTS

A number of friends and kindly colleagues
gave me most generous co-operation with
the compilation of this new theatre annual.
I would like to thank:
Yvette Morgan-Griffiths of W H Allen for
her expert guidance,and for the courage she
inspired at times when daunting difficulties
appeared.
Peter Hepple, Raymond Marriott and
Maureen Taylor of *The Stage*, who were ever
ready with advice, suggestions and other
practicalities.
Douglas Blake for patiently listening to half-
baked ideas and helping to mould them into
acceptable shape and for his much
appreciated expert proof-reading.
John Goodwin of the Royal Shakespeare
Company and Craig Macdonald of the
National Theatre Company for their
valuable assistance in providing colour
pictures for the dust-jacket.
Neil Crawford, Don Ross, Peter Watkins
and Rhona Thorndike for lending me rare
prints of the Houston Sisters, Hetty King,
Harry Hanson and Russell Thorndike.
Press Officers of the Association of London
Theatre Press Representatives and of
independent theatres throughout the country
for their generous co-operation in keeping
me regularly supplied with press releases
and photographs.

FOREWORD
Eric Johns

It has been my intention to prepare a nostalgic chronicle of the theatrical year, covering the period from May 1, 1972 to April 30, 1973, using a generous number of illustrations to enhance and expand the text. A picture book of theatre achievements recalls nights of enjoyment – or disappointment – for those who actually saw the productions under review on the pages. It also helps those who never saw the shows to get a fairly accurate idea of what they missed.

A brief comment on the plays, complete with cast-list and in most cases production pictures, helps to produce a book which never really becomes dated. An attractively illustrated record of any period of theatre activity becomes more and more fascinating with the passing of time, in that it stirs forgotten memories and produces evidence of small-part artists who may have become internationally famous stars in less than a decade.

Such a publication cannot claim to cover every production presented during any specific twelve-month period and readers are bound to wonder why some plays have been included, while others have not merited attention, but every effort has been made to present a broad cross-section of the most significant plays seen on the London stage, at leading regional theatres and at the drama festivals of Stratford-upon-Avon, Chichester and Pitlochry.

Lunchtime productions have increased to a remarkable degree during the period covered by this review. It would not be possible to cover so large a number of productions individually, but Douglas Blake, who has probably seen more London lunch-hour plays than any other professional critic, has dealt with the significance of this comparatively new movement in a single feature. He draws attention to individual shows which he considered of outstanding merit and assesses the value of this trend of play presentation which has replaced the disappearing try-out theatres which served as a shop-window for so much new talent in the past.

Other features concentrate upon various topics which came under discussion during the 1972–73 period of time, such as Sybil Thorndike's ninetieth birthday; *The Mousetrap* coming of age; Laurence Olivier's ideas on the new National Theatre; Marcel Marceau's quarter of a century of silence; Peter Daubeny's decade of World Theatre Seasons; plans for a Bankside Globe Playhouse in Southwark; the Romans at Stratford-upon-Avon; nudity in the theatre; rock musicals; the magnetism of the Minstrels and new theatres in the regions. Knowing how play-goers enjoy poring over prints of old shows, I have included some scrap-book pages of scenes from productions of the past forty years. Some of the players are no longer with us, some of the small-part people have become great names on the contemporary scene and some pictures remind us of actors in parts we forgot they ever played. This is just an outburst of that same shameless nostalgia which has kept the theatre thriving ever since those early professional players first trod the boards of James Burbage's theatre in Finsbury Fields almost four hundred years ago.

OBITUARIES

The world of entertainment lost the most loved eccentric comedienne in living memory when **Margaret Rutherford** died on May 22, 1972, at the age of eighty. In a strange way her highly successful career was something of a disappointment to her. She considered Juliet had been given some of the most beautiful lines in the language, yet with her own particular face, she could only hope to be cast for the Nurse. In her autobiography she admits she felt sad at times through having allowed herself to be typed into eccentric parts, when she really wanted to have a go at the stronger stuff.

She was thirty-three by the time she placed a foot on the professional stage at the Old Vic in *Little Jack Horner* and was forty-one when she reached the West End in *Wild Justice* at the Vaudeville. Then her career became an unbroken succession of memorable triumphs. Her characterizations were highly individualized, when one recalls Bijou Furse in *Spring Meeting*, Mrs Danvers in *Rebecca*, Miss Prism and Lady Bracknell in *The Importance of Being Earnest*, Madame Arcati in *Blithe Spirit*, the White Queen in *Alice Through the Looking Glass*, the Headmistress in *The Happiest Days of Your Life* and Mrs Candour in *The School for Scandal*. These parts covered a wide range of humour and pathos and Margaret Rutherford was mistress of both. So superbly unaffected was Margaret Rutherford's acting, she often gave the impression of devising comedy situations on the spur of the moment. She seemed to be behaving rather than acting.

In 1945 she married the actor, Stringer Davis, and he remained her 'dearest friend and helper' for the rest of her life – and fortune did not smile upon them all the time. Margaret Rutherford was made a Dame of the British Empire in 1967.

Jack Strachey, the composer of light music, died in Brighton on May 26, 1972, aged seventy-eight. His best-known song was 'These Foolish Things', for which Eric Maschwitz wrote a perfectly matching lyric. It was originally heard in a radio revue and later sung by Dorothy Dickson in *Spread it Abroad*, a revue at the Saville Theatre in 1936.

After starting as a concert-party pianist, Jack Strachey contributed numbers to several Charlot and other intimate revues as well as writing the score of *Belinda Fair* at the Saville in 1949.

Esme Church, the actress, director and teacher, died on May 31, 1972, aged seventy-nine. She first appeared in London with George Alexander and worked with the Lena Ashwell Players, appearing in 150 parts in eight years. In spite of being a valuable actress, her greatest achievement lay in her ability to teach and to organize. She joined the Old Vic as head of the School of Acting and she directed a number of Old Vic and H M Tennent productions. She was Director of the Bradford Civic Playhouse.

Elizabeth Whitworth Scott, who designed the Shakespeare Memorial Theatre at Stratford-upon-Avon – now the Royal Shakespeare Theatre – died on June 19, 1972, aged seventy-four. Her design was chosen in 1928 as the best of many submitted in a competition for a suitable theatre to replace the Stratford playhouse that was destroyed by fire. The present theatre was opened in 1932, but has undergone a number of structural alterations and modernizations since that time.

Ronald Frederick Delderfield, the dramatist, died at Sidmouth, on June 25, 1972, aged sixty. Formerly a journalist, he turned to playwriting and scored a tremendous popular success with *Worm's Eye View*, the farce of Army life, in which Ronald Shiner scored the outstanding success of his career.

He was fascinated by historical research and one of the results of his studies was *The Mayerling Affair*, which was presented at the Pit-lochry Festival Theatre in 1957. He became a prolific writer of saga-type novels, but in the theatre never eclipsed the success of *Worm's Eye View*, which ran for more than 2,000 performances.

Nicholas Hannen, one of the most distinguished leading actors of our time, died in London on June 25, 1972, aged ninety-one. Starting as an architect, he then studied for the stage under Rosina Filippi and first appeared at the Vaudeville in 1910 in *The Girl in the Train*. As a member of George Edwardes's companies he appeared in such musicals as *The Count of Luxembourg*, *Gipsy Love* and *The Dancing Mistress*.

He then became attracted to the straight stage and went to America with Granville Barker to play Louis Dubedat in *The Doctor's Dilemma* and the Emperor in *Androcles and the Lion*. After the First World War he was seen in London at the Garrick, playing Christian in Robert Loraine's historic production of *Cyrano de Bergerac*. He joined Lewis Casson and Sybil Thorndike to appear in *Candida*, *The Trojan Women* and *Medea* at the Holborn Empire in 1920.

During a long and distinguished career of some sixty years he was in such memorable productions as *The Dover Road*, *The Gay Lord Quex*, *In the Next Room*, *Tiger Cats* (an early Edith Evans success), *The Madras House*, *The Skin Game*, a long succession of classical roles at the Old Vic, *Tiger at the Gates*, *The Rape of the Belt* and *Teresa of Avila*, with Sybil Thorndike.

He was married to Athene Seyler.

Emrys Jones, the actor, died at the age of fifty-six on July 10, 1972 in Johannesburg, where he was appearing as Sir Winston Churchill in *A Man and His Wife*. The production was a popular success and there were plans for him to go to America and then London in the same part; but he was a victim of an influenza epidemic.

After learning his craft in Donald Wolfit's Company, Emrys Jones played Malcolm in *Macbeth* at the Piccadilly, when Gielgud and Gwen Ffrangcon-Davies appeared as the Macbeths.

His great success – and what turned out to be the triumph of his career – was his sensitive performance as the tragic Lachlen McLachlen in *The Hasty Heart* at the Aldwych in 1945. He never quite recovered from the disappointment of not being chosen to play the part on the screen.

He was later seen in *Dial M for Murder* and on a trip to South Africa was seen in *The Mousetrap* and *Carrington VC*. In Australia he scored a personal success in *Double Image* in 1957. Emrys Jones never enjoyed the stardom he deserved in London.

Buddy Bradley, the dancer and dance director, died in New York on July 17, 1972, aged sixty-four. He made his début as a dancer in the Florence Mills' Revue in New York in 1926 and was first seen dancing in London in Cochran's 1931 *Revue* at the Pavilion. Until 1967 he had a studio in London and produced the dances for such successful musicals as *Evergreen*, *Blackbirds*, *Anything Goes* and *Sauce Tartare*.

Eleanor Powell, Ruby Keeler and Adele Astaire were among those who used his early routines.

Pierre Brasseur, the French actor, died in Italy while filming on August 14, 1972, at the age of sixty-seven. He was born into a theatrical family in Paris and went on the stage while still a child to gain valuable experience in numerous small parts before scoring a sensational success in *Le Sexe Faible*.

After a long career in films he returned to the stage in *Le Bossu* and was in the first production of the Claudel classic, *Partage de Midi*. He gave a spectacular virtuoso performance in the name-part in *Kean* by Jean-Paul Sartre, and made a deep impression on the French stage as the father in *The Homecoming* by Harold Pinter.

Viola Lyel, the actress, died in London on August 14, 1972, aged seventy-one. She started her career as a student at the Old Vic, where she first appeared in 1918 playing small parts and understudying. Her earliest West End appearances were in the Birmingham Repertory Theatre productions of *The Farmer's Wife* at the Royal Court Theatre and *Yellow Sands* at the Haymarket.

In later years she had a most active career, making an outstanding success in comedy roles, such as Miss Gossage in *The Happiest Days of Your Life*. Her relaxed, angular figure was ideally suited to hilarious parts of this type. On the other hand, she made a memorable Queen in *Hamlet* and Nurse in *Romeo and Juliet* at Stratford-upon-Avon and was a tense Emily Creed in *Ladies in Retirement* at the St Martin's

Theatre. A more recent West End success was as Lady Cleghorn in *The Reluctant Peer* by William Douglas Home at the Duchess Theatre.

Benn Toff, one-time technical director of London Festival Ballet, died in London on August 31, 1972. When Julian Braunsweg first launched Festival Ballet, Benn Toff devised ingenious ideas for staging their productions. Mr Toff was principally responsible for giving the Royal Festival Hall a 'theatre look' by designing a false proscenium which was used year after year for the company's regular autumn and Christmas seasons.

After leaving Festival Ballet he was concerned with a company specializing in stage sets and exhibition stands.

Walter Johnstone Douglas, singer, pianist and producer, died in August 1972 at the age of eighty-five. He will be remembered for his performance in Rutland Boughton's opera, *The Immortal Hour* in London in the 1920s and for his own production of *Cosi Fan Tutte* at the Royal Court Theatre. He became interested in teaching and helped to found the Webber-Douglas Academy of Dramatic Art. His pupils included Audrey Mildmay, Stewart Granger, Michael Denison and Dulcie Gray.

Roger Furse, one of the outstanding stage designers of his time, died in August 1972 in retirement in Corfu. He started designing for the theatre in 1934 and created a number of memorable stage pro-

ductions for the London stage including *Anna Christie*, *Victoria Regina*, *Spring Meeting*, *Goodness How Sad!*, *Design for Living*, *Venus Observed*, *Look After Lulu*, *Daphne Laureola*, *Antony and Cleopatra*, *Caesar and Cleopatra* and two very famous thrillers, *Arsenic and Old Lace* and *The Mousetrap*. He also mounted a number of productions at the Old Vic, Stratford-upon-Avon and Covent Garden.

Val Parnell, the impresario, died in London in August 1972, aged seventy-eight. As a teenager he joined the staff of the Walter de Freece music-hall circuit and ultimately became Managing Director of Moss Empires Ltd and chief executive of Associated Television. Under his guidance the Palladium became the most famous variety theatre in the world and on television *Sunday Night at the Palladium* was a top-viewing feature for many years. Val Parnell created the Crazy Gang and staged six Palladium shows for them. His father was Fred Russell, the popular ventriloquist, who lived to the age of ninety-five.

Alfred Sangster, actor and dramatist, died in New Zealand in August 1972 at the age of ninety-two. He trained as a painter and exhibited at the Royal Academy. He went on the stage at the age of thirty-one at the St James's Theatre in *Eccentric Lord Comberdene*, and played the Sea Captain in *Twelfth Night* on the historic occasion when Sadler's Wells Theatre reopened in 1931. He was also seen at the Old

Vic and he played the Rev. Patrick Brontë in his own play, *The Brontës* at the Royalty Theatre in Dean Street, Soho, in 1933. For some years he was a leading member of the Liverpool Repertory Company.

Margaret Fraser, the actress, died in London on September 1, 1972, aged ninety-six. She was in the chorus of *In Town*, the first musical comedy, when it transferred to the Garrick in 1893. With George Edwardes's productions she toured America and was at Daly's and the Gaiety at the turn of the century.

With Seymour Hicks and Ellaline Terriss, Margaret Fraser appeared in *Bluebell in Fairyland* at the Vaudeville in 1901 and then worked for the Frohman management as a straight actress. She understudied Irene Vanbrugh in *The Admirable Crichton* and played in Barrie's *Little Mary* and in *Peter Pan* as Tiger Lily. She left the stage in 1908 to get married.

Jean-Jacques Bernard, the playwright, died in Paris on September 21, 1972, aged eighty-four. In this country he was best known for three plays – *Martine*, *The Sulky Fire* and *The Unquiet Spirit*, all seen in London in the 1930s. Victoria Hopper played Martine; Donald Wolfit was in *The Sulky Fire* and Tyrone Guthrie directed *The Unquiet Spirit*. Jean-Jacques Bernard had a sensitive understanding of unrequited love, which so often served as a theme for his plays. *Martine* was in the repertoire of the Comédie Française.

Henry de Montherlant, the French dramatist, shot himself in his Paris home on September 21, 1972, at the age of seventy-six. He had lost one eye and feared he might go completely blind. By the time his first play was staged he was forty-six and according to the example of French classical playwrights, he chose historical themes.

Donald Wolfit directed a translation of Montherlant's *The Master of Santiago* and played the leading part of Don Alvaro at the Lyric Theatre, Hammersmith, in 1957. Montherlant's finest work, *La Ville dont le Prince est un Enfant*, based on his own schoolboy love affair with a priest, was played in London by Le Théâtre Michel during the 1971 World Theatre Season at the Aldwych. In translation his *Port-Royal* and *The Queen After Death* were also seen in this country.

John Burrell, director of plays, died on September 28, 1972, at Champaign, Illinois, aged sixty-two. Having studied art, he joined Michel Saint-Denis at the London Theatre Studio in 1937 as producer and director of décor.

He won praise for his now legendary production of *Heartbreak House* at the Cambridge Theatre in 1943 and a year later went to the Old Vic, where among other plays he directed *Saint Joan*, *The Government Inspector* and *Arms and the Man*.

Mr Burrell went to America in 1950 to direct Jean Arthur in *Peter Pan*, and from 1957 to 1967 he was Executive Art Director for

Hetty King in one of her early
numbers as a curate

CBS Television in New York.
At the time of his death he was
Director of the Krannert Center of
the Performing Arts, which is
affiliated to the University of
Illinois in Champaign.

Hetty King, the music-hall star,
died in a Wimbledon hospital on
September 28, 1972, aged eighty-
nine. She was the last of the
legendary male impersonators,
having rivalled both Vesta Tilley
and in her time, Ella Shields. After
making her début at the Old Mo
music-hall in 1897 she enjoyed an
unbroken career until 1972, when
she was seen in a Christmas show
at the Wyvern Theatre in Swindon.
It is doubtful that any other artist
in British stage history has been
able to boast of an unbroken span
of seventy-five years on the boards.
   As character studies for her songs
she favoured drunken swells and
jolly-jack tars. Her most famous
numbers were 'Piccadilly' and 'All
the Nice Girls Love a Sailor'.
Throughout Hetty's career her
sister Olive served as her dresser.

Billie Houston, the music-hall
artist, died in hospital at Walton-
on-Thames on September 30, 1972,
aged sixty-six. With her sister
Renée, billed as the Houston
Sisters, they topped variety bills in
London and the provinces from
1920 to 1935, when the partnership
was dissolved on account of Billie's
prolonged illness. In their act
Billie favoured a blond Eton crop;
Renée chose a more feminine stage
personality.

Jack Gatti, former owner of the
Vaudeville and the Adelphi
Theatres in London, died at
Angmering-on-Sea on October 1,
1972, aged seventy-three. He was
the son of Sir John Gatti who
founded, with his brother Rocco,
one of the most popular supper
haunts of Edwardian London, the
famous Gatti Restaurant. Gaiety
Girls were often entertained there
by their admirers.

Colin Gordon, the actor, died in
London on October 5, 1972, aged
sixty-one, after being taken ill
while playing in South Africa. He
gained his first stage experience in
repertory at the Watford Palace
Theatre and made his West End
début as the hind-legs of a horse in
Toad of Toad Hall at the Royalty
Theatre in Dean Street. At the
same theatre he played in *Frolic
Wind,* a distinguished failure.
   His first spectacular stage success
was in *The Happiest Days of Your
Life* at the Apollo in 1948, giving a
performance which earned for him
the Clarence Derwent Award. This
was followed by appearances on
the West End stage in *The Love of
Four Colonels, The White Carnation,
Misery Me!, Alibi for a Judge* and
Relatively Speaking. His comedy
was strengthened by the relaxed
style of his acting.

Felix Felton, the actor, died in
October 1972, at the age of sixty.
He was interested in the theatre
while at Oxford when he became
President of the Oxford University
Dramatic Society in 1933. He
joined Val Gielgud's group of radio

12

producers at Broadcasting House and made a significant contribution to the development of drama on radio. He moved over to the script side in the 1960s, often collaborating with his wife Susan Ashman.

In the theatre he was recognized as a highly gifted character actor. One of his finest performances was as Mr Spettigue in the musical version of *Charley's Aunt*, presented at the Palace Theatre under the title of *Where's Charley?* in 1958, with Norman Wisdom as Charley.

Charles Leno, the actor, died in London in October 1972, at the age of sixty-four. He was one of those useful actors whose work in supporting roles so often lent lustre to a production as a whole. He was a member of the Old Vic Company in residence at the New Theatre at the end of the Second World War. Of his later commitments, those who saw him in *Look Homeward Angel* and *Hostile Witness* will recall his intelligent acting at its best.

Jack Melford, the actor, died in October 1972, aged seventy-three. Born into a well-known theatrical family, he first appeared on the stage in Birmingham in *The Silver King* at the age of thirteen. A versatile artist, he played in musical comedy, music-hall sketches and in the classics. He was with the Astaires in *Stop Flirting* in 1923, with Tallulah Bankhead in *Her Cardboard Lover*, with Binnie Hale in *Mr Cinders* and he appeared with the Oliviers at the St James's in 1951 in *Antony and Cleopatra* and *Caesar and Cleopatra*. In *Carousel* at

Drury Lane, he played the Heavenly Friend.

Geoffey Ost, director of productions, died in October 1972, while on holiday in the Cotswolds. As Director of Productions at the old Sheffield Playhouse from 1937 to 1964, he was responsible for hundreds of plays, ranging from West End after-dinner trifles to sensitive Chekhov masterpieces. He frequently designed the settings as well. On retiring from Sheffield Playhouse, he became a freelance and did fine work at the Pitlochry Festival and just before his death at the Bolton Octagon Theatre.

Harry Hanson, the actor and manager, died in London on November 1, 1972, aged seventy-seven. Born in Cape Town, he made his first appearance there as an actor with Matheson Lang's Company in *Westward Ho!* in 1912. He came to London in 1913 and played in various stock companies in this country. Having made his first appearance on the London stage as a speciality dancer in *Pick-A-Dilly* at the London Pavilion, he then toured in revue and was in *The Nine O'clock Revue* at the Little Theatre.

In 1932 he went into management and founded the Court Players at Hastings and later established similar repertory companies at Leeds, Sheffield, Peterborough, Penge, Nottingham, Richmond, Stockton, Chester, Bradford and elsewhere. He was in partnership with George Black.

The Court Players flourished in

the heyday of weekly repertory. The productions were often rough and ready, but the artists gained invaluable experience, playing every night and rehearsing the following week's play every day. Hundreds of dedicated actors, many well known in the profession, look back on their Harry Hanson days with gratitude and affection.

Sidney Jarvis, who had a distinguished career as resident designer at Oxford Playhouse, Watford Palace and the Leatherhead Theatre, died on November 4, 1972, aged sixty-two.

Russell Thorndike, actor and author, died at Foulsham, Norfolk, on November 7, 1972, aged eighty-seven. The younger brother of Sybil Thorndike, he first appeared on the London stage in 1905 in *The Eternal City.* He joined the Ben Greet Company and stayed with it for three and a half years, and then toured with Matheson Lang in an extensive repertoire of plays before joining Miss Horniman's famous repertory Company at the Gaiety Theatre in Manchester, with Sybil Thorndike and Lewis Casson.

He was a distinguished member of the Old Vic Company during several seasons, playing Hamlet, King Lear, Richard II and III, Falstaff, Shylock and Bottom, as well as many other parts. In 1920 he joined the Cassons for their Grand Guignol season at the Little Theatre. He appeared in his own play, *Dr Syn* at the Strand Theatre in 1927 and was Smee in *Peter Pan*

from 1950 to 1960 at the Scala Theatre. Sybil Thorndike appeared with him in his lurid melodrama, *The House of Jeffreys,* at the Playhouse in 1942.

Russell Thorndike possessed a magnificent voice of compelling power which made him an asset to every company he joined, including the Open Air Theatre Company in Regent's Park in 1941, 1944, 1946, 1951, 1952, 1955, 1956 and 1960. He wrote a biography of his sister in 1929 and with her he wrote a memoir of Lilian Baylis in 1938.

Margaret Webster, actress-daughter of Dame May Whitty and Ben Webster, died in London on November 13, 1972, aged sixty-seven. She first appeared on the stage in 1924 in the Chorus of *The Trojan Women* with Sybil Thorndike and the next year was seen as the Gentlewoman when John Barrymore played Hamlet at the Haymarket. She understudied Sybil Thorndike in *Saint Joan* and was with the Macdona Players in their Bernard Shaw repertory. She joined the Old Vic in 1929 and was the Player Queen when Gielgud played Hamlet for the first time.

She was in *Musical Chairs* at the Criterion Theatre and played the Countess of Derby in *Richard of Bordeaux* at the New Theatre in 1933. Other notable productions in which she appeared were *Queen of Scots, Viceroy Sarah, Parnell* and in America she was seen as Emilia in *Othello* when Paul Robeson played the Moor.

In later years she directed a number of productions on both

sides of the Atlantic, including Shakespeare and opera. She directed *Aida* and *Simon Boccanegra* at the New York Metropolitan Opera House. In 1960 she was in London to direct Noël Coward's *Waiting in the Wings*, a play about aged actors in a rest home, presented at the Duke of York's. She made numerous lecture tours based on the works of Shakespeare and Shaw and devised a solo recital called *The Brontës*. She published scholarly books on Shakespeare, and her own memoirs under the title of *The Same Only Different*.

Gerard Heinz, the actor, died in London on November 20, 1972, aged sixty-eight. Born in Hamburg, he first appeared on the stage in 1921. He played all over Germany and Austria, founding his own company in 1932. He was arrested by the Gestapo in 1933 and imprisoned in a concentration camp. After emigrating to Czechoslovakia he resumed his acting career at the Zürich Schauspielhaus.

He arrived in England in 1938 and broadcast with the BBC European Service during the Second World War. He made his stage début in London at the Apollo in 1942 as Count Skriczevinsky in *Flare Path*. He was in *Appointment with Death* at the Piccadilly and in 1948 played Papa in *I Remember Mama* at the Aldwych Theatre. He had a long run with Yvonne Arnaud in *Dear Charles* at the New Theatre in 1952–53. His later career was more concerned with films and television than the theatre.

His last appearance was in *A Touch of Purple* at the Globe Theatre, which opened a month before his death.

Douglas Young, the entertainer, died at Dorking on November 29, 1972, aged seventy-one. With his glamorous blonde wife Nan Kenway he formed a comedy team which was enormously popular during the Second World War years. They frequently topped music-hall bills, were heard on the radio and toured with ENSA parties at that time. He wrote all his own scripts and coined the 'Very tasty, very sweet!' catch-phrase.

He made his stage début in Liverpool in 1926 and took part in Princess Elizabeth's sixteenth birthday party celebrations at Windsor Castle in 1942.

Rudolf Friml, composer of more than thirty operettas died in Hollywood in November 1972, aged ninety-two. Born in Prague, he studied the piano under Jiránek at the Conservatoire there and became accompanist to the famous violinist, Jan Kubelik, from 1900 to 1902. He went to America and settled there permanently in 1906.

Rudolf Friml had a flair for writing tuneful musicals, starting with *The Firefly* in 1912 and continuing with *High Jinks* in 1914, *Katinka* in 1915, *The Ziegfeld Follies* of 1921 and 1923, *The Blue Kitten* in 1921, *The Wild Rose* in 1926 and *The Three Musketeers* in 1928.

His two most successful shows were *Rose-Marie*, which he composed with Herbert Stothart, completed in 1924, and *The Vagabond King* in 1925. They were staged with enormous success all over the world and were filmed as early talking pictures. They are still very much in demand by amateur operatic societies and the tunes are continually played on light music programmes on the radio. Mary Ellis was the original Rose-Marie in New York in 1924; Edith Day created the part in London at Drury Lane the following year.

Reginald Owen, the actor, died in Idaho, in November 1972, aged eighty-five. Although the most impressive part of his career was devoted to Hollywood films, he started as an actor in this country. He studied at Tree's Academy of Dramatic Art, where he won the first Bancroft Gold Medal for Acting in 1905. He played small parts under Tree's management at His Majesty's Theatre and then joined the Benson Company.

In 1911 he was the original Saint George in *Where the Rainbow Ends*,

15

of which he was part-author. Among his later stage successes were *Our Betters*, *The Charming People*, and in America, *Caprice*, *Petticoat Influence*, *Affairs of State* and *Not in the Book*. He started his film career in 1929.

Derek Patmore, the author, died in November 1972, aged sixty-four. Great-grandson of the poet Coventry Patmore, he is chiefly remembered in the theatre for the comedy, *French for Love*, which he wrote with Marguerite Steen soon after the outbreak of war in 1939. It was seen at the Criterion Theatre with Delysia, Athene Seyler and Cecil Parker in the cast.

Bernard Grun, composer and conductor, died in London on December 21, 1972, aged seventy-two. Born in Czechoslovakia, he studied music under Weingartner and Alban Berg and composed tuneful and popular music for some thirty musical shows. His first success in this country was *Balalaika*, the Eric Maschwitz play, for which Bernard Grun and George Posford wrote the music in 1936. Also with George Posford he wrote the music for *Paprika* in 1938 and the show was later called *Magyar Melody*, when Binnie Hale appeared in it at His Majesty's Theatre in 1939.

With Richard Tauber he wrote the music for *Old Chelsea*, in which the famous tenor appeared as a struggling composer and sang the popular number, 'My Heart and I'. The show opened in London at the Princes Theatre in 1943 and moved to the Winter Garden the following

year. Dr Grun arranged Chopin music for *Waltz Without End* in 1942 and the music of Dvořák for *Summer Song* in 1956. He conducted performances of *The Great Waltz*, the musical based on the life of Johann Strauss at Drury Lane in 1970. Earlier in his career in the mid-thirties he composed a musical based on the life of Fanny Elssler, the ballerina, and another about Gaby Deslys, the French music-hall artist whose jewels gave rise to much colourful gossip.

Eugene Berman, the Russian-born American stage designer, died in Rome in December 1972, aged seventy-three. Born in St Petersburg, he made his reputation in America with designs in the tradition of Berain and the Bibienas, but seen through contemporary eyes. In London he was best known for the Royal Ballet production of *Ballet Imperial* which evoked the glitter of Petersburg at the time of the Romanovs. The Balanchine ballet was staged at Covent Garden in 1950.

Jacques Deval, the French dramatist, died in December 1972, aged eight-two. He was a popular playwright in France from 1924, when he wrote *Le Bien Aimé* and he continued writing until the early 1960s. His plays provided good entertainment and excellent parts for leading actors. His two outstanding London successes were *Tovarich*, with an English text by Robert Sherwood, seen at the Lyric Theatre in 1935 with Cedric Hardwicke as the Prince and

Eugenie Leontovich, making her London début as the Archduchess; and *Mademoiselle*, adapted by Audrey and Waveney Carten, directed by Noël Coward at Wyndham's Theatre a year later, with Isabel Jeans, Madge Titheradge, Greer Garson, Nigel Patrick and Cecil Parker in the cast. Emlyn Williams played the name-part in *Etienne*, a comedy by Deval seen at the St James's Theatre in 1931, with Mary Clare, Margaret Webster, Una O'Connor and David Horne in the cast.

Dave Willis, one of Scotland's most popular comedians, died on January 1, 1973, at the age of seventy-eight at his home at Peebles. He appeared regularly in Howard & Wyndham pantomimes and in their summer shows in Scotland. Impersonation was one of his great gifts. At the time of the Munich crisis he impersonated Hitler with great success. The German Ambassador complained to the Foreign Office and Lord Inverclyde was sent to the comedian to advise him to remove the offending passage from his act. He did so.

Gandhi provided a subject for another uncanny impersonation, until a deputation of Indian students asked him to refrain. He had made enough money to retire at the age of fifty-six, but lost his fortune through buying a hotel at Rothesay, which proved to be a disastrous venture. His son, Denny Willis, is a popular comedian today.

Leonard Henry, the comedian, died in London on January 6,

1973, aged eighty-two. In the early days of radio he was the most popular comic on the air, usually writing his own material and broadcasting as a solo act.

He went on the stage as the result of going to the sea-side to convalesce, while he was still very young. He met a friend who happened to be in a concert party who persuaded him to entertain at the piano, more or less as a joke. As a result of this engagement he played under André Charlot's management at the Prince of Wales Theatre and wrote a number of revues. Later he appeared in several pantomimes, but it is as a pioneering radio comic that he will be remembered. As he was only five feet in height, microphones at the BBC had to be specially adjusted for him.

16

Michael Weight, one of the most striking and successful stage designers of the past forty years, died in Rome on January 14, 1973, aged sixty-six. Born in South Africa, he came to London to study at the Slade School. His first assignment in the theatre, designs for a revival of *Dandy Dick* at the Lyric Theatre, Hammersmith, attracted immediate attention and set him on the road to success. Cochran invited him to design his 1931 revue, and he did numerous shows for André Charlot.

Then came three Emlyn Williams plays – *The Corn is Green, The Light of Heart* and *Spring 1600*, followed by *The Winslow Boy, Clutterbuck, Little Lambs Eat Ivy, French Without Tears, Castle in the Air, Seagulls Over Sorrento, The White Sheep of the Family, Affairs of State, Witness for the Prosecution, The Manor of Northstead, Separate Tables, The Bride and the Bachelor, Farewell, Farewell Eugene* and *Aunt Edwina*, to name some of his outstanding achievements in a long and busy career.

Jon Rose, cabaret artist and writer, died in London on January 10, 1973. More than twenty years ago he appeared in cabaret with Sandy Wilson, author and composer of *The Boy Friend*.

Bill Nagy, the actor, died in London on January 19, 1973, aged fifty-one. Born in Hungary, he went to Canada as a child and subsequently studied for the stage at the New York Dramatic Workshop. He came to England in 1950 and the following year played Stewpot in *South Pacific* at Drury Lane and in 1959 he took over the part of Alvaro Mangiocavallo from Sam Wanamaker in *The Rose Tattoo* at the New Theatre. He was married to the actress Janet Macfarlane, who was playing in the London production of *Brigadoon* when he met her.

Ria Mooney, the Irish actress, died in Dublin in January 1973, aged sixty-nine. She made a tremendous impression in 1926 when she played Rosie Redmond, the prostitute, when *The Plough and the Stars* by Sean O'Casey was first seen at the Abbey Theatre in Dublin.

She was well known as a director of Irish plays and produced at the Abbey from 1948 to 1963. She was much in demand in London and America by managements who insisted upon their productions of Irish plays being given an authentic touch.

Jack MacGowran, the Irish actor who became the most famous interpreter of the works of Samuel Beckett, died in New York on January 30, 1973, at the age of fifty-four. He died of influenza in the hotel where he had been staying while playing in *The Plough and the Stars*.

After appearing in Dublin at the Abbey and Gate Theatres from 1944 to 1950, he made his first appearance in London at the New Lindsey Theatre as the Young Covey in a revival of *The Plough and the Stars* in 1954. He made a deep impression in 1958 at the Winter Garden as Harry Hope in *The Iceman Cometh* and played Clov in Beckett's *End Game* the same year at the Royal Court Theatre. At Stratford-upon-Avon in 1960 he played Old Gobbo, Christopher Sly and Autolycus in *The Winter's Tale*.

He became increasingly interested in the work of Samuel Beckett and devised and appeared in a solo programme of his writings called *Beginning to End* in Dublin in 1965. He specialized in readings and lectures on Beckett and O'Casey in later years, and his early mime training in Paris made his solo appearances vivid theatrical experiences.

Tex McLeod, the American cowboy who became a popular music-hall act in this country, died in Brighton on February 1, 1973, at the age of eighty-three. He was famous for his humorous stories and rope tricks. On retiring in 1957 he settled in Brighton where he ran a hostel to help down-and-outs.

Caryl Jenner, a leading pioneer for children's theatre in this country, died in London on January 29, 1973, aged fifty-four. She began her professional career at the Gate Theatre in London in *Karl and Anna,* a production for which she was also assistant stage manager. She was stage manager for a number of West End managements until 1938 when she became resident director at the Amersham Playhouse repertory theatre for Sally Latimer, producing more than 200 plays in ten years.

In 1949 she launched Mobile Theatres Ltd, developed from the Amersham Schools Mobile Unit to play in isolated towns and villages lacking any form of theatrical activity. By 1960 one touring company for adults and four for children had been formed and she devoted the rest of her career to providing theatre for the young. In 1962 she created the Unicorn Theatre for Young People which made its base at the Arts Theatre in London and sent out tours to various parts of the country. She also organized performances for young audiences of visiting companies presenting dance-theatre, puppets and films from this country and abroad.

She established a loyal and enthusiastic public of 3,500 members for her Unicorn Theatre productions at the Arts, aged between four and seven. Undeterred by bad weather in the depth of winter, they invariably turned up and filled the house. She never played down to children and they respected her regard for them as intelligent young folk. She provided them with entertainment, which was uncannily geared to their particular age group. Her Unicorn Theatre gave up to 800 performances a year and travelled some 40,000 miles.

Dudley Foster, the actor, was found hanged in his London home on January 8, 1973, aged forty-eight. He was known to millions through his regular performances on television, but did some notable stage work in the early productions of Joan Littlewood's Theatre Workshop at the Theatre Royal, Stratford, in London's East End. His widow, Eileen Kennally, was rehearsing a Theatre Workshop production, *Is Your Doctor Really Necessary?*, at the time of her husband's tragic death.

Max Adrian, the actor, died at his home near Guildford on January 1973, aged sixty-nine. Born in Ireland, he made his first appearance on the stage in the chorus of *Katja the Dancer* at the Gaiety in Douglas, Isle of Man, at the age of twenty-two. He walked-on in London, joined Tod Slaughter's Company and gained valuable early experience at the Northampton Repertory Theatre. He was in Terence Rattigan's first play, *First Episode*, at the Comedy Theatre in 1934 and in 1939 played the Dauphin in an Old Vic revival of *Saint Joan.*

His great chance came when John Gielgud cast him as Jeremy in the 1943 production of *Love for Love* at the Phoenix Theatre. From that moment he was recognized as an actor with an unrivalled flair for satire. The timbre of his voice and his biting attack made him an outstanding figure on the comedy stage, especially in such famous intimate revues as *Tuppence Coloured, Oranges and Lemons, Penny Plain* and *Airs on a Shoestring.*

He was a sterling player with the Royal Shakespeare Company and also with the National Theatre Company, playing such parts as Feste in *Twelfth Night*, Polonius, and the Inquisitor in *Saint Joan.* He frequently appeared at the Yvonne Arnaud Theatre in Guildford and devised two one-man shows – *An Evening with G.B.S.* and *Gilbert and Sullivan* which he toured in this country and abroad with great success. Just before his death he read satirical verse at the Fanfare for Europe Gala staged at

Covent Garden in the presence of the Queen.

In intimate revue he had no equal, apart from Hermione Gingold, who had a similar taste for withering wit. His voice was unique and instantly recognizable and he knew how to use it so that every line was a laugh in the comedies in which he excelled.

Bruce Walker, actor and author, died on March 7, 1973, aged sixty-six. In the days of the Teddy Boys he scored a considerable success with his play concerning a young delinquent. Called *Cosh Boy*, it was first seen at the Embassy Theatre in Swiss Cottage in 1951 and later moved to the Comedy Theatre under the title of *Master Crook*. James Kenney scored a spectacular success in the name-part.

Cyril Raymond, the actor, died in his seventies at Lewes in March 1973. In 1915 he played William Bagot in *Trilby* with Tree at Finsbury Park Empire. He was what is known in the profession as a useful actor, responsive to the director's demands and capable of creating individual characterizations from the flimsiest of scripts. He had a unique stage personality.

Among the many successes in which he appeared were *There's Always Juliet, The Shining Hour, Short Story, The Constant Wife, Tony Draws a Horse, Under the Counter, September Tide, Waters of the Moon, Aunt Edwina, Signpost to Murder* and *Inadmissible Evidence*. He was married to the actress Iris Hoey and later to Gillian Lind.

Katina Paxinou, the imposing actress who became the *grande dame* of the Greek stage, died in Athens on February 22, 1973 aged seventy-three. After starting life as an opera singer, she made her first appearance as an actress in 1924 and after two and a half years in repertory became leading lady of the Athens Royal Theatre. During a number of years she played leading parts in the Greek classics, in Shakespeare and in English and American plays which she translated into Greek, and also produced. Her outstanding successes were in *Anna Christie, Desire Under The Elms* and as Mrs Alving in Ibsen's *Ghosts*.

She first appeared in London in 1939 with the Royal Theatre of Greece, playing the name-part in *Electra*, the Sophocles tragedy translated into modern Greek at His Majesty's Theatre. The following night she played with the same company as Gertrude to the Hamlet of her husband, Alexis

Minotis. The following year she played in English for the first time at the Duchess Theatre in London, as Mrs Alving in *Ghosts*, with John Carol as Oswald and Nicholas Hannen as Pastor Manders. In New York she was seen as Hedda Gabler, Hecuba and Jocasta.

She returned to London in 1966 with the Greek National Theatre, as part of the World Theatre Season at the Aldwych Theatre, playing the title role in *Hecuba* and Jocasta in *Oedipus Rex*, but time had begun to take its toll and her performances were not as electrifying as they had been in the days when she held multitudes spellbound on summer nights in the vast open-air theatres in Greece. In those days she was the greatest authority on Greek classic drama and her every appearance was something of an occasion.

She did not approve of the modern approach Karolos Koun brought to his Greek Art Theatre productions of *The Birds* by Aristophanes and *The Persians* by Aeschylus. She regarded this popularizing of the Greek classics as something akin to sacrilege.

Hugh Beaumont, Managing Director of H M Tennent Ltd, died suddenly in London on March 22, 1973, aged sixty-four. Known throughout the profession as Binkie, he was the most powerful theatrical manager of his time and was responsible for the presentation of more superbly cast stylish productions than any other impresario in the history of the British theatre, having a monopoly over a number of years of the cream of the profession and the most fashionable theatres in the West End.

He started his career as an assistant manager in Cardiff under Howard & Wyndham in 1924 and was later business manager at Barnes Theatre under Philip Ridgeway. After working at the Little Theatre and the Duke of York's he joined Moss Empires of which he subsequently became a director.

His memorable work stemmed from the time he became Managing Director of H M Tennent Ltd and a director of the Company of Four. The productions were staged between 1936 and the present time.

Such stars as Marie Tempest, Edith Evans, Noël Coward, Vivien Leigh, the Lunts, Emlyn Williams, Sybil Thorndike, John Gielgud, Margaret Rutherford, Isabel Jeans, Peter Ustinov, Paul Scofield, Eileen Herlie, Peggy Ashcroft, Gladys Cooper, Rex Harrison, Ruth Draper, Ralph Richardson, Celia Johnson, Hermione Gingold, Mary Martin and Yvonne Arnaud scored some of their most sensational successes under the Tennent banner, under the leadership of Binkie Beaumont.

Notable productions that come to mind include *George and Margaret*, *Dear Octopus*, *Design for Living*, *Rebecca*, *Blithe Spirit*, *While the Sun Shines*, *Private Lives*, *The Skin of Our Teeth*, *Tuppence Coloured*, *The Happiest Days of Your Life*, *Oranges and Lemons*, *The Heiress*, *The Lady's Not For Burning*, *A Streetcar Named Desire*, *Ring Round the Moon*, *Waters of the Moon*, *The Deep Blue Sea*, *A Day by the Sea*, *Hotel Paradiso*, *Nude with Violin*, *The Potting Shed*, *Duel of Angels*, *Irma La Douce*, *Ross*, *A Man For All Seasons*, *The Private Ear and The Public Eye*, *At the Drop of a Hat*, *Hello, Dolly!*, *Vivat! Vivat! Regina!*, *Oklahoma*, *West Side Story* and *My Fair Lady*.

The death of Binkie Beaumont marks the end of an era in the West End theatre. Times have changed. No one could ever repeat his achievement at a later date, with different plays and different stars. He was unique and was responsible for a tremendous achievement.

David Bauer, the American actor, died at his London home in February 1973, aged fifty-five. A familiar figure in American films and television, he came to this country in 1958 to play Doc in *West Side Story*. He returned to join the National Theatre Company in 1972 to appear as Sheriff Hartman in *The Front Page* at the Old Vic. The directors were so impressed by his work they invited him to play Sir Toby Belch in *Twelfth Night* at the Old Vic. He was married to Stella Tanner, one of the popular Tanner Sisters act, a singing group popular in light entertainment.

Bob Bahl, the American stage designer, died in Toronto on February 15, 1973, aged thirty-four. He came to Europe about ten years ago and became Sean Kenny's general assistant and was working with Mr Kenny at the Irish Arts Theatre in Toronto at the time of his death.

In London he worked on *Blitz*, *Maggie May*, *King Priam* and the sets for the D'Oyly Carte Opera Season at the Royal Festival Hall. He was consultant designer for the Bankside Globe Playhouse where he was solely responsible for the décor of the *Hamlet* which presented Keith Michell in the name-part. He also supervised the erection of the 1972 temporary theatre on Bankside.

Melville Cooper, the actor, died in Hollywood in March 1973 at the age of seventy-six. He was with the Birmingham Repertory Company from 1919 to 1924 and was first seen in London in their productions of *Back to Methuselah* and *The Farmer's Wife*, in which he played Samuel Sweetland. At the London Pavilion he was in two famous revues, *One Dam Thing After Another* and *This Year of Grace*. He made his name in 1929 as Trotter in *Journey's End* at the Savoy in the sort of comedy part which Ronald Shiner made so popular in later years.

He was in musicals and revues in London, as well as *Laburnum Grove* at the Duchess, before he went to America to make films from 1937 to 1943. Apart from one brief return to London in the Victor Herbert operetta, *Romany Love*, in 1947, he spent the rest of his career on the American stage in such shows as *The Merry Widow*, *Pygmalion*, *An Inspector Calls*, *Escapade*, *My Fair Lady*, *The Importance of Being Earnest*, *Camelot* and *Hostile Witness*. He was at one time married to Rita Page, the musical comedy actress.

Frederick W Bromwich, who died suddenly at the end of March 1973, had a lifetime association with the theatre on the managerial side. For many years he looked after the business interests of the Ballet Rambert and was instrumental in pioneering longer and wider tours which enabled the ballet to be seen and appreciated in towns off the normal touring circuit.

A year or two before his death he looked after The Place at Euston, where so many different kinds of theatrical presentations were presented under his authority. Though not a famous actress, his mother appeared as a child player with Ellen Terry in *Olivia*, a

Left: Ursula Jeans
Right: Noël Coward. *Photograph by The Press Association*

popular dramatization of *The Vicar of Wakefield* by W G Wills.

Ursula Jeans, the actress, died in a Hertfordshire nursing home on April 21, aged sixty-six. One of the most accomplished actresses of her time, she first attracted attention in Galsworthy's *Escape* and in Miles Malleson's controversial *Fanatics* at the Ambassadors. She was with Marie Tempest in *Passing Brompton Road* and *The First Mrs Fraser*. After playing Flaemmchen in *Grand Hotel* at the Adelphi and appearing with Ivor Novello in *I Lived With You*, she joined the Old Vic Company to get a ground-

ing in the classics in 1933. She gave memorable performances as Viola, Anne Bullen and Cecily Cardew in *The Importance of Being Earnest*. She was Olivia when the Old Vic opened with *Twelfth Night* after the war and later played Mistress Ford and Lady Cicely Waynflete.

She frequently toured in this country and abroad with her husband, Roger Livesey and they will both be remembered for their polished acting in *An Ideal Husband* at the Strand Theatre in 1965.

Noël Coward, actor, dramatist and composer, died suddenly at his home in Jamaica on March 26, 1973, aged seventy-three. Known in the profession as The Master, he was quite the most versatile man of the theatre of all time. He was an accomplished actor, a highly successful dramatist, a top-rank cabaret star, a composer of lilting light theatre music, and an astute director of productions. His name had a magic which held sway over several generations. At the time of his death, two of the most successful productions in London were a revival of his *Private Lives* at the Queen's Theatre, and *Cowardy Custard*, a pot-pourri of his successful revue numbers, at the Mermaid Theatre.

Born in Teddington, he made his first appearance on the stage at the age of ten in *The Goldfish*, a children's fairy play, which also had Micheal MacLiammoir in the cast. In the same year he appeared with Charles Hawtrey in *The Great Name*.

He was Slightly in *Peter Pan* in 1913 and 1915 at the Duke of York's Theatre, and in 1920 played Bobbie in his own play, *I'll Leave It To You* at the New Theatre.

His first tremendous success came in 1924 at the Everyman Theatre in Hampstead in his own play, *The Vortex*, a powerful mother-and-son drama, in which he appeared with Lilian Braithwaite. He never looked back after that historic first night, and he became the darling of the sophisticated London and New York stage. He then played Lewis Dodd in *The Constant Nymph*, followed by a series of brilliant performances in his own productions.

He appeared in his own revue, *This Year of Grace*, at the Selwyn Theatre in New York in 1928, and in 1930 he opened at the Phoenix Theatre in London with *Private Lives*, playing opposite Gertrude Lawrence; like his *Hay Fever*, the play is now regarded as a classic and never fails to pack theatres. Again with Gertrude Lawrence, and also at the Phoenix, he played in a series of short plays called *Tonight at 8.30*. He gave amusing performances in *Blithe Spirit*, *Present Laughter*, *This Happy Breed*, *Sigh No More*, *Nude With Violin*, and his last appearances on the London stage were at the Queen's Theatre in a collection of three plays called *Suite in Three Keys*. By that time his health was failing and the brilliance was beginning to dim.

In 1931 *Cavalcade* made history at Drury Lane and *Bitter Sweet* (1929) has a nostalgia which still

lingers on after more than forty years. None of his music written after that time had the same glorious sentimental melodiousness. Marie Tempest will never be forgotten in *Hay Fever*, nor will Tallulah Bankhead and Edna Best in *Fallen Angels*. One recalls Yvonne Printemps in *Conversation Piece*, the Lunts in *Quadrille*, Fritzi Massary in *Operette*, Margaret Rutherford, Kay Hammond and Fay Compton in *Blithe Spirit*, Gladys Cooper in *Relative Values*, Sybil Thorndike, Marie Löhr and Edith Day in *Waiting in the Wings* . . . wonderful nights at the theatre with the most dazzling stars of the twentieth century.

Strangely enough, one of Noël Coward's most brilliant performances was not in his own play. It was as King Magnus in the Haymarket Theatre revival in 1953 of *The Apple Cart* by Bernard Shaw, with Margaret Leighton as the glittering Orinthia. They all but eclipsed the original creations by Cedric Hardwicke and Edith Evans. The critics said the part of Magnus might have been written expressly for Coward.

Noël Coward had a glorious sense of humour. During an exhausting tour of overseas Forces camps during the war, an actress in the party rang Coward one morning – 'How do you look today, my darling?' He replied, 'Like a very old Chinese washerwoman.' He loved the profession and gained enormous pleasure from writing about his fellow artists, such as the down-trodden vaudeville duo in *Red Peppers* and the spoilt matinée

idol in *Present Laughter*.

He was knighted at the time of his seventieth birthday, and the Queen Mother arranged a private birthday lunch for him at Clarence House. At the last moment she could not play hostess on account of a sudden indisposition. From her bed she telephoned her apologies to her guest of honour, adding 'My daughters will take care of you.'

THE MAGNETISM OF THE MINSTRELS

The Black and White Minstrels are an outstanding theatrical phenomenon of our time. They are now in their fourteenth year and during that time their stage shows have been seen by some 25,000,000 people in this country and overseas. Inspired by television, they started in quite a modest way.

George Inns produced the first Black and White Minstrel show on BBC Television at the Earls Court Radio Show of 1957. It included the George Mitchell Singers, whose business affairs were handled by the Robert Luff Organization. When Robert Luff saw this production he considered it to be the first television show capable of being translated successfully to the live stage. George Inns and George Mitchell were of the same opinion, so they set about devising a theatre version.

It was geared to play a fourteen-week summer season at Scarborough in 1960, presented by Robert Luff, in association with George Mitchell. They arranged an eight-week tour to run-in the show on the road before the Scarborough opening, but those early days were anything but encouraging. The tour started in Bristol to bad business and went on to Newcastle, Glasgow, Edinburgh, Birmingham and Hanley, but by the time it reached Scarborough, Robert Luff had lost some £12,000 on the venture.

To use his own words, the production caught fire the moment it opened in Scarborough and the box-office receipts soared to what became record-breaking

heights right from the start. Business was phenomenal and a further eight-week tour, planned at the end of the summer season, to visit Stockton, Leeds, Shrewsbury, Nottingham, Glasgow, Brighton, Blackpool and Cardiff was a smash hit.

Robert Luff knew he had an excellent money-making property in his possession, a worthwhile show capable of filling the largest theatres for as long as he cared to tour it. He has been touring various versions of the production ever since and also filling the Victoria Palace in London for years on end. Following the last Crazy Gang Show, the first Victoria Palace season ran for seven years; the second, called *The Magic of the Minstrels*, ran for three years, and now a third show at the New Victoria Theatre looks like following suit.

What is the secret of this unique money-spinner? Robert Luff puts his faith in nostalgia and melody. The audience hears snatches of some hundred songs during the two-hour show, songs which they love because they evoke precious memories for them. Melody is the most potent magnet of the Minstrels. Mr Luff has no time for what he calls brittle and aggressive music, so he turns to soothing melodies, most of them having been composed in the last half-century. The audience find them irresistible.

Glamour is another trump-card of the Minstrel shows. The girls are the contemporary equivalent of Cochran's Young Ladies. The Minstrel Maids and the

Television Toppers smile in such a way that the audience warms towards them; superb lighting enhances their beauty, as do tasteful décors and glittering costumes. For each girl chosen, about two hundred are auditioned, so the standard is remarkably high.

Robert Luff has never relied upon stars. His leading artists are billed as featured soloists, not as star performers. No name appears above the title of the show. Since the unparalleled success of the Minstrel shows, several stars have indicated a desire to join the Minstrels for guest seasons. But it would never work. They would want far too much money and far too much time. They would demand a thirty-minute spot in the programme, which is not Robert Luff's idea of a Black and White Minstrel show.

No one is allowed to hog the stage. Spectacular song and dance scenes alternate with individual acts in the Minstrel shows. There is no moment when everything stops to allow a star to monopolize the stage for a quarter of the running time. Stars would find no place in the team-work principle upon which the Minstrel shows are devised. There is a decided family atmosphere about the companies, which accounts for the fact that close on seventy Minstrel couples have been married since the shows were first seen in the theatre.

A strict watch is kept on every performance, so that the remarkably high standard is proudly maintained. There is never any question of a Minstrel show having a tired look. No one ever sees laddered tights or scuffed shoes; nor does one see performances which are less sparkling than they were on the opening night. Private jokes shared between artists on stage would never be tolerated in a Minstrel show, nor would the jaded artist who attempted to walk-through a performance.

In this way Robert Luff hopes that people will feel a sense of occasion when they attend one of his shows. More than half the acts are visual; 'business' comedy is preferred and the specialities on the bill are sight acts. In consequence, thousands of foreign tourists who flock to this country every summer, without knowing even a smattering of English, enjoy the entertainment provided by the Minstrels, with no fear of boredom as a result of being confused by what is happening on the stage.

Robert Luff sets out to provide family entertainment at a price which the average family can afford. He prefers to make a smaller profit and thus obtain a longer run, than charge the best part of £3 each for stalls, knowing full well that only a minority audience can afford such a crippling price. Entertainment for the millions at a price within their pockets remains his objective. A new policy has been adopted this year by Robert Luff, who does not intend to run his Black and White Minstrel shows in the West End for years at a stretch. He has now decided to present his London shows for shorter seasons of between thirty and forty weeks at a time. After each of these seasons a television series is to be arranged; the company will be quite fresh to cope with work in the studio because the Minstrels will not be appearing in the theatre every evening. Only after the television series has finished will they return to the London stage.

Tours carry on as usual for an average of forty-four weeks a year and there are plans for a third tour of Australia and New Zealand, to be extended to take in Singapore, Manila, Hong Kong, Bangkok and possibly Tokyo.

NUDITY WITHOUT PROTEST

R. B. Marriott

The nude came into the theatre when the censor went out. That was in 1968. And with the nude came hitherto forbidden words, gestures and themes, even types of character. This led to a lot of naked fun, most of it, and to the surprise of some people, harmless, practically innocuous. But it also led to serious work, in which nudity played a significant part. Thus we had *Hair*, the first production with what one might describe as free-wheeling nudity, *Oh! Calcutta!*, a show for voyeurs, *The Dirtiest Show in Town*, anti-pollution propaganda plus tangles of nakedness, and *Pyjama Tops*, with swimming nudes, as well as *Abelard and Héloïse* and *The Changing Room*, both works on a high level of seriousness, with nudity as part of the development; in fact, nudity from the Whitehall to the Royal Court.

To the question, Is nudity box-office?, I think there are two main answers. In the first flush of freedom for nudity, I believe it was indeed an attraction in itself. On the other hand, as nudity becomes more and more familiar on our stages it will do less and less in itself, and will have to be part of a really good show, if the production is to succeed. One instance is *Pyjama Tops*, at the Whitehall. A farce adapted from the French, it had as its big attraction a huge water-filled glass tank in which naked girls swam. The show was pretty mediocre, but the tank and the novelty of the nudes were a real attraction. I surmise that future shows of the sort will have to offer more than tank nudity: dashing farce, too.

In *Abelard and Héloïse*, at Wyndham's,

Diana Rigg and Keith Michell had a nude scene which perfectly fitted the action of a celebrated drama of a great love. This was interesting, even fascinating, but the play was much more than the nudity, and almost certainly would have been a success without it. *Hair*, at the Shaftesbury, brought in nudity as an expression of love of life by those of mankind who aim to free themselves of destructive and limiting conventions of thought and action. It contained a beautiful, moving scene of many naked people, a scene with poetry and humanity. There was no offence, and no outcry.

The Changing Room, at the Royal Court, a drama-documentary of local footballers in their private room behind the scenes, had men going through their normal bathing ablutions and horse-play, their nakedness giving sharpness, starkness and veracity to an impressive story of ordinary people. Indecency never came to mind. Indeed, protests about indecency, obscenity, corruption and so forth have been very few, and then only from a tiny minority.

In *Oh! Calcutta!*, at the Round House and the Royalty, there were things which might have put the producers in prison a few years ago; yet the show packed out, and was allowed to run freely in its own way.

It is not merely a question of a 'permissive' society, but of changing society. There was a time when some of Ibsen's great plays, notably the highly moral *Ghosts*, were condemned as vile, obscene and a danger to the community.

Perhaps nudity has gone down so well, I

mean without trouble, because in its two principal spheres it has been used 'properly'. In light entertainment, it has been used to entertain, to titillate, to provoke, as a response to a demand, indeed to a need, among a certain section of the population, who want to see and enjoy the movement of the naked body. In serious work, it has been used as an integral part of a drama, to help to explain a situation, to further reveal a character. The 'proper' use of the nude seems now to be justified and accepted. At the Mermaid a nude Desdemona was a fiasco simply because it was out of place, even silly. The attitude of the artist towards working in the nude, and to the use of the nude in the theatre, of course varies considerably. Actors in the past have rebelled, because of their principles, against playing murderers. Margaret Rutherford thought hard before taking the part of Miss Marples, Agatha Christie's detective, because of the crime involved in her work. We do have the artist who would be against appearing in the nude. But, generally, the artist is ready to play almost any part in almost any play, not only for the money – though this is important to thousands of artists – but because he will be practising his craft and doing his job of entertaining the public. Narrowing down the matter, however, one does find artists who have become sick of exploiting their bodies when the object has been more or less only exploitation.

So far there is really no problem. With the coming of the nude was the notion that the whole of the theatre would be besieged by

The nude *pas-de-deux* from *Oh! Calcutta!*, seen in London at the Round House in Chalk Farm and later at the Royalty Theatre. *Photograph by Chris J Arthur, Trans World Eye*

nakedness. This was not so. The vast majority of shows are still without nudes, and will continue to be, for a very good reason: nudes are not needed in them and would be ludicrous.

One surprise has been the fact that so few nude shows or shows with nudity have been put on in the provinces. When the censor went, many people expected the stages of the nation, big and small, in the open or hole in corner, to be filled by nude shows. This did not happen. In one year in the thirties there were far more cheap 'girlie' revues on tour than all the post-censor nudity shows put together. Another surprise has been the behaviour of audiences at shows containing nudity. People have been known to walk out; people have been seen to be embarrassed; men have been seen to be enjoying themselves while their women friends looked down. Yet this kind of reaction has been rare, at least in the London theatre. There has been nothing that could even remotely be called a 'protest'. So one must conclude that audiences generally are not embarrassed. One even suspects that the sharing in nudity by people who have never done so before, may have a salutary effect. Understanding may be broadened, frankness encouraged. It is impossible to know for sure, but I would hazard that those who really do not fancy nudity on the stage, just do not go to see it.

Is the novelty of the nude wearing off, or will it wear off? No. There will always be a natural interest in nudity but, as I have said, it will have to be presented in new and

The cast of *The Dirtiest Show in Town* at the Duchess Theatre, just before they stripped to play the last twenty minutes of the show in total nudity.
Photograph by Laurie Asprey

striking ways if it is to continue as a novelty attraction in light entertainment. In the serious, or more serious theatre, one supposes nudes will come and go, as the occasion demands. It seems unlikely that managements will exploit the nude recklessly, wantonly, seeing that this has not already been done. There may be the odd transgressor, there usually is, but he is not really of importance.

For years before the censor vanished, there were, of course, nudes to be seen in public places. In the sleazy clubs of Soho and provincial cities, in the gaudy, plush, expensive clubs, they flourished, as they do now, sleaziness sometimes being covered up by gorgeous plumes and glittering spangles. But this is not the theatre. It is hardly, I was going to say, barely entertainment. It is pandering to a certain demand. And as most psychologists would declare, on the whole it probably performs a useful function, as a safety-valve. Though a few artists have graduated to the theatre from this odd world, it remains apart, reflecting theatre only in the dancers and acts pushed in between the nude displays.

No doubt there is further exploitation of the nude to come, as well as original use within a seriously defined context. It is difficult to visualize just what form this is likely to take. We can have nudes jumping off high platforms, swinging on trapezes, running about the auditorium, even receiving the customers in the foyer or at the box-office. But this kind of thing is merely an extension of now familiar nudity in the theatre.

The arrival of nudes in the theatre in 1968 was something quite new, something which had never before happened in this country. What can happen with nudes which has not happened before? An extension into sexual activity is, again, only an extension of present nudity. So perhaps it is a case of a nude is a nude is a nude; the rest always being trimmings.

The astonishing and very good thing to happen since nudes came, is the non-arrival of another form of censorship. No great protest; not even the Longford Report bashed at the theatre, which came out of it extremely well. No social turmoil, the Church unworried, apparently accepting nudes as it has accepted Jesus Christ *en fête* in musicals.

There may well be all-nude shows, everyone nude throughout in light entertainment; yet, as I suggest, future nudes will have as it were to be clothed in something – wit, glamour of a fresh kind, comedy, revelry – in short, additional entertainment. Serious plays will be written in which the nude has a part, but it is impossible to foresee nude productions of Shakespeare or Ibsen, Shaw or O'Casey: there would simply be no point. Looking over the years since 1968, one thing is most notable: every single West End manager has behaved with a sense of responsibility regarding the new freedom for nudes. The best shows – the serious plays and musicals – have deployed nudes for obvious good reason. The lighter shows have deployed them for another sort of good reason, as a legitimate form of diversion designed to appeal to a particular audience – not necessarily to a perverted or puerile audience – but to the audience which at one time patronized the scantily dressed innuendo shows, and which naturally welcomes less dress or no dress and less double-meaning, rather liking frankness, a bit of honest vulgarity, and a touch of the crudity common in everyday life.

In short, it would seem that the theatre, far from suffering through the arrival of the nude, has benefited: a few windows have been opened, and in have blown fresh ideas of flesh and blood.

30

THE ROMANS AT STRATFORD

The Romans at Stratford

Trevor Nunn, artistic director of the Royal Shakespeare Company, devoted the 1972 season at Stratford-upon-Avon to the Romans – a daring and imaginative conception which was crowned with success. He hit upon the idea of performing a cycle of Shakespeare's four Roman plays – *Coriolanus, Julius Caesar, Antony and Cleopatra* and *Titus Andronicus*. Never at any time or in any other theatre in the world had these plays ever previously been presented as a group. Though each play is complete in itself, together they showed the birth, achievement and collapse of a civilization. During the winter preceding the opening of the Roman Season with *Coriolanus* in April, radical alterations, designed by Christopher Morley, were made to the auditorium of the Royal Shakespeare Theatre. They included improvements to benefit the public, providing seventy-six extra seats. Elaborate hydraulically-operated staging was installed, making possible closer contact between actor and audience. These developments were designed to bring the Stratford auditorium nearer to the 'one-room' relationship between actor and audience already planned for the RSC's new London theatre, now being built by the City of London in the Barbican, to which the Company will eventually move from the Aldwych Theatre.

These £90,000 alterations at Stratford, paid for partly out of the RSC repair funds and partly out of the increased revenue in future years from the extra seats, have provided the theatre with a new concept in stage design; one of the most variable stage systems in the world. The design incorporates a complex of movable sections which enables an extremely wide range of stage settings. The changes to the stage area contributed to the flexible 'stone'-textured basic setting for the Romans and Rank Strand Electric's new computer stage lighting system was put into action for the first time.

After seeing *Coriolanus* on the Opening Night of the Roman Season, which proved a significant milestone in the history of the home of the Royal Shakespeare Company, one critic wrote, 'Visually, Rome looks like a collection of vast cement biscuit-boxes. To mark the scene changes, walls rise or fall, unexpected flights of steps appear and even flaming furnaces sprout from nowhere. Or the whole floor tilts forward, while slabs of masonry revolve.'

Tasteful and imaginatively designed back-cloths are projected on to the vast expanse at the back of the stage, so we can be transported from Rome to Athens or to Alexandria in a matter of seconds and confronted by a stage setting drenched in appropriate atmosphere. This speeding up of scene changes cancels out those dreary waits which so often separated scenes in earlier Shakespeare productions.

This new system is completely noiseless, which is a boon on those occasions when backstage operations have to be carried out while actors are still on stage finishing a scene. The installation of hydraulic pumps has reduced noise to a minimum at Stratford. Trevor Nunn was responsible for directing all four plays in the Roman cycle, assisted by Buzz Goodbody, John Barton and Euan Smith. Christopher Morley, assisted by Ann Curtis, was responsible for the designs and the music was by Guy Woolfenden who has provided music for more than forty RSC productions.

The Company at Stratford-upon-Avon, under the Trevor Nunn régime, is a team of sterling players, without any star system complex. To them, 'the play's the thing', and there is no question of any artist being glorified and raised to star status. Superstar is an expression ridiculed at Stratford. A good all-round versatile player, capable of doing justice to any part, no matter how long or small, is the actor who earns respect on the banks of the Avon.

As an example of his casting, Trevor Nunn chose Ian Hogg to play Coriolanus, Margaret Tyzack for Volumnia, John Wood as Brutus, Patrick Stewart as Cassius, Richard Johnson as Antony, Janet Suzman as Cleopatra and Colin Blakely as Titus Andronicus. The season lasted thirty-six weeks and also included the internationally popular Clifford Williams production of *A Comedy of Errors*, which lent a touch of light-hearted gaiety to what might have otherwise been considered a heavy season. The Romans opened a five-month season at the Aldwych Theatre on July 7, 1973, with few casting changes

Left: Ian Hogg as Coriolanus and Patrick Stewart as Tullus Aufidius in *Coriolanus*. *Photograph by Reg Wilson*
Right: Ian Hogg as Coriolanus, arriving triumphantly in Rome. *Photograph by Joe Cocks*

CORIOLANUS

Trevor Nunn opened his Roman cycle at the Royal Shakespeare Theatre, Stratford-upon-Avon, with *Coriolanus*; the new stage made a favourable impression, in view of the fact that Mr Nunn showed his special flair for dealing with crowds, whether they be Romans or Volsci. The audience was involved from the outset. The impact was sensational.

Margaret Tyzack's impressive Volumnia gained the acting honours of the production. Ian Hogg's Coriolanus lacked nobility; his delivery was undistinguished and he failed to match up to his distinguished predecessors in the part.

The crafty Menenius of Mark Dignam, the exotic Aufidius of Patrick Stewart and the impressive Tribunes of Raymond Westwell and Gerald James were memorable performances.

A revival of a play by Shakespeare. Presented by the Royal Shakespeare Company at the Royal Shakespeare Theatre, Stratford-upon-Avon on April 11, 1972, as the first production of the Roman Season. Designed by Christopher Morley with Ann Curtis. Music by Guy Woolfenden.

Cast included :

Coriolanus	*Ian Hogg*
Menenius	*Mark Dignam*
Cominius	*Clement McCallin*
Volumnia	*Margaret Tyzack*
Virgilia	*Rosemary McHale*
Sicinius Velutus	*Raymond Westwell*
Junius Brutus	*Gerald James*
Tullus Aufidius	*Patrick Stewart*

Directed by Trevor Nunn with Buzz Goodbody assisted by Euan Smith

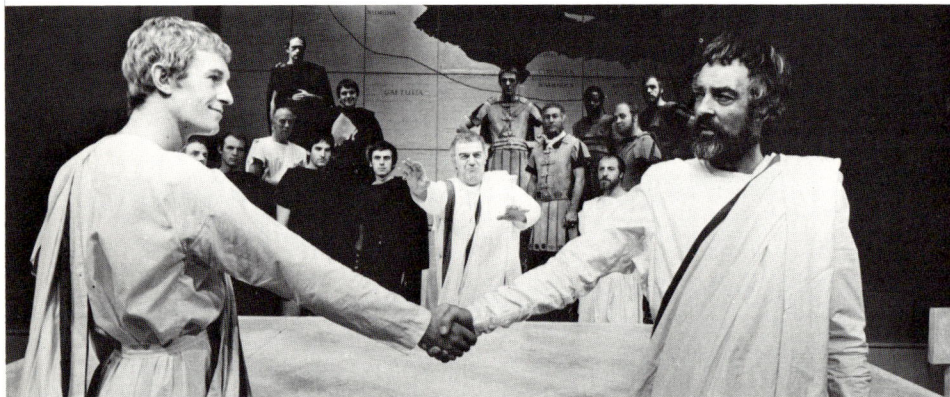

Top: Corin Redgrave as Octavius Caesar, Raymond Westwell as Lepidus and Richard Johnson as Antony in *Antony and Cleopatra*, the third play in the 1972 Roman Season at Stratford-upon-Avon
Bottom: Patrick Stewart as Enobarbus and Janet Suzman as Cleopatra in *Antony and Cleopatra*.
Photographs by Reg Wilson

TITUS ANDRONICUS

The Royal Shakespeare Company concluded their Roman Season with *Titus Andronicus* which Trevor Nunn, assisted by Buzz Goodbody and Euan Smith, presented as a chronicle of realistic horrors.

The actors delivered their lines with a blood and thunder approach which suited the Grand Guignol style of the production. John Wood was most impressive as the neurotic emperor, so was Margaret Tyzack as his terrifying wife. Colin Blakely played the desperate Titus and Janet Suzman the poignant, mangled Lavinia.

A revival of a play by Shakespeare. Presented by the Royal Shakespeare Company at the Royal Shakespeare Theatre, Stratford-upon-Avon on October 12, 1972, as the fourth play in the Roman Season. Designed by Christopher Morley, with Ann Curtis, William Lockwood and Gordon Sumpter. Music by Guy Woolfenden.
Cast included:

Titus Andronicus	.	.		*Colin Blakely*
Marcus Andronicus	.	.		*Mark Digman*
Lucius	.	.	.	*Ian Hogg*
Demetrius	.	.		*Geoffrey Hutchings*
Aaron	.	.	.	*Calvin Lockhart*
Chiron	.	.	.	*Philip Manikum*
Bassianus	.	.	.	*Tim Pigott-Smith*
Lavinia	.	.	.	*Janet Suzman*
Tamora	.	.	.	*Margaret Tyzack*
Saturnius	.	.	.	*John Wood*

Directed by Trevor Nunn with Buzz Goodbody and Euan Smith

34

Top Left : Mark Dignam as Marcus, Colin Blakely as Titus and Janet Suzman as Lavinia in *Titus Andronicus*, the last of Shakespeare's four Roman plays presented by the Royal Shakespeare Company during their 1972 season at Stratford-upon-Avon

Bottom left : Margaret Tyzack as Tamora and John Wood as Saturnius in *Titus Andronicus*
Right : Ian Hogg as Lucius and Calvin Lockhart as Aaron in *Titus Andronicus*. *Photographs by Reg Wilson*

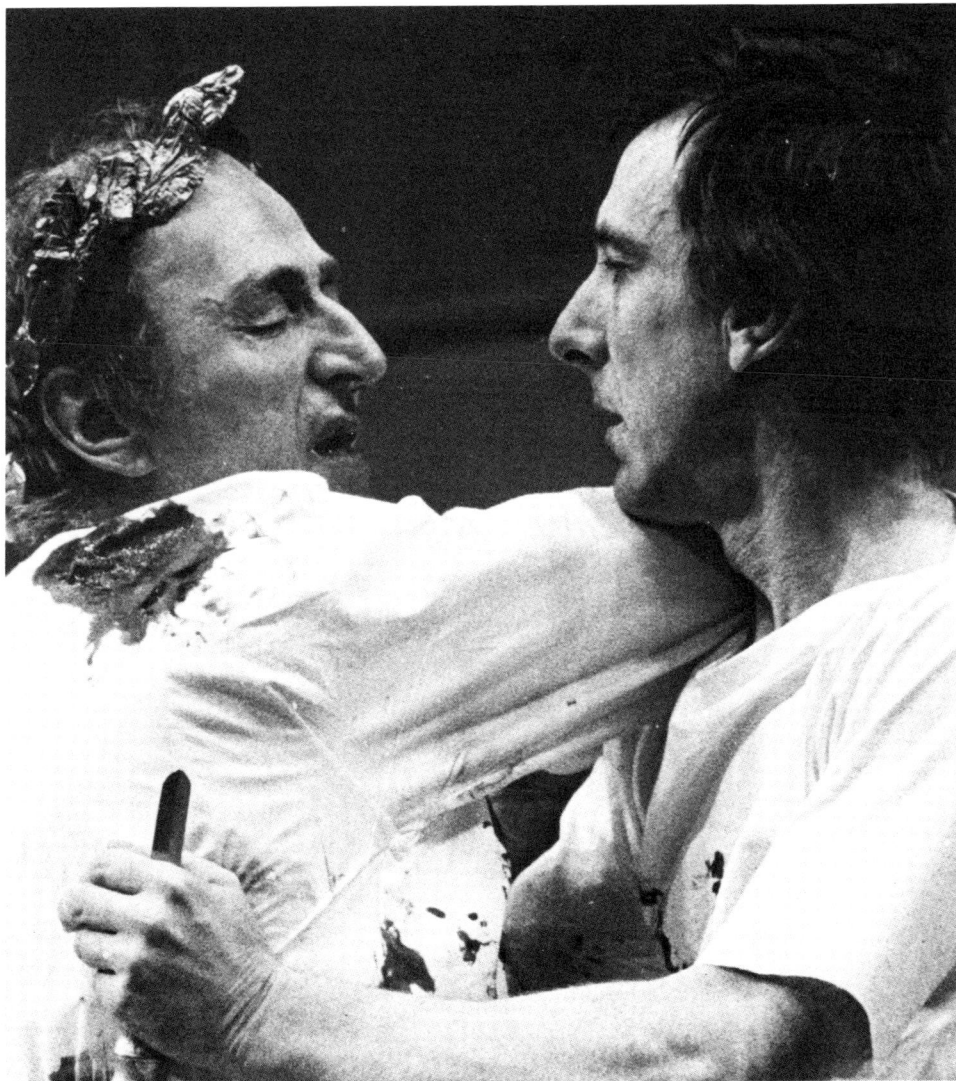

Mark Dignam as Caesar and John Wood as Brutus in Trevor Nunn's production of *Julius Caesar*, the second play in the Royal Shakespeare Company's Roman Season at Stratford-upon-Avon.
Photograph by Reg Wilson

JULIUS CAESAR

Blazing fanfares and royal red carpet ushered in *Julius Caesar*, the second play in the Roman cycle, presented by the Royal Shakespeare Company at Stratford-upon-Avon.

John Wood as the cold-blooded Brutus gained the acting honours of this production. He was hailed by John Barber as a major heroic actor, 'with a twisted face that could belong to an El Greco saint'. Mark Dignam's Caesar was an impressive tyrant; Patrick Stewart's likable Cassius smiled unduly; as Antony, Richard Johnson's funeral oration was splendidly flamboyant and Corin Redgrave's Octavius was icily supercilious.

A revival of a play by Shakespeare. Presented by the Royal Shakespeare Company at the Royal Shakespeare Theatre, Stratford-upon-Avon on May 2, 1972, as the second play in the Roman Season. Designed by Christopher Morley with Ann Curtis. Music by Guy Woolfenden.

Cast included:

Julius Caesar	.	.	*Mark Dignam*
Brutus	.	.	*John Wood*
Cassius	.	.	*Patrick Stewart*
Casca	.	.	*Gerald James*
Mark Antony	.	.	*Richard Johnson*
Octavius Caesar	.	.	*Corin Redgrave*
Portia	.	.	*Margaret Tyzack*
Calpurnia	.	.	*Judy Cornwell*

Directed by Trevor Nunn with Buzz Goodbody, Euan Smith and John Barton

Top left: Richard Johnson as Mark Antony addressing the Citizens in *Julius Caesar*
Bottom left: Phillip Manikum as Decius Brutus, Mark Dignam as Caesar and Judy Cornwell as Calpurnia in *Julius Caesar*
Right: Richard Johnson as Mark Antony with the body of Caesar (Mark Dignam), in *Julius Caesar*.
Photographs by Reg Wilson

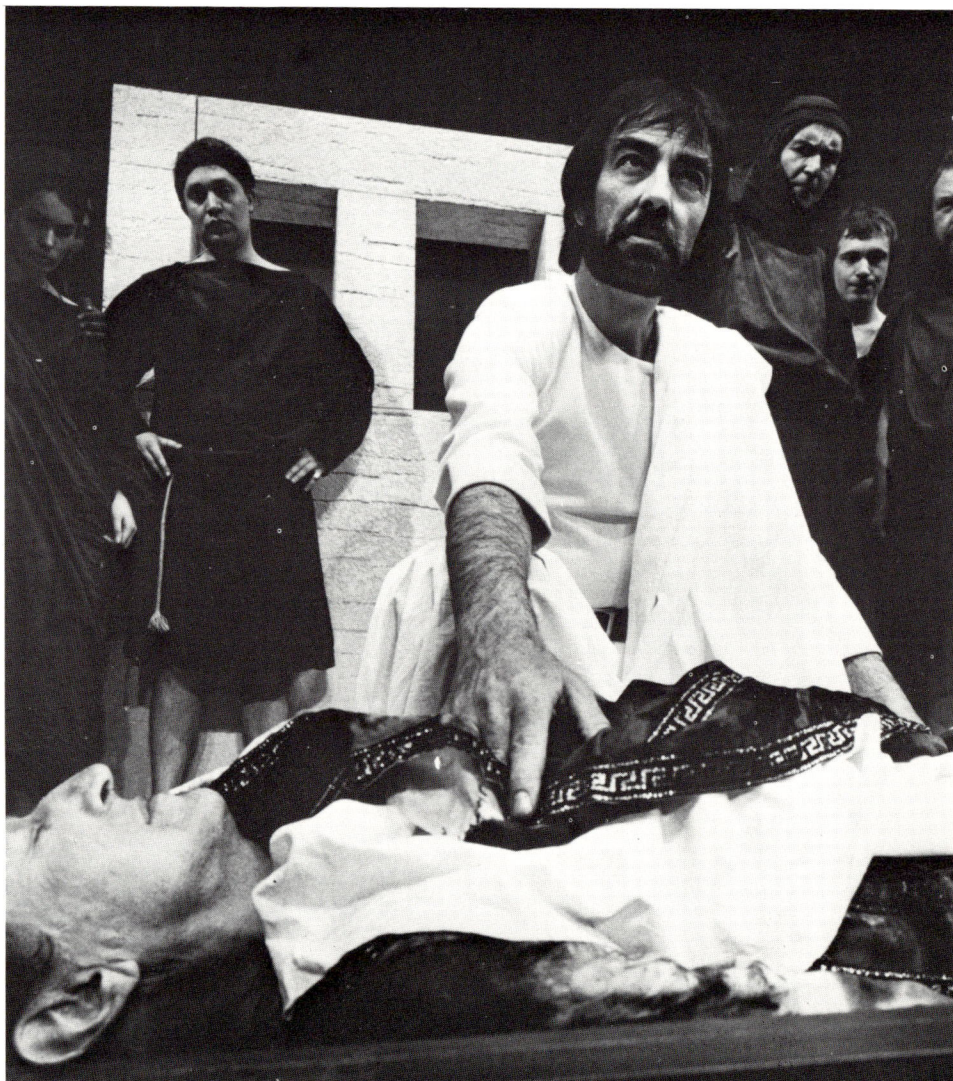

ANTONY AND CLEOPATRA

The brazen din of Trevor Nunn's production of *Antony and Cleopatra* made it one of the most impressive plays in the Roman Season at Stratford-upon-Avon. The designs by Christopher Morley, with purple costumes for the Romans and gold-encrusted rainbow shades for the Egyptians, were seen to fine advantage against the clinical white setting of the new stage. Janet Suzman's uninhibited Cleopatra twisted the ageing Antony round her little finger. She could and did behave like a sex kitten, but at heart she was a creature of supreme intelligence, a fine strategist in the game of power politics. She enhanced the stage picture and introduced some splendid touches of dramatic action into her performance.

Richard Johnson's Antony fell below expectations, but rose to impressive heights in his death-scene. Patrick Stewart, speaking the sublimely beautiful lines allotted to Enobarbus, made this piece of casting one of the highlights of the production. Corin Redgrave's Caesar was too petulant, but Raymond Westwell's Lepidus made a deep impression.

A revival of a play by Shakespeare. Presented by the Royal Shakespeare Company at the Royal Shakespeare Theatre, Stratford-upon-Avon on August 15, 1972, as the third production in their cycle of four Roman plays. Designed by Christopher Morley, with Ann Curtis, William Lockwood and Gordon Sumpter. Music by Guy Woolfenden.

Cast included:

Mark Antony	.	.	*Richard Johnson*
Enobarbus	.	.	*Patrick Stewart*
Cleopatra	.	.	*Janet Suzman*
Charmian	.	.	*Rosemary McHale*
Octavius Caesar	.	.	*Corin Redgrave*
Octavia	.	.	*Judy Cornwell*
Lepidus	.	.	*Raymond Westwell*
Sextus Pompeius	.	.	*Gerald James*

Directed by Trevor Nunn with Buzz Goodbody and Euan Smith

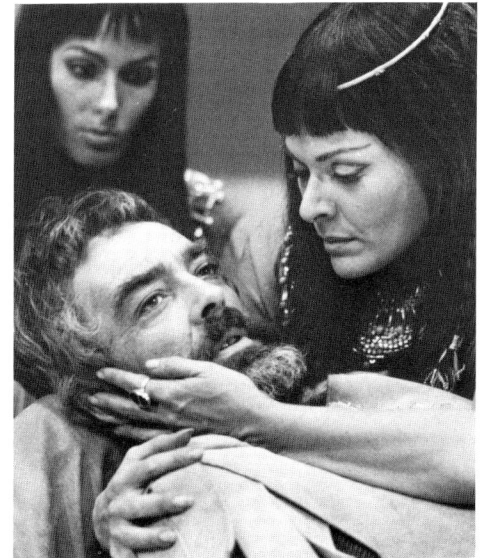

SYBIL THORNDIKE IN HER NINETIES

Eric Johns

I am fortunate to have enjoyed Sybil Thorndike's friendship for more than forty years. The date she celebrated her ninetieth birthday – October 24, 1972 – was a milestone in theatre history. Since making her first professional appearance sixty-eight years ago in the grounds of Downing College, Cambridge, playing Palmis in *The Palace of Truth* in the afternoon and walking-on the same evening in *The Merry Wives of Windsor* with Ben Greet's Pastoral Players, she has never stopped working. Even now, in her ninety-first year, she is playing a prominent part in public life, giving dramatic recitals quite regularly. She is a living legend and a very active one at that.

Once the ninetieth birthday celebrations began to ebb, but before the bouquets had begun to fade, I made my way to her flat high above the roofs of Chelsea for a cosy nostalgic gossip about her remarkable career, which I had followed personally since she first played Shaw's Saint Joan almost a half-century ago.

I wondered when she considered she had 'arrived' as an actress. 'I never felt I had arrived', she protested, 'but I got my first thrill when a distinguished writer on the theatre indicated that England had at last produced a tragedienne.'

Her most rewarding theatrical experiences have been playing Joan, Medea and Hecuba in *The Trojan Women*, but she is quick to add that proud as she is of Joan, she does not place her above the Greeks. When she played Medea and Hecuba during a 1920

matinées-only season at the Holborn Empire – a variety theatre destroyed in the Second World War – she recalls that play-goers converging on the theatre stopped the dense lunchtime traffic – quite a remarkable event in those days – long before London lionized Danny Kaye, Marlene Dietrich and the Beatles. At that time George Robey was topping the evening variety bill and his first line was, 'I can sniff the air of Greece'.

Joan, of course, was a new part and that made it different from the Greek roles. The idea of playing Joan of Arc had always appealed to her and together with her husband, Lewis Casson, she discussed the idea with the poet, Laurence Binyon, and he agreed to write a play for her. Soon afterwards, to the consternation of the Cassons, they read in the Press that Bernard Shaw was writing a play about Joan. Lewis Casson wrote to Shaw about their plans and in reply received one of the famous postcards saying, 'Of course Sybil plays my Joan'. And he named another actress who could play Binyon's. Binyon gallantly withdrew and his play was never written. It then transpired that for some time Mrs Bernard Shaw had been trying to persuade her husband to write a play about Joan and had done valuable research for him by way of encouragement. He hesitated to start writing because he knew no actress who could play the part. Eventually he saw Sybil Thorndike in *The Cenci* and rushed home to Mrs Shaw with the news that he could start writing *Saint Joan* because he had at last seen the actress capable of playing her.

Sybil loves to recall how Shaw helped the cast during rehearsals for the first production. 'He would supervise rehearsals in the mornings and Lewis would take over in the afternoons. Shaw was a better actor than anyone in the cast. He read the play to us with a rich variety of sound. He went through the script with me and indicated the intonations of every single line, so that even now I can read the play like a musical score. We worked together as one person. Almost instinctively I knew what he wanted to say and how he wanted me to say it.'

Sybil Thorndike is very generous with her comments on actresses who played Joan after her. 'There was much to admire in these performances, but they were not Shaw's Joan. Joan Plowright came nearest to it, but she did not have the Belief behind her. The actress playing Joan must be aware that Shaw was a deep and profound believer. Shaw's Joan cannot be played just as a magical theatre part. The Greeks – Medea and Hecuba – are no more than theatre parts, but Joan goes much deeper.'

Shaw, according to Sybil Thorndike, cherished every word he had written. He hated actors to walk about the stage because he thought movement would distract the audience who would therefore miss the full significance of the text. It was left to Lewis Casson in the afternoon rehearsals to inject some action into Shaw's static ideas of production. Shaw even resented the glowing stage pictures designed by Charles Ricketts, feeling they would also tend to distract. He

was at his happiest when members of the
cast were lined up on the stage, speaking
lines without moving or dressing up in
costume. Some sort of compromise was
reached and the opening night turned out to
be the crowning achievement of Sybil
Thorndike's career. 'It is the only time I've
ever been nervous on a first night,' she
admitted, 'but I thought I was on wings, up
in heaven!'

By way of a postscript, Shaw sent her a copy
of the play inscribed – 'To Saint Sybil
Thorndike from Saint Bernard Shaw'. She
has never been a hoarder and has a grand
clear-out of her flat every few years, but this
autographed copy of *Saint Joan* survives and
always goes back on the shelf, being the
most cherished of all her possessions.

'Big tragedy is enormously rewarding,'
maintains Sybil Thorndike, 'but a really good
part is a joy to play, whether it is comedy or
tragedy. When I played Hecuba at the
Holborn Empire just after the First World
War, the old girls from the Waterloo Road,
who had followed my career at the Old Vic
during the war, came to see me and were
deeply moved. They, too, had lost their
husbands and knew what the Greek play
was all about. They identified their own grief
with Hecuba's.'

When playing some of the great classic roles,
such as Lady Macbeth, Jocasta or Volumnia,
I wondered if Sybil Thorndike ever read
accounts of how they had been played by
famous actresses of the past, who had
triumphed in them long before her time. It is
interesting, she agreed, to discover how

Top: Sybil Thorndike with Agatha Christie at a party to celebrate the tenth birthday of *The Mousetrap* at the Ambassadors Theatre. Dame Agatha was being presented with the original script of her play enclosed in a gold cover. *Photograph by Planet News Ltd*
Bottom left: Anna Neagle and Sybil Thorndike congratulating Evelyn Laye on her seventieth birthday in 1970. *Photograph by The Press Association Ltd*

Bottom right: Sybil Thorndike as Isabel Brocken in *The Foolish Gentlewoman* by Margery Sharp at the Duchess Theatre in 1949. *Photograph by Houston Rogers*

Mrs Siddons regarded Lady Macbeth. 'But when I study a part which has been played by other actresses I prefer to approach it quite freshly. You've got to work out your own way first. Then, and only then, is it advisable to research into what contemporaries may have written about earlier performances.'

Elizabeth I is Sybil Thorndike's only unfulfilled ambition. She would love to have played her on the stage. Apart from *Will Shakespeare*, in which Haidée Wright played Elizabeth, Clemence Dane wrote another play about Elizabeth which Sybil Thorndike would like to have played. There were times when it was on the brink of being produced, but something always happened to frustrate the plans. Lewis Casson used to say that from the 'Other Side' Elizabeth herself made sure it would never be staged! Sybil Thorndike and Lewis Casson often performed extracts from this yet-to-be-staged play in those drama recitals they gave all over the world. She much admired the poignant death-scene and Elizabeth's stirring speech to Parliament.

Looking back on changes she has seen in the theatre during her career of nearly seventy years, Sybil Thorndike deplores the deterioration of speech. 'It has changed for the worse,' she says. 'Today actors are more closely identified with the characters they play. Ellen Terry could have done extraordinarily exciting things, had she got away from her own personality, but it never happened because the public would not have accepted her. Times have changed now and

acting is more natural, but in the process words are far too often lost. It is too heavy a price to pay.

'Actors underplay because they are afraid of not being natural. They lose sight of the fact that the theatre is theatrical. Art, like theatre, is bigger than life. It is anything but natural, but it must sound natural. London play-goers first heard natural poised speaking at the Court Theatre during the Granville Barker season at the turn of the century. Actors of today have lost sight of this art.' She considers projection and audibility to be the prime essentials of anyone purporting to be an actor. 'When I used to go to the theatre as a girl I cannot remember a single occasion when I was unable to hear the words spoken on the stage. Much as I hate to say it, because I admire so much that is being done by the younger generation of actors today, they are not as vocally efficient as beginners in my day. They are too afraid of being called ham. That is the root of the problem. What good is an actor incapable of projecting his lines and failing to communicate to the audience? He might just as well play his part in a locked room with the blinds drawn.'

Sybil Thorndike greatly admired John Gielgud and Ralph Richardson in David Storey's *Home*, as two patients in a mental home. They used their imagination brilliantly and gave amazingly natural performances, but in her opinion this would not have been possible without the long years both these actors spent playing the classics. Discussing John Gielgud, she considers his first Hamlet at the Old Vic in 1930 to be the ultimate one.

A painful arthritic complaint handicaps Sybil Thorndike's mobility these days; she has considerable difficulty in lowering herself into a chair and in getting up again, but she refuses to be defeated by it. When I entered her flat for our chat, she called out a cheery welcome, even before I reached the open door of her sitting-room, adding 'I can't get up to greet you, dear, because it would take me half-an-hour and another half-hour to get down again!' Her blue eyes sparkled and she was obviously well aware of what was

45

happening in the world and retained the infectious enthusiasm of a young girl.

She still takes an active part in public life. She goes to all the West End plays likely to interest her; she is even content to sit on the hard wooden seats at the Young Vic because 'that is my kind of theatre'. She goes as far afield as the Sheffield Crucible Theatre to see what is happening in the regions. Nothing deters her.

She misses foreign travel, which meant so much to her in her younger days. On the night she and Lewis Casson celebrated their fiftieth year on the stage they left the cast of *A Day by the Sea* at the Haymarket Theatre for a four-year recital tour which covered 60,000 miles, taking them to Australia, New Zealand, South Africa, India and Turkey. At that time she was seventy-two and her husband was seventy-nine.

'We were always strolling players at heart and enjoyed being on the road much more than playing in a comfortable long run in the West End. I always had a passion for travel and our drama recitals meant I could realize my ambition and let the expense be paid by a theatre management. It meant I could see the sun rise over Everest and admire the skyline of Istanbul, which held a magic spell for me, ever since my girlhood when it was called Constantinople.'

During the Second World War, with a handful of barn-storming enthusiasts, the Cassons took *Macbeth* and *Medea* to the Welsh mining towns, playing one-night stands, often in places where there was no such thing as a conventional theatre. In some towns there was not even a hotel, so they had to be 'put up' by local bigwigs, who entertained them to supper with other local celebrities. The Cassons were expected to sparkle at table, even though they were often dropping with fatigue and had to face another long and uncomfortable journey the following day, only to face the same ordeal all over again. Even so, they never complained. They were never happier; they were together and they were taking drama to theatreless towns in the middle of the War. What could be more worth while?

'I want to go on. I don't want to hark back!' insisted Sybil, after reminiscing about her early career, and immediately proceeded to consider which items to include in a drama recital she had agreed to give at St Thomas's Hospital, some time after her ninetieth birthday. There was no question of resting on her laurels in the friendly Chelsea flat which had been her home for so many years.

Just before her ninetieth birthday, she sang my praises at a lunch arranged by close friends to surprise me on the occasion of my retirement from the editorship of *The Stage*. She gave a tremendous oration, much to the delight and amusement of the guests. We drove back to Chelsea together afterwards and I suggested she would probably welcome a quiet afternoon with her feet up. 'Oh, no!' she protested. 'I think I'll read *The Trojan Women* in the original Greek!' In other words, she intends to go on! And no one is going to stop her.

THE ALBERY THEATRE

The New Theatre in St Martin's Lane was renamed the Albery Theatre on New Year's Day, 1973, as a tribute to the memory of Sir Bronson Albery who presided over the fortunes of that famous West End theatre for so many years. Sir Bronson was the son of the popular Victorian dramatist James Albery and his actress-wife, Mary Moore, who later married Sir Charles Wyndham. It was Sir Charles Wyndham who built what is now the Albery Theatre in 1903 on a piece of land at the back of Wyndham's Theatre, which he had built four years earlier. Both Mary Moore and Charles Wyndham appeared in the revival of *Rosemary* by Louis N Parker and Murray Carson which opened the New Theatre seventy years ago. At one time she directed the management, which was later relegated to her son Bronson. Today Bronson's son and grandson, Donald and Ian Albery, are responsible for the business side of this house which has such a distinguished past.

Johnston Forbes-Robertson was seen there in the early days in *The Light That Failed*, the famous Edwardian tear-jerker. Fred Terry and Julia Neilson presented the first London performance of *The Scarlet Pimpernel* in 1905 and proceeded to play it in and out of London for more than twenty years.

Few play-goers in this country realize the great American actress, Katharine Cornell, played on the London stage. She did, at the New Theatre in 1919, when she appeared as Jo in a matinées-only season of *Little Women* while Lilian Braithwaite was playing in a different production during the evenings.

She insisted upon Katharine Cornell using her dressing-room for the four or five matinées a week when *Little Women* was performed. The dressing-rooms were very crowded because the crinolines of the Louisa M Alcott play took up so much space and the wardrobes were already full of costumes being used by the players appearing at night. London never saw Cornell again. Her two great Broadway triumphs were Shaw's Saint Joan and Elizabeth Moulton-Barrett in *The Barretts of Wimpole Street*. Both these parts had been immaculately played in London by Sybil Thorndike and Gwen Ffrangcon-Davies respectively and no doubt Cornell feared to challenge comparison. When John Gielgud played Macbeth in London in 1942 he invited Cornell to appear as Lady Macbeth in his own production, but she refused because she feared crossing the Atlantic in the middle of the Second World War.

The year after the one and only Cornell Season Noël Coward appeared at the New Theatre in *I'll Leave It To You*, the first play of his to be produced. Mary Moore presented the play which only ran for five weeks, but it gave the young dramatist enormous confidence. Soon afterwards, Matheson Lang took over the theatre with such memorable productions as *Carnival*, *Othello*, with Hilda Bayley as his Desdemona, *Blood and Sand* and *The Wandering Jew*. Perhaps the most historic first night in the history of the New was March 26, 1924, when London first saw Sybil Thorndike in Bernard Shaw's *Saint Joan*, which proved to

be the crowning achievement of her career. 'It is the only time I have ever been nervous on a first night,' she confessed. 'I thought I was on wings, up in heaven!'

Two years later *The Constant Nymph*, with Edna Best in the name-part, was the great draw for almost 600 performances. Noël Coward played Lewis Dodd, the hero, but at that time he was suffering from nervous exhaustion, due to over-work. He played one of the performances through tears which he could not control, to the astonishment of the audience and the horror of his fellow-players. When he finally collapsed after the show, the part was taken over by John Gielgud.

Gielgud more or less moved into the New Theatre in the 1930s. He drew the town with Gwen Ffrangcon-Davies in *Richard of Bordeaux* and in 1934 played Hamlet to the Gertrude of Laura Cowie, Ophelia of Jessica Tandy, Polonius of George Howe, Claudius of Frank Vosper, Laertes of Glen Byam Shaw and the Osric of Alec Guinness. The following year came Gielgud's own production of *Romeo and Juliet*, in which he and Laurence Olivier alternated the roles of Romeo and Mercutio to the Juliet of Peggy Ashcroft and the Nurse of Edith Evans. Alec Guinness played the small part of the Apothecary. To round off the thirties, Edith Evans was seen on the New stage as Agatha Payne in *The Old Ladies*, that macabre Hugh Walpole story dramatized by Rodney Ackland, Rosalind in *As You Like It* and Katherine in *The Taming of the Shrew*. During the Second World War the New

Theatre housed the Old Vic Company and the Sadler's Wells Ballet, as the home theatres of both these organizations had been bombed. Robert Helpmann turned actor and played the Prince of Denmark in *Hamlet* and Beryl Grey on her fifteenth birthday in 1943 danced Odette-Odile in the full-length *Swan Lake*. Before the Old Vic Company left the New to return to the Old Vic after the War Laurence Olivier and Sybil Thorndike played Oedipus and Jocasta and Olivier was seen as Lear, with Pamela Brown as Goneril, Margaret Leighton as Regan, Joyce Redman as Cordelia and Alec Guinness as the Fool.

In more recent years Australia sent her best play, Ray Lawler's *Summer of the Seventeenth Doll* to the New. Yvonne Arnaud was there in *Dear Charles*, Charles Laughton was in *The Party*, with young Albert Finney, and Katharine Hepburn made her first appearance on the London stage as The Lady in *The Millionairess* by Shaw, with Robert Helpmann as the Doctor. Lionel Bart's Dickens musical, *Oliver!*, broke lots of New Theatre records during its run of 2,618 performances. The Royal Shakespeare Company's production of *London Assurance* by Dion Boucicault, with Donald Sinden at his most amusing, was the last long run enjoyed at the New before the name changed to the Albery Theatre at the beginning of this year.

NEW THEATRE:
THE MERCURY THEATRE AT COLCHESTER

On a fine May evening in 1972 Colchester play-goers attended the opening night of their new £250,000 Mercury Theatre to see a sparkling production of the Restoration comedy *The Recruiting Officer* by George Farquhar.

The people of Colchester obviously wanted a theatre and it was because hundreds of residents were determined their town should possess one that the enchanting Mercury Theatre came into being. This modern playhouse has been erected on the crest of the hill, nestling cosily between Jumbo, the picturesque Victorian water-tower, and the Balkerne Gate, which has miraculously survived from the days of the Roman Occupation of Britain. It was the comparatively small sums of money subscribed by local people which made it all possible.

In 1937 Robert Digby and Beatrice Radley founded the Colchester Repertory Company, then housed in a converted art gallery at the top of the High Street. By the time of the War it had become a well-established weekly repertory theatre, drawing audiences not only from the town, but from outlying rural areas and surrounding country towns. It flourished under the able leadership of Robert Digby for twenty years and was a founder member of the Council of Repertory Theatres. Television began to affect attendances in the early 1960s. A time of crisis came in 1963, with the untimely death of Robert Digby, and when David Forder came from Coventry to administer the company, the

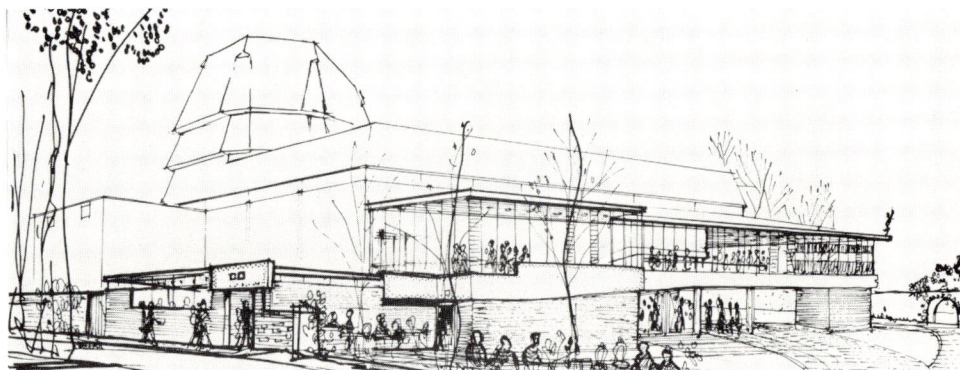

future of the theatre looked very bleak. Under David Forder's leadership, attendances doubled within two years and a change was made to three weekly productions, but even so, it became apparent that a new theatre building was the only hope of long-term salvation. A campaign for a new theatre was sparked off in 1966 by the loss of all backstage premises at the theatre, apart from dressing-rooms, as a result of neighbouring development. A new era dawned when Colchester Borough Council granted a site for the new Mercury, in the centre of the town at a peppercorn rent and they also granted £60,000, providing a similar sum could be raised from public appeal – just to prove Colchester residents really wanted a theatre. The Colchester New Theatre Trust came into being under the chairmanship of Lord Alport and plans for the new playhouse were drawn up by the Colchester architect, Norman Downie, with Christopher Morley, Head of Design for the Royal Shakespeare

Company, acting as Theatre Consultant. The Arts Council stepped in with a contribution of £80,000 making an initial budget of £200,000.

The prospect fired the imagination and the enthusiasm of the local population, who contributed their £60,000 in less than a year. Colchester has almost no industry; there were no big businesses to be coaxed into giving princely sums towards the new venture. The fund consisted mostly of small sums and in many cases contributions were given by residents who rarely get an opportunity to go to the theatre because of the nature of their work. But they believed a theatre would make Colchester a more attractive place in which to live.

The Mercury, still under the guidance of David Forder, Managing Director, has large picture windows, commanding spacious views of the surrounding countryside and a large paved forecourt provides space for an open-air café, with sunshade tables in the summer months. Inside, the Mercury has a

Left: David Forder, managing director of Colchester's new Mercury Theatre with Norman Downie, the architect, Christopher Morley, the theatre consultant, and Olga Richards, the theatre manager, admiring the figure of Mercury poised on the roof of the playhouse

Right: Brian Walton as Captain Brazen, Gillian McCutcheon as Silvia, Michael Robbins as Sgt. Kite and Matthew Long as Captain Plume in George Farquhar's *The Recruiting Officer*, David Buxton's opening production at Colchester's Mercury Theatre

restaurant, coffee-bar and exhibition space, as well as an attractive studio to serve as a rehearsal room and as a centre for young people's theatre activities, experimental work and studio productions by interested local amateurs.

The design of the stage and auditorium makes a flexible actor–audience relationship possible. The form of the auditorium and its relationship with the stage can be altered, giving either an open stage, with no proscenium at all and some degree of thrust into an audience of 500, or an end stage with wings and curtain with a narrower opening, facing an audience of about 410.

The seating is what has become known as Continental in style – in single tier with unbroken rows. The rows are sufficiently wide apart to make it unnecessary for an already-seated member of the audience to have to stand up to allow anyone to pass him in order to occupy a seat beyond.

THE BANKSIDE GLOBE PLAYHOUSE

In view of the fact that Sam Wanamaker is Chicago born, it may seem remarkable to find him the leading spirit of a movement to build a unique permanent theatre on the bank of the Thames at Southwark, more or less on the site of the original Globe Playhouse which opened in 1599 and saw the world premières of most of Shakespeare's plays.

Since becoming an established leading player on both sides of the Atlantic, Sam Wanamaker has played only two Shakespearean roles – Iago at Stratford-upon-Avon in 1959 and Macbeth in Chicago five years later. So it comes as something of a surprise to discover he played some 800 times in various Shakespeare plays at the beginning of his acting career in America as a member of the Globe Shakespearean Theatre Group.

In Cleveland, Ohio in 1937, an Elizabethan Globe Theatre was reconstructed at the Great Lakes Fair and a repertoire of nine Shakespeare plays was directed by B Iden Payne. Sam Wanamaker appeared in all of them, but his most vivid recollections are of *A Midsummer Night's Dream*, *Henry VIII*, *The Taming of the Shrew*, *As You Like It* and *The Comedy of Errors*. As a result of this engagement he became intensely interested in Elizabethan playhouses.

In the 1930s there were several other reconstructed Globe Theatres in America in such cities as San Francisco, San Diego, Dallas and Chicago. So when Sam Wanamaker came to London to make his début on the English stage as Bernie Dodd in *Winter Journey* at the St James's Theatre in 1952, he took the first opportunity to go to Southwark to see what we had erected on the site of the theatre which saw the first performance of *Hamlet* with Richard Burbage in the name-part in 1602. He was amazed and disappointed to discover nothing more than a plaque marking the site.

As a result of this unrewarding pilgrimage, Sam Wanamaker thought he would like to mark the existence of Shakespeare's Globe in a more spectacular and permanent fashion and that is how, in the course of time, he became the Executive Director of the Globe Playhouse Trust, which intends to reclaim the Thames bank at Southwark.

The Trust took its first step in July 1972, when a temporary playhouse called the Bankside Globe, seating 700 people, was erected near the original sites of the sixteenth century Globe Theatre and the Bear Gardens.

Thanks to the generosity of John Player & Sons of Nottingham, the first season ran from July 1 to September 9 and was known as the John Player Season. The Greater London Council also contributed a welcome £5,000. So encouraging was the public response, Players agreed to provide an increased guarantee of £35,000 to enable the Globe Playhouse Trust to present a second and longer season in 1973.

The temporary Bankside Globe Playhouse is Sam Wanamaker's first step towards realizing his dream of building a permanent theatre on the site of the original Globe, which was destroyed by fire in 1613 as the result of a cannon being fired during a performance of *Henry VIII* and setting light to the thatched roof over the stage and galleries. It was rebuilt the following year with a tiled roof, so Wanamaker's Globe will be the third theatre to rise on the bank of the Thames at Southwark.

The 1972 season opened with the Sheffield Crucible Theatre Company playing *The Shoemaker's Holiday* by Thomas Dekker, with Douglas Campbell taking the leading part of Simon Eyre. Later in the season the Crucible Company were seen in Douglas Campbell's production of *A Man For All Seasons* by Robert Bolt.

The Northcott Theatre Company from Exeter brought the fourteenth century *Cornish Passion Play*, adapted by Kevin Robinson; the Phoenix Opera Company performed *The Beggar's Opera*, and there were performances of *Brief Lives*, Roy Dotrice's one-man triumph, adapted and directed by Patrick Garland; the National Theatre mobile production of John Ford's *'Tis Pity She's A Whore*, with Diana Rigg, Anna Carteret and Nicholas Clay in the cast; and *Pleasure and Repentance*, a light-hearted look at love, devised and directed by Terry Hands, with Brenda Bruce, Adrian Harman, Brewster Mason and Ian Richardson in the cast of this Royal Shakespeare Company's Theatregoround production. The season closed with a new production of *Hamlet*, directed by Peter Coe with Keith Michell as the Prince.

Peter Coe chose to stage his *Hamlet* in modern dress because he believes this is the

A model of the Bankside Globe Playhouse erected on the banks of the Thames at Southwark near the site of the original Globe which flourished in Shakespeare's day. The new temporary theatre, seating 700 people, presented a ten-week season in 1972, when Keith Michell played Hamlet in modern dress

Douglas Campbell as Simon Eyre in the Sheffield Crucible Theatre's production of *The Shoemaker's Holiday*, which opened the ten-week John Player Season at the temporary Bankside Globe Playhouse at Southwark

only way to present Shakespeare. 'It is simply a question of finding a place where the events of the play could happen today.' So he decided upon a military state and when his production of the play opened, Claudius had engineered a *coup d'état* and seized power by military means, thus preventing Hamlet from succeeding his father.

In Peter Coe's opinion *Hamlet* is relevant to Man's dilemma in the twentieth century; his total frustration and impotence in the face of world events. Claudius was played by Donald Houston, Gertrude by Helen Cherry, Ophelia by Carolyn Seymour, Horatio by Gary Raymond, Laertes by Peter Harlowe and the Ghost by Ralph Nossek. Ron Moody doubled as Polonius and the First Gravedigger. Robert Bahl

designed the setting and Ingeborg the costumes.

It was gratifying to discover at the end of the season some 85,000 enthusiasts attended cultural events on the Southwark Bank, where the ten-week John Player Season at the temporary Globe Playhouse was the chief attraction.

The end of the first season seemed an appropriate moment for Sam Wanamaker to remind us of the nine specific aims of the Globe Playhouse Trust, which in essence are:

1 To reclaim Southwark's Thames Bank from a wilderness of warehouses.
2 To propose a redevelopment plan to promote Bankside into becoming an area of culture, education and entertainment.
3 To construct a third Globe Playhouse on or near its original site.
4 To produce the plays of Shakespeare and his contemporaries in the third Globe Playhouse and elsewhere.
5 To found and administer a world centre for Shakespeare studies as a higher educational institute.
6 To establish a library and museum, containing relevant material on the Elizabethan theatre and its dramatic achievements.
7 To encourage and facilitate the study of music from the fifteenth to the seventeenth century.
8 To establish a Shakespeare Birthday Fund which would commission new works of music, poetry, drama and art.
9 To promote and organize in London, particularly in Southwark, plays, concerts, musicals, theatre, exhibitions, film festivals, lectures, recitals and performances relating to Shakespeare, his period, the Elizabethan theatre and the history of England.

Sam Wanamaker regarded the first John Player Season and other artistic events of 1972 in Southwark as a giant step towards achieving the various goals outlined in the nine aims of the Globe Playhouse Trust and the events of that first summer demonstrated their ability to contribute creatively to the cultural and educational fabric of the community.

As far as the permanent Bankside Globe Playhouse is concerned, after much discussion between scholars, architects and

The temporary Bankside Globe Playhouse where
the first John Player Season was presented during
the summer of 1972.   *Photograph by Peggy Leder*

Donald Houston as Claudius, Helen Cherry as Gertrude and Keith Michell as Hamlet in Peter Coe's modern dress production of *Hamlet* at the Bankside Globe Playhouse during the 1972 season. *Photograph by Peggy Leder*

men of the theatre regarding the ideal shape and size, Sam Wanamaker assures us the ground will be broken at the end of 1974 and the theatre will present its first season in the winter of 1975.

Sam Wanamaker hastens to explain he has no intention of making a theatrical home for himself at the new Globe or becoming its artistic dictator. The theatre will be run by the Trust by appointed artistic directors. If they care to invite Mr Wanamaker to act there or to direct productions, he will be delighted to consider their suggestions in the light of his other professional commitments.

Being an American, Wanamaker is rather modest about playing Shakespeare on the English stage. John Barrymore is still regarded as one of the finest Hamlets seen in London within living memory, but Mr Wanamaker is quick to point out he is no Barrymore, but he is encouraged to observe Richard Chamberlain, another fine American actor, has been accepted as Hamlet over here, even without the blazing Barrymore genius.

Antony in *Antony and Cleopatra* and Coriolanus are two parts Sam Wanamaker would consider playing, but he admits he no longer has the same passion to act as he had in his younger days. Producing interests him far more. On his own admission he could never have played Lear, but he would dearly love to direct a production of this tragedy which has fascinated him throughout his adult years. *The Tempest* is another play he would enjoy directing.

Ron Moody rehearsing his part as the First
Gravedigger in Peter Coe's production of *Hamlet*
at the Bankside Globe Playhouse

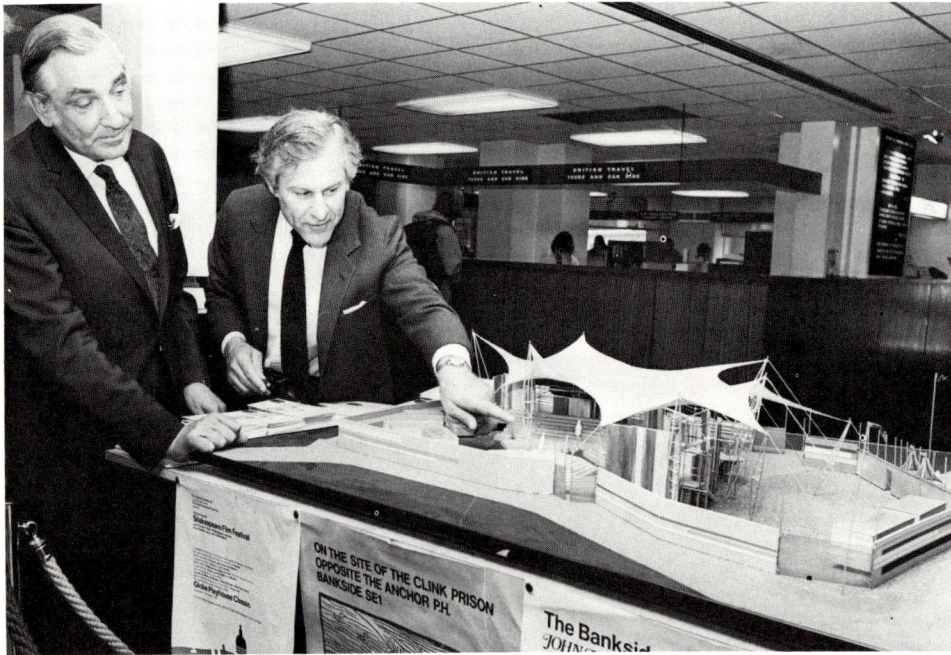

Martin Agnew of the American Express with Sam Wanamaker who is explaining a model of the temporary Bankside Globe Playhouse. *Photograph by Keystone Press*

Each season at the permanent Bankside Globe he would like to arrange for the presentation of a fairly well-researched reconstruction of a sixteenth century production of a Shakespeare play, using similar costumes, props and mode of speech. He considers it would be of immense interest academically and to the play-going public. It would unashamedly be a museum-piece and no more than one play would receive this treatment during any one season. A different play could be chosen every year until most of the Shakespearean repertoire had been covered.

Henry VIII would be the ideal choice for the play to open the new Globe, since it is historical and relates to London, Mr Wanamaker likes to think that Henry used to go to Southwark to see the bear-baiting, as did his daughter Elizabeth. It was also the last play to be performed at the original Globe.

Fascinated by Peter Brook's world-famous Royal Shakespeare Company production of *A Midsummer Night's Dream*, Sam Wanamaker would like to see modern reinterpretations of the classics on the Bankside Globe stage. Ben Jonson's

Bartholomew Fair would be ideally suitable to combine the best of sixteenth century presentation with our modern equivalent and in relation to Southwark Fair it could be seen as a romp and an improvisation. London will eventually have three arts complexes, with the National Theatre and the concert halls on the South Bank, the Royal Shakespeare Company and yet another concert hall in the Barbican and the Bankside Globe at Southwark. Sam Wanamaker is full of admiration for the large number of excellent actors in this country and does not need to be reminded that there are more than enough not under contract to either the National Theatre or the Royal Shakespeare Company, to make an impressive team at the Bankside Globe, where the repertoire would consist entirely of the classics and modern reinterpretations of them.

The future looks rosy enough. The novelty has worn off television, now an accepted part of our way of life. Gone are the days when people remained at home, glued to their sets lest they missed anything. They are now ready to go out in the evening and going to the theatre is one of the most enjoyable of all social activities.

Shaftesbury Avenue and Broadway prove that the theatre feeds on a multiplicity of theatres and the South Bank, the Barbican and Bankside are likely to offer an abundance of cultural activity, in three specific areas of London which will become the unquestioned artistic capital of the world.

58

THE NEW LONDON THEATRE AND BERNARD DELFONT

Photograph on the previous page of the New London Centre in Drury Lane which contains the New London Theatre, restaurant, flats, showrooms, shops and multi-storey underground car park

Photo below and on opposite page illustrate two aspects of the New London Theatre in Drury Lane, showing the conventional auditorium and stage and the front stalls transposed on the giant revolve to form a complete theatre-in-the-round

One of London's lost theatres, the Winter Garden in Drury Lane, which closed in 1959, was replaced by the New London Theatre which opened on the same site on January 11, 1973, with Peter Ustinov playing the leading part of the Archbishop in his own play, *The Unknown Soldier and His Wife*, which he also directed.

The Winter Garden occupied a site of genuine historic interest, having in its turn replaced the Middlesex Music Hall. Before that the Old Mo, the Great Mogul Tavern, stood on the same spot and there had been licensed premises at 167 Drury Lane since the reign of the first Elizabeth – an unbroken tradition of singing and dancing for more than 400 years. Nell Gwynn lived close by before she became an orange-wench at Drury Lane's Theatre Royal where she turned the head of Charles II.

Upon this historic patch of theatreland the New London Theatre, which carries on rich stage traditions, is part of an elaborate complex which includes a playhouse seating 911, a multi-storey car park to accommodate 500 vehicles, a 400-seat restaurant, numerous bars and lounges, together with shops and flats.

Described as Europe's most modern new theatre, the New London embodies revolutionary concepts in theatre design, and is administered by EMI under the personal supervision of Bernard Delfont. An escalator conveys the public from the street level to the theatre's main reception foyer, immediately beneath and behind the rake of the auditorium. Here there is a vast comfortable lounge area where patrons can drink and chat before taking their seats. The New London has been described as a theatre that moves. Stage, seats, lights and even the walls can be made to change position. Consequently, totally different types of production can be presented in entirely different ways within a matter of hours of each other. Directors of theatre productions will not be restricted by the limitations of either proscenium or in-the-round premises because at the New London the use of modern technology makes both possible.

Almost one-third of the theatre floor is built on a 60-feet-wide revolve which accommodates the stage, the orchestra pit and the first eight rows of the 911 seats. The walls along more than half the theatre length are faced with movable panels extending from floor to ceiling. These are made to track and pivot in such a way that the shape of the auditorium can be completely changed. In a normal proscenium setting, those at the edge of the stage turn to form the wings and proscenium opening, while the remainder open out into a trumpet shape, merging with the walls of the main auditorium.

At the throw of a switch, all these elements –

stage, seats, orchestra pit and walls –
silently change their position to transform
the theatre into an amphitheatre.

In a matter of four minutes the revolve turns
through 180 degrees, bringing the stage to
the centre of the auditorium and the front
stalls to where the back-drop had been. All
of these 206 seats are then raised by
electrically operated screw-jacks to a
steeper angle of raking. The wall panels slide
and pivot into an unbroken half-circle at the
back of the theatre. The ceiling, composed of
louvered panels like a horizontal Venetian
blind, can be opened up to allow lights to
project through and scenery to be lowered

onto any part of the stage below.
Everything on the main revolve is movable.
The orchestra pit across its centre is made
up of three simple elevators, any of which,
when raised to floor level, can reduce the
size of the pit for smaller groups of musicians.
Accommodating just over 900 people, the
New London is not a small theatre, but by
massing the seating radially around the focal
point of the stage, the designers have
achieved an atmosphere of intimacy that
belies the size of the auditorium.

No seat, including those in the circle, is
remote from the stage, and carefully defined
sight-lines will ensure that the audience will

have a clear, uninterrupted view of the
performance.

Dressing-rooms are arranged on four floors
at one side of the theatre, with a lift giving
access across to the stage. The star dressing-
rooms, together with a spacious Green
Room, are at stage level.

A night out at the New London can start in
the underground car park. With a straight
drive-in it prevents the frustration of trying
to find street parking space; something that
can mar the enjoyment of an evening,
especially on a wet night. Parking space can
be booked at the same time as theatre seats
are reserved. From the car park, lifts carry
patrons to the main entrance foyer, where
cloakrooms and box-office are situated.
From this level an escalator reaches up to
the main reception foyer.

A late-night meal at the New London Centre
Restaurant completes a night out, all under
the same roof. Midnight cabaret, featuring
one notable artist, rather than a production
show, adds to the occasion.

While Sean Kenny and Ernest Chew were
involved in the production and development
of the theatre design, the architect in charge,
with ultimate responsibility for the theatre
and restaurant, was Michael Percival. The
architect of the New London Centre, of
which the New London Theatre is a vital
part, was Paul Tvrtkovic, who trained at the
University of Zagreb.

For the opening production, Bernard
Delfont decided upon the London
première of *The Unknown Soldier and His Wife*,
Peter Ustinov's exposure of the futility of

Bernard Delfont, Director of the New London
Theatre

war, presented in a series of episodes from the times of the Romans to our own day. It was directed by Mr Ustinov who made an impressive figure as the Archbishop who had so much to answer for in the name of war. Highly delighted with his new toy, Bernard Delfont says it is the most exciting theatre he has ever controlled, and without being able to give any hard and fast details of future plans, he has definite ideas regarding policy. His aim is to keep seat prices low enough to prevent theatre-going from becoming a luxury. He insists upon catering to various income groups so that those only able to budget a modest amount for entertainment can still afford to buy a seat at the New London.

He has given consideration to the idea of putting a permanent company into the New London and creating what he calls a commercial national theatre. This could be effected without state aid because the New London is partly subsidized by being used for conferences and for other purposes during the daytime when most playhouses are lying idle and not helping to earn their own keep. These daytime activities in no way interfere with theatre-goers because they are over long before the curtain rises for the evening performance.

The geographical position of a theatre, in Mr Delfont's estimation, is no longer as important as it used to be. The old Winter Garden, which occupied the New London site, was considered off the beaten track towards the end of its existence, but cars have now put all theatres on the map and the New London caters to car-owner-patrons by offering parking facilities under the same roof as the theatre itself.

In the past *Witness for the Prosecution* and *No Room at the Inn* were both popular successes at the Winter Garden, but Mr Delfont has an idea they were presented at the then out-of-the-way theatre at the top of Drury Lane only because no other stage was available. In the new mechanized age, he likes to think managements will choose Drury Lane's New London Theatre because it is an attractive playhouse with its own unique atmosphere and not because it is the only place which happens to be vacant. The Common Market countries open up new possibilities, and Mr Delfont is confident that excellent light entertainment from the Continent can be presented at the New London, as well as more serious fare. This need not queer the pitch of the World Theatre Seasons of Peter Daubeny when he resumes his role of London's leading international impresario after taking a much needed rest at the end of his tenth season in 1973.

ANGELS AND THEIR MONEY

John de Lannoy

Sometimes plays become such popular successes they take root and occupy the same theatre for years at a stretch. Apart from the phenomenal *Mousetrap*, which enters its twenty-second year at the Ambassadors Theatre this winter, there have been several remarkably long runs in the West End in recent years – *Sleuth*, *Hair*, *Canterbury Tales*, *There's a Girl in My Soup*, *The Secretary Bird*, *How the Other Half Loves*, *The Black and White Minstrel Show*, *Boeing-Boeing* and *My Fair Lady*. Some of these shows have earned fantastic fortunes, comparable with bumper wins on the Pools, particularly when swollen by film rights amounting to tens of thousands.

Who benefits from the financial results of a smash-hit in the theatre? Apart from the author, the actors and the management? What about the backers – the so-called 'Angels' – who put up the money in order that the play can be seen in the first instance? Who are these people who enjoy having a flutter in the theatre, just as others like slipping along to the betting-shop?

Whenever a story appears in the Press concerning a show making a fortune, many wonder just who puts up the money and how an outsider could get a chance to invest a few pounds in a promising new show. In most cases, the names of Angels who back shows are a closely guarded secret. They are not normally publicized by the management who invite them to invest. Private backers might be described as a group of fairly wealthy people who happen to be bitten by the theatre bug. Few of them invest more than £500 in a show, but they may put money into more than one show at a time. They are mostly regular theatre-goers, but before they decide to part with money they must be inspired by the name of the author or the star who has agreed to play the leading part. In other words, the management must have something to offer which looks like a potential success. A new play by an unheard-of author without the support of a well-known actor or actress is not likely to attract a penny, but if as good a box-office name as Robert Morley is seen to appear in the show, there will be little difficulty in raising the money to put it on. The management cannot rely entirely upon this comparatively small group of affluent people to put up all the money for a new production. Leading theatre managements, such as Howard & Wyndham, might be sufficiently interested to contribute quite a considerable sum. And then there are people in what might be called the leisure industries who may have made money out of, shall we say, recordings, and have thus acquired a pool of capital. As a case in point, last Christmas David Frost presented *Once Upon a Time . . .*, a new children's play based on nursery rhyme characters, at the Duke of York's Theatre, though he took no personal part in the actual show.

Rival managements often invest £200 to £300 in a new show. This sort of contribution might be called spy-money in the profession because it is a means of other organizations getting their hands on a copy of the box-office figures to learn just how well or badly the new production is doing. Big industry might be expected to invest surplus profits in the theatre, but this is only a rare occurrence, possibly because it is difficult to get company board members to agree to such a step. Shareholders could protest vehemently.

There is no question of making a regular living out of investment in the theatre. It is as much a gambler's world as horse-racing. Backers are people prepared to write off their money the moment they sign the cheque and forget all about it. If they make any money, it comes as a pleasant surprise. It is just like having a bet on the horses, only in show-business the punter gets a longer run for his money.

In other words, it is not possible to go into business to back shows because any losses could not be offset as a working loss and this would naturally lead to tax difficulties. The manager, who is in an accepted form of business and hopes to make a living out of the presentation of plays, takes 40 per cent of the profits and the backers get 60 per cent, but they are not regarded as a business concern. They are just people with money to spare who take a gambler's chance to make a little extra.

Even a regular and seasoned investor usually only breaks even. If he could be certain of making money there would be no problem in getting backers. Luck plays too big a part in the theatre to place any degree of certainty in backing shows. Investors really do little more than buy fun, but they pay for the indulgence.

Buying a ticket at the Vaudeville Theatre box-office to see *Move Over Mrs Markham*, a Peter Saunders success which paid handsome dividends to the backers. *Photograph by Dezo Hoffmann*

None of the established West End managements advertises for capital when deciding to stage a new production. I am asked by people who would like to have a share in a show how they could go about it. When is a chance likely to present itself? I can only suggest they write to the leading managements and inquire about prospects. But I ought to point out that such a request is useless unless they are prepared to part with at least £200. Mini-Angels, as small-sum backers have been called, are doomed to failure. A man offering to invest no more than £25 can obviously not afford to part with more than £25 – and he is afraid of losing that! In consequence he takes too close an interest in the preparation and launching of the show and in the box-office receipts during the early weeks of the run. He would naturally have to be furnished with figures at regular intervals and for so small a sum, his contribution would be more bother to the management than it was worth.

A real West End success makes a backer's gamble well worth while. Suppose a management discovers an attractive straight play, acquires a star name to head a cast of modest proportions and has the luck to find a vacant West End theatre of the right size. It would cost about £15,000 to mount such a show these days, but if it caught the public fancy and became a hit from the start, it would take no longer than a couple of months to get back the production costs. Such a show could make a gross profit of £2,000 a week – about £100,000 a year. In other words, the backer could make 400 per cent on his money in a single year. If film rights were sold the figure might rise to 500 per cent. A post-London tour might bring in diminishing but nevertheless acceptable returns.

A musical might present more fantastic results. But such shows are harder to come by and they take longer to show results. A musical would cost at least £100,000 to put on, which means it would take far longer to get the money back. It might take as long as six months to pay off production costs, even if the show got off to a flying start. In the long run, the rewards would be greater and well worth waiting for.

The profits on an imported musical would not be so great. So many of our musicals are American imports these days and people on the other side of the Atlantic take a large slice of the profits before British investors begin to benefit.

Years ago quite a reasonable living was possible from presenting shows on tour. At that time there was a comprehensive touring circuit and out-of-town audiences were content to see plays which had enjoyed long West End runs, even without the original Shaftesbury Avenue stars. Times have changed and people in the regions cannot be lured into what few theatres are left standing outside London unless there are dazzling star names to attract them. Today very few names are cast-iron box-office and they have no desire to go on the road for long periods, just for the sake of touring. They rarely consider a tour of longer than eight weeks, purely as a means to an end, in order to lick the production into shape. Once the tour has served its purpose they are ready for London.

Television has brought top-flight stars into every sitting-room and unless the local theatre can compete with TV names in a big way no one is going to spend money at the box-office. They cannot be blamed for staying at home and seeing bigger names for free.

It all boils down to luck, that ingredient which is quite indispensable in the theatre. There is an element of luck in finding a good play; in discovering just the right star at liberty to play the lead; in finding a vacant theatre of the right size at the right moment. There are a hundred and one other elements which need luck in order to fuse at the precise moment. Even the backer needs luck to be given the chance to become an Angel with the opportunity to put a hundred or two into the proceedings.

THE PLAY-GOER'S SCRAPBOOK

Photographs on previous page – *Top left*: 1934, John Gielgud as Hamlet and George Howe as Polonius in the revival of *Hamlet* at the New Theatre. Directed by John Gielgud.
Top right: 1934, Cathleen Nesbitt as Elizabeth and Peter Glenville making his first appearance in London as Richard in Leontine Sagan's production of *Richard III* at the Regent's Park Open Air Theatre.   *Photograph by J. W.*

Debenham. Bottom: 1934, Bernard Shaw visited the Open Air Theatre, Regent's Park, and met Clare Harris after a performance of his *Androcles and the Lion* in which she played Megaera. *Photograph by Sasha*

Left: 1955, John Gielgud as Lear and Claire Bloom as Cordelia in the Stratford-upon-Avon

Shakespeare Memorial Company's London season at the Palace Theatre. Directed by George Devine
Top right: 1953, John Mills and Joan Greenwood in *The Uninvited Guest* by Mary Hayley Bell at the St James's Theatre.   *Photograph by Houston Rogers*
Bottom right: 1935, Phyllis Neilson-Terry as Oberon and Fay Compton as Titania in *A Midsummer Night's Dream* at the Open Air Theatre in Regent's Park.   *Photograph by Cyril Mathews*

Left: 1959, Peggy Mount and Margaret Rutherford played sisters in *Farewell, Farewell Eugene* adapted by Rodney Ackland from the American original by John Vari, at the Garrick Theatre. As the curtain rose on the first act, the sisters were discovered singing the hymn 'Stand Up, Stand Up for Jesus'. *Photograph by Angus McBean*

Top right: 1933, Leslie French as Ariel and John Drinkwater as Prospero in the Regent's Park Open Air Theatre production of *The Tempest*
Bottom right: 1937, Nigel Patrick and Jane Baxter in *George and Margaret*, the Gerald Savory comedy which ran for 799 performances at Wyndham's Theatre. *Photograph by Peter Clark Ltd*

Top left: 1959, Kenneth Williams and Fenella Fielding in *Pieces of Eight* by Peter Cook at the Apollo Theatre. *Photograph by David Sim*

Top centre: 1935, Isabel Jeans, not normally associated with musical productions, played Lucy Lockit in *The Beggar's Opera* at the Criterion Theatre

Top right: 1935, Phyllis Neilson-Terry as the Princess of France and Fay Compton as Rosalind in *Love's Labour's Lost* at the Regent's Park Open Air Theatre. *London News Agency Photos Ltd*

Bottom left: 1934, Marie Tempest as Fanny Cavendish in *Theatre Royal* at the Lyric Theatre. Written by Edna Ferber and George S Kaufman, the play was based on the Barrymore Family, regarded as the Royal Family of the American stage. *Photograph by George Dallison*

Bottom centre: 1934, Anna Neagle as Olivia in *Twelfth Night* at the Regent's Park Open Air Theatre. Until she played Rosalind and Olivia in the Park, she had spent most of her time gaining valuable experience in the chorus of such West End hits as *Rose Marie*, *The Desert Song* and *This Year of Grace*. *Photograph by J. W. Debenham*

Bottom right: 1963, Peter O'Toole as the Prince of Denmark and Rosemary Harris as Ophelia in *Hamlet*, which was the National Theatre Company's inaugural production at the Old Vic, directed by Laurence Olivier. *Angus McBean*

Far left, top: 1934, Jack Hawkins as Orsino and Anna Neagle as Olivia in the Regent's Park Open Air Theatre production of *Twelfth Night*. *Sasha*
Top left: 1929, Ivy St Helier made the outstanding success of her career as Manon la Crevette in Noël Coward's *Bitter Sweet* at His Majesty's Theatre
Top right: 1933, Alice Delysia as Josephine Pavani in *Mother of Pearl*, the Oscar Straus musical, adapted from the German by A. P. Herbert, at the Gaiety Theatre. *Photograph by Sasha*
Far right, top: 1957, Sophie Tucker in her apartment at the Savoy made contact with old friends when she returned to London for a cabaret season. *Central Press Photos Ltd*
Bottom Left: 1956, Kay Hammond as Lydia Languish and Laurence Harvey as Captain Absolute in *The Rivals*, which John Clements presented at the Saville Theatre. *Photograph by Houston Rogers*
Bottom centre: 1930s, an early picture of Emlyn Williams when he was enjoying his first success as actor and author on the London stage
Bottom right: 1953, Vivien Leigh and Laurence Olivier as Mary Morgan and the Prince Regent of Carpathia in *The Sleeping Prince* by Terence Rattigan at the Phoenix Theatre. *Photograph by Angus McBean*

Left: 1958, after an absence of 22 years, Charles Laughton returned to the London stage at the New Theatre in *The Party* by Jane Arden, with Joyce Redman as his wife and Ann Lynn as his daughter. Albert Finney, at the age of 22, made his West End début in the same production.

Right: Peggy Ashcroft as Juliet, Laurence Olivier as Romeo and Edith Evans as the Nurse rehearsing the now legendary production of *Romeo and Juliet* at the New Theatre. Gielgud played Mercutio and during the run he alternated the part of Romeo with Olivier. *Photograph by London News Agency Photos Ltd*

OLIVIER AND THE NATIONAL THEATRE

Eric Johns

Irving refused a knighthood way back in 1883, feeling the unique fellowship which exists between actors would be impaired by the elevation of one member above another. Twelve years later his outlook changed and when Queen Victoria said she was very, very pleased as she laid the sword upon Irving's shoulder, he realized that through him the monarch was conferring an honour upon the calling to which he had devoted his life, and every member of the acting profession would benefit and be advanced by the distinction he had been given.

In the course of time Victoria's great-great-granddaughter gave Sir Laurence Olivier a Life Peerage for his services to the theatre, and he thus became the first actor to be elected to the House of Lords. Olivier is overawed by titular glory and honours; he does not consider he has deserved them all personally, but has accepted them in the name of the actor's profession. 'My seat in the House of Lords, it was explained to me, means I can work for other causes.' As director of the National Theatre and a Peer, Olivier is automatically regarded as the leader of the English stage, but it is a title he strongly resists and discourages.

It comes as something of a surprise to discover that Sir Laurence, as he prefers to be known, has been on the stage more than fifty years, without any tremendous fanfare having been sounded to herald his jubilee. It was in 1922 at the Shakespeare Festival Theatre, Stratford-upon-Avon, that he made his first stage performance in a special boys' performance of *The Taming of the Shrew*, in

which he played the part of Katherine. Now, as director of the National Theatre, he holds much the same position on the contemporary stage as did Irving at the Lyceum during the eighties and the nineties. But there is a vast difference between them.

The actor-knights of today – Olivier, John Gielgud, Ralph Richardson, Alec Guinness and Michael Redgrave – shun the superstar attitude. They have all tried to develop a less selfish approach towards their work than was expected of the Victorian actor-manager. At the Lyceum, Irving was the great dictator, and he was expected to dominate every production, usually with Ellen Terry as his leading lady. A Lyceum production without Irving at the head of the cast was a real case of *Hamlet* without the Prince.

Olivier's attitude is totally different. During his ten years as director of the National Theatre, seventy productions have been presented, he having appeared in only nine and directed eight. He has never regarded the National Theatre Company as Olivier's troupe of players. He never considered himself the indispensable star attraction and no one was more pleased when the National Theatre Company acquired sufficient lustre to be capable of packing the theatre night after night with productions in which Olivier had no part. It gave him definite proof that the company could continue to thrive when he was no longer with them.

His main regret during his first ten years in office at the National Theatre was that he had not been able to get closer to the company. He would like to have directed

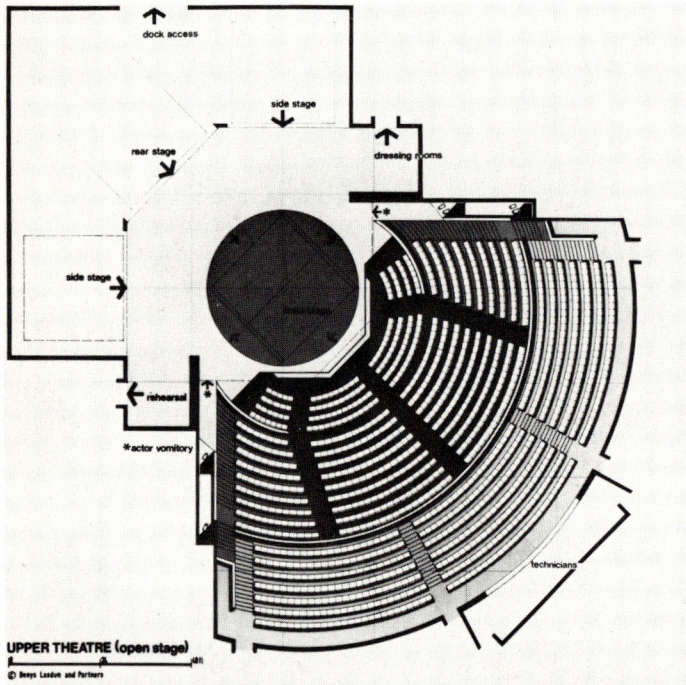

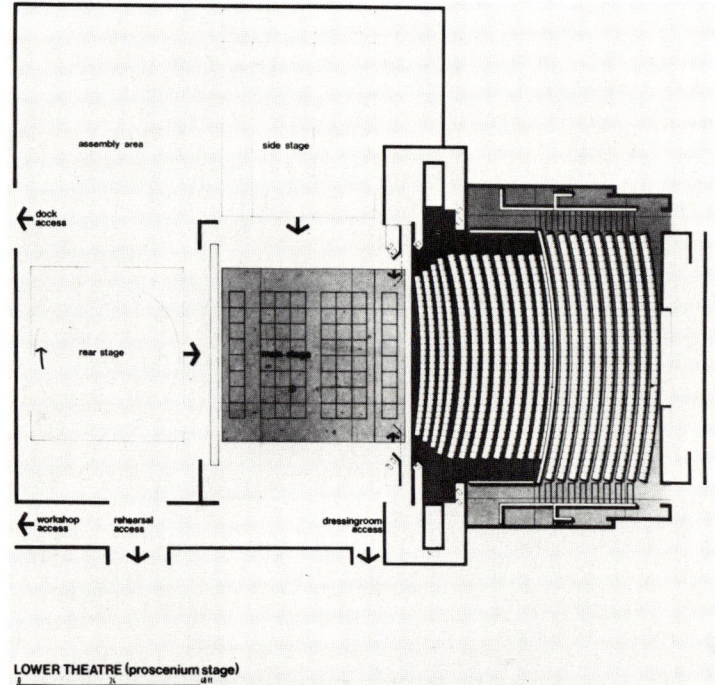

Model of the National Theatre on the South
Bank, seen from the river

75

more productions and have worked hand in hand with his colleagues to a greater extent than had been possible. Opportunities he could have seized for himself he has time and time again unselfishly given to others, often with an anxious eye to the succession. Should he not be able to continue in office, he wanted to leave an experienced ensemble, capable of presenting productions worthy of a National Theatre.

He has only played parts which he felt no one else could play under the circumstances, parts such as Othello, Shylock, Edgar in *The Dance of Death* and James Tyrone in *Long Day's Journey Into Night*. He hates being called an actor-manager. 'I want to be a fellow student, but a leading one.'

Before he agreed to play Shylock in the National Theatre production of *The Merchant of Venice*, he offered the part to at least three actors of the highest renown. Rather than play it himself, he was eager to have more time at his disposal to spend with the company. Once he decides to play a major role he knows he will be locked away for two or three months preparing his performance and spending lunch hours and late evenings in his office to catch up on administrative matters.

This year he felt it was time to go and decided to relinquish the directorship of the National Theatre. He agreed to stay on with the company as an associate director and appear in leading parts in three productions. After sabbatical leave, to start in the Spring of 1974, he will return to the company in good time for the opening of the £10,000,000

National Theatre building on the South Bank in the summer of 1975.

Peter Hall, firm friend of Olivier for some fifteen years, joined him as co-director of the National Theatre on April 1, 1973, and assumed full directoral responsibility from the beginning of November.

'I am willing to come back in whatever capacity I can be useful,' stated Olivier. 'I would not want to work anywhere else and I look forward to coming back both as actor and director. I like the feeling of being a member of the company; I like the repertoire system, as opposed to the drudgery of appearing in the same play for a long run and I know I shall enjoy being "one of the boys" in the theatre I have helped to create.'

Olivier has decided ideas about the part the National Theatre should play outside London. He promised years ago there would be no Second Eleven for the provinces. He has committed the National Theatre to sending out the First Eleven in productions which find favour in their South Bank headquarters, either in the large or the smaller of the two theatres which will occupy the riverside site.

The old-style touring days seem to be numbered, when a company goes regularly on the road, often compelled to play in vast theatres really only suitable for opera, ballet and musicals. Such theatres demanded operatic-style acting which strained the voice and facial expressions of the actor to a point beyond plausibility.

Olivier is convinced there is a degree of hypnotism in every actor's technique and as

In the National Theatre production of Somerset
Maugham's *Home and Beauty*, Laurence Olivier
played Mr A B Raham to the Miss Montmorency
of Jeanne Watts.   *Photograph by Reg Wilson*

Laurence Olivier as Titus, Vivien Leigh as
Lavinia and Alan Webb in the Stratford-upon-
Avon production of *Titus Andronicus*, directed by
Peter Brook in 1955

no actor can hope to hypnotize more than a thousand people 'at one go', he considers no auditorium should be much larger than that for straight plays. The larger auditorium on the South Bank – to be called the Olivier Theatre – holds just over a thousand. Splendid civic theatres are flourishing in our leading cities, such as the Crucible at Sheffield, Nottingham Playhouse and the Bristol Old Vic, with two playhouses functioning simultaneously. These establishments accept the National Theatre's achievement as a challenge and these theatres and others of the same calibre are doing excellent work which London gets very little chance to see. Instead of touring, Olivier suggests the National Theatre should exchange productions with the finest civic theatres outside London. Let the regional players come to the South Bank while the National actors visit the theatres which have been vacated by their home companies. The existence of what Sir Laurence calls underprivileged theatres is no longer possible. Every seat in the house should be a good one, commanding an excellent sight-line and be close enough to the stage to enable play-goers to observe with ease the expression on the actors' faces.

Acting is no longer a virtuoso performance, as in the days of Kean, when the star could go to Bath or some other popular provincial playhouse as a guest star and hastily arrange the existing stock company round his performance, where his own inventions had broken with tradition. Since those days the

Laurence Olivier as Etienne and Maggie Riley as Lucienne in the Feydeau farce, *A Flea in her Ear*, which Jacques Charon directed for the National Theatre. *Photograph by Zoë Dominic*

director has emerged to control tempo and rhythm and inject a point of view into the production. The ensemble is what counts today and that can be safeguarded by Olivier's exchange theory replacing the old touring system.

Looking back on his own half-century as an actor, Olivier regards Archie Rice, the declining music hall artist in *The Entertainer* by John Osborne as providing the most rewarding experience of his lifetime. He played it in London at the Royal Court and Palace Theatres, he took it to Broadway, he toured it in this country and also made a film, but never ceased to enjoy it and never got tired of it. Other parts which gave him immense pleasure are Tattle in *Love for Love* and Astrov in *Uncle Vanya*. He describes Othello as . . . . 'cruelty to animals, the enormity of its demands making it the most difficult of all parts to play.'

There are no special parts Sir Laurence has been hankering to play all his life, but he would love to be cast in a screamingly funny play by a contemporary dramatist some time in the future. Comedy has a strong appeal for him and he considers tragedy is better played by an actor who is also a comedian, rather than by one who tends to specialize like the old-time tragedian used to do. Disguise fascinated him at the beginning of his career when he had a flair for wearing false noses on stage. He feels he must have been the first juvenile to use a false nose when playing Romeo. At the age of twenty-eight when he alternated Romeo and Mercutio with John Gielgud at the New Theatre, he made his Romeo more handsome and more Italian-looking by moulding a false nose. His Henry V, Macbeth and Coriolanus all wore false noses. His heaviest make-up job was for Oedipus, followed by *The Critic*. As an actor gets older, in Olivier's opinion, he gets more like the characters he plays and the characters get more like him. Consequently the player tends to economize and simplify his make-up. When he first played Richard III he found nothing of the part within himself; he had to look about him for a suitable walk, a way of speaking, physical appearance and uses of facial expression.

Years later when Olivier played Edgar in *The Dance of Death* by Strindberg he admits he did not have to draw upon his imagination at all. By then he felt there was little he did not know about marital relationships or had recognized about his own failings – his own life having taught him so much about the character – and through practising his craft for years he found wiser ways of doing

Laurence Olivier in his favourite part of Archie Rice in *The Entertainer* by John Osborne, first seen in London in 1957. He sang and danced as the ageing music-hall trouper and went to two of London's last surviving variety theatres – Collins on Islington Green and the Chelsea Palace – to study the authentic background. *Photograph by P. A. Reuter*

things from a technical point of view and employed them in the actual performance of the part.

When faced with the problem of playing a man who has actually lived, such as Richard III or Henry V, Olivier spends much time in outside research, quite apart from a close study of the author's text. This is not always an advantage. From his own research, for instance, Olivier has come to the conclusion that Richard III was an efficient man and quite a good king. But Shakespeare's villain could not be played that way. The actor had no choice but to follow the legend. Incidentally, he has no intention of ever playing that great part again, though it was one of his most spectacular successes. As he played it on and off for four years and also made a film of it he feels the field should be left for others.

It was the intention of the National Theatre to stage *Guys and Dolls* a year or two ago, a project which had to be abandoned because of Olivier's ill-health at the time, so one wonders whether we are likely to see musicals on the South Bank when the new theatre opens. 'There is nothing we won't do' is Olivier's emphatic reply to that question. Every form of theatrical art should be seen in the course of time on the stages of those two theatres, and distinguished players, designers and directors from all over the world be invited to work there; a national and an international theatre.

QUARTER OF A CENTURY OF SILENCE

Universally acclaimed as the finest mime within living memory, Marcel Marceau can now look back on a career of twenty-five years – during which time he has played to packed theatres all over the world without ever uttering a single syllable. By way of marking this unique achievement, the French Ministry of Culture is to put a Paris theatre permanently at his disposal in 1974. Marceau intends to play there four months a year, devoting the rest of the time to international touring.

Although Marceau has never spoken a word on stage, he is a highly eloquent conversationalist at other times, teeming with ideas for cultivation and preservation of the art of mime. It is to Marceau that we owe a renaissance of mime in our time. Just after the Second World War, as a young man of twenty-two, he joined Jean-Louis Barrault's company in Paris, where he attracted considerable attention as Arlequin in *Baptiste*. The following year he abandoned conventional acting to concentrate upon the study of mime, basing his work on the character of the nineteenth-century French Pierrot and thus evolving his now internationally famous Bip, a white-faced clown with sailor trousers and striped jacket.

In effect, he recreated a new medium, influenced by the mime of the Greeks, the Romans, the Commedia dell'Arte, Charlie Chaplin and Buster Keaton, as well as by statuary, ballet and the work of Jean-Louis Barrault. He first attracted attention at the Théâtre de la Poche in Paris where he established a company of fifteen actors and five technicians. Under Marceau's direction they created a repertoire of mimodramas – plays without words – the most famous of which was *The Overcoat* by Gogol. The company flourished from 1947 to 1960, when it had to be disbanded because it was impossible to carry on without a subsidy, which was not forthcoming from the French Government. They played to full houses, but box-office receipts did not cover the expense of running so large a company. So Marceau went on alone and his one-man show became enormously popular in many different countries. The public lionized him and he became a magnetic solo star, equally popular outside France because his appeal did not rely on any language. After four years he recruited another company, based in Paris, where they played *Don Juan* in an expensive and elaborate production. Outside opera *Don Juan* was not popular at that time and after three months the company had to be disbanded yet again. Marceau set off on his solo travels once more.

The boon of air travel and the invention of films and television have made Marcel Marceau the best-known mime of all time. In his own words, 'I am more widely known in the world than were either Molière or Shakespeare in their own day!' He has appeared on the stage in sixty-five different countries, and television – to which his work is ideally suited – has made his white face familiar to millions all over the world. Clowns have added another dimension to the art of stage playing. Through Marceau mime

it has become more popular than it has ever been before. Great players such as John Gielgud have paid tribute to Marceau and are first to admit that mime has affected stage acting in projecting psychological feeling and conveying emotion through physical situations. In short, the actor is less likely to rely entirely on the spoken word after realizing how much can be expressed in total silence by an artist of Marceau's calibre. Marceau has had the satisfaction of realizing, during the comparatively short span of his career, just how strongly mime now appeals to the general public. Ten years ago he would not have dared to take his one-man show to provincial theatres in Britain, but now he can go to such places as Liverpool, Nottingham and Brighton and people are turned away at every performance. He was extremely gratified to discover that 80 per cent of his recent London audiences consisted of young people. Princess Anne attended his first night at Sadler's Wells Theatre and went backstage to congratulate him and to ask significant questions about mime, which she had never before seen so eloquently performed.

Having reached the age of fifty, Marceau hopes he has a third of his life yet to live and when he moves into his Paris theatre in 1974 to make it his artistic home, he will recruit yet another company and open a mime school, thus preserving the art which he has done so much to popularize. A film studio will be attached to the theatre, so that the mimodramas can be preserved for all time, just as certain ballets have been recorded.

Some of the films will be directed so that they can be shown on cinema and television screens, and others will be made specially for the archives so that students will be in a position to see just how Marceau speaks volumes out of silent gestures.

When Marceau appears with a company of mime artists he uses stage properties, scenery and costumes and does not put on a white face. When appearing alone he performs on a bare stage and uses white face make-up. As he puts it, the visible becomes invisible and the invisible becomes visible. He lets the audience into a few mime secrets. He walks against the wind where there is no wind. He walks upstairs where there is no staircase and he walks the tightrope where there is no high wire. The audience, intrigued by this trickery, is agog for more. The programme proceeds by using mime satirically. Adopting his white face, Marceau becomes sexless. He can be man or woman; he can be an animal or a plant or just a symbol. Finally, he devotes a section of his one-man show to Bip, the clown of his own creation. Bip is essentially a man and cannot change sex or become plant or symbol. He always appears alone because, according to Marceau, the presence of other characters would only destroy the magic.

Marceau is quick to maintain that solo mime is in no way superior to concerted mime. It is merely a question of difference of material. *The Overcoat* calls for a company and could not be performed by a solitary artist, whereas *The Mask-maker* is a dramatic mimodrama created expressly for a single

Marcel Marceau – a camera study. *Photograph by Shuhei Iwamoto*

player. Plays without words are necessarily shorter than plays which employ speech. With one gesture the mime can convey so much in a matter of seconds; using words communicating the same idea would require a much longer space of time. Marceau's solo mimodramas last between four and nine minutes. Similarly, Edith Piaf used to create a complete drama in four minutes of song. The plays performed by a company of mime artists vary between twenty and fifty minutes. Marceau likens them to short stories by Maupassant or Chekhov, which, despite their brevity, capture the essence of a particular situation.

There are some eighty numbers in Marceau's repertoire. In his own estimation the most famous are *The Mask-maker*, *The Cage*, *Hands*, *Side Show*, *The Creation of the World*, *The Dream* and *The Trial*. The most popular Bip items are *The Butterfly-catcher*, *The Lion Tamer*, *The Skater*, *The Soldier*, *High Society* and *The Public Garden*. Discussing their creation, Marceau says an idea can often lie at the back of his mind for as long as two years. Suddenly it leaps to life and in a matter of three days a mimodrama could be created and ready for public performance.

Every time Marceau presents one of his solos, he claims to give an identical performance each time because the movements and expressions are codified, just as if they had been crystallized into memorized words. He is convinced the illusion of mime can be more powerful than reality. For instance, he has appeared as a real wire-walker in public and in one of his most popular mime numbers he pretends to walk a tightrope. Even though his feet remain firmly on the boards of the stage, his mime suggests he might lose his balance at any moment. This thrills the audience even more than if they watched him actually walking a wire.

He deplores the fact that the public is sometimes subjected to inferior mime artists, whose work is no better than cabaret mimicry. There is nothing the onlooker can do about it. On the other hand, if a play-goer sees a poor production of Shakespeare or Chekhov he can always go home and read the words. Those who see poor mimes are denied such compensation. Mime demands perfection and Marceau is never prepared to make allowances.

He reckons he gives some 300 performances every year, but throughout his career he has only missed two shows – in Paris in 1965 during an influenza epidemic. There is no understudy for Marceau and without him the show has to be cancelled.

'We clowns are a large family,' he says. 'I have met Chaplin, Buster Keaton, Stan Laurel and Harpo Marx, who are among the greatest within living memory, and in my dreams I have met Grock, Dan Leno and Grimaldi.'

ROCK AND THE THEATRE

Peter Hepple

When *Hair*, describing itself as a 'tribal love-rock musical', burst upon London in the autumn of 1968, the Press and public were more interested in the fact that for a brief, dimly-lit period some male members of the cast appeared in the nude than in the more important fact that *Hair* was a harbinger of a revolution in the theatre. As revolutions do, it started with a bang and has now settled down to a kind of acceptance. But it has taken place all the same. A glance through the list of new American musicals produced during the 1972–73 season, on and off Broadway, shows that the vast majority are at the very least rock-influenced, while some are out-and-out rock.

The fact that rock or rock flavouring has now found a place upon the stage is proof enough to some of its most ardent disciples and pioneers that it has sold out to commerce. Rebellion is no longer attractive when its cause has been taken up by the general public, and some of rock's erstwhile fervent adherents have switched to other fields of music.

To my mind, no perfect definition of 'rock' has yet been formed but, possibly for the first time in history, a culture or life-style was created around a type of music. As to who invented it or propelled it along, no one seems quite sure. Historically, of course, it belongs to the United States and perhaps it took shape, at least in a literary form, in the fifties with the 'beat' poets and writers such as Jack Kerouac, Allen Ginsberg and Gregory Corso. They in turn could have been influenced by such earlier writers and performers as Woody Guthrie, wandering minstrels of the thirties and forties with a social conscience and consequently an instant appeal to the young, especially when it was combined with a 'back to the roots' or, more strictly, 'rootless' approach to life. The essence of rock, then, is a species of rebellion, a turning of the back upon materialism. The music just happened to be at hand. Bill Haley and his Comets, pilloried as instigators of the seat-slashing violence of nearly twenty years ago, may well have been a more important cultural influence than we give them credit for. Their souped-up mixture of Country and Western and the Blues, which came to be known as 'rock 'n roll', contained in its two strands both the musical elements of the rock revolution – the Country and Western part, which sent people back to genuine C & W, which in turn led back to folk, and the Blues, which again turned interest towards the original. In addition, Haley's stage act had its moments of intense theatricality and even high drama which were eventually taken up by protagonists of the new culture.

It is hard to escape the conclusion that there have been some shrewd business brains behind rock culture, sharp manipulators of the young masses who saw the effect of the music and teamed it up with the natural yearning of youth to escape from the fetters of their elders.

This, then, is the background to rock – how and when did it come into the theatre? George Melly, author of that excellent book

One of the highspots in the London production of
Hair at the Shaftesbury Theatre

Revolt Into Style, denies that it has come into the theatre at all, stating that in his opinion all the theatre has done is to adapt rock, and pop, to its own conventions. While this is undoubtedly true up to a point, it ignores the fact that there are a number of artists and writers, basically brought up on rock, who have found that the theatre offers them a better means of communication, and a smaller but more significant group, among them David Bowie, Rod Stewart and The Faces, The Who and even the fearsome Alice Cooper, who seem to be going in more and more for visual, theatrical presentation, drawing from such fields as classical mime, Eastern mysticism, Grand Guignol, music-hall and opera, in addition to employing all the latest electronic instrumental and visual aids, such as synthesizers and the most advanced methods of slide and film projection.

To tell the truth, there was nothing of note in the rock theatre before *Hair*, though some might put in a claim for *Your Own Thing*, which opened and, soon after, closed at the Comedy around the same time. Hal Hester and Danny Apolinar, the composers and writers of this charming little show, credited themselves with bringing the rock beat to the American musical theatre. But the rock beat was about all they did bring. Their background is night-clubs and in *Your Own Thing*, which is a version of *Twelfth Night*, they trailed around echoes of the previous year's 'flower power' and 'gentle people' and put them into a bandbox theatre format.

Hair, for all its detractors, is the nearest thing yet to the genuine rock article. The yards of microphone cable snaking across the stage, the real rock band in full view of the audience, the coltish amateurism of most of the cast, the informal dress – all these give it a stamp of originality. To many people in its audience it is their first, and possibly their only, look at rock culture. Ignore its somewhat meretricious attempt to embroil the audience in its 'tribal love-rock' credo by persuading them to dance on the stage with the cast after the show, and you still have a good production, which may be performed by near-amateurs, but nevertheless has a firm directorial control somewhere in the background. Do not forget either that *Hair* is packed with excellent tunes from its composer Galt MacDermot – 'Aquarius', 'Good Morning Starshine', 'Where Do I Go', 'Let the Sun Shine In'.

Galt MacDermot has so far failed to follow up the success of *Hair*. The second show of his to be seen in London, *Isabel's a Jezebel* at the Duchess, with book and lyrics by William Dumaresq, was everything a rock musical should not be – puerile, hysterical and somehow obsessed with sex and ecology, both of these being important subjects which the rock musical is in danger of turning its audiences away from.

One might say that rock's infiltration into the theatre has been in spite of the material. Because of its association with youthful revolt, sexual freedom, conservation and

anti-authoritarianism, the rock musical has tended to restrict itself, often with unsatisfying results. *Mother Earth*, for instance, was an ecological revue with a talented company and some reasonable songs. Yet it was ruined by callow sketch material by authors who appear to think that they alone are aware of the state of the world. Arrogant supposition of this nature will do the rock theatre no good at all and it is worth pointing out that the 'committed' playwrights of the thirties, equally if not more concerned with people's welfare, went to some pains to present a reasoned statement rather than an hysterical outburst.

Nor is it a lot of use when rock writers deliberately override convention and usage by giving us rock classics, particularly when something of the sort has been done before – and better – as in the case of *Carmen*. *Carmen Jones*, seen only on film in this country, had the virtue of novelty as well as exceptional dramatic and lyrical ability with its Negro version of Bizet's opera. The same cannot be said of its 1972 successor *Rock Carmen*, an incredibly muddy and muddled affair set on the campus of an American college. Shakespeare is a likely sufferer in the future and even Greek tragedy has been through the rock mill.

Why, then, you might say, should the Bible have survived the transition to rock musical so well? For the biggest hits of the new genre during the past couple of years have undoubtedly been *Godspell* and *Jesus Christ Superstar*. It is partly, I think, because the Bible remains the greatest work of

inspiration in the whole of literature, saying practically all there is to be said on the very themes which the rock culturists have clasped to their collective bosom.

But an even more important reason is that the two works represent the first flowering of a new generation of writers and composers prepared to merge the rock idiom with theatrical requirements. Stephen Schwartz, the composer of *Godspell*, is a worthy inheritor of the mantle of all the great American composers of musicals, apart from which the show is tightly conceived and sternly directed. It is a small-scale production, devised strictly within theatre terms, and it is almost certain to survive.

So, too, I believe, is *Jesus Christ Superstar*, though this stems from a different tradition. It may seem strange to say so, but I detect in the work of Andrew Lloyd Webber and Tim Rice not only a certain affinity with the grand oratorios which have been the backbone of many an English music festival, but with Gilbert and Sullivan, in that the words and music are entirely complementary. This facet is perhaps more noticeable in Webber's and Rice's earlier work, *Joseph and the Amazing Technicolor Dreamcoat*, which takes liberties with the Old Testament but is highly successful within its modest limits. Talking with Andrew Lloyd Webber, I was impressed to discover that, like Gilbert and Sullivan, he is essentially a theatre man. Much has been made of the fact that *Jesus Christ Superstar* started life as a record, but Andrew Lloyd Webber explains that this was really to pre-sell the music and thereby

create a demand for a stage production. The various productions of *Superstar* in all parts of the world have differed widely, but Andrew Lloyd Webber makes no secret that his dearest ambition is to see *Jesus Christ Superstar* staged at Covent Garden with the orchestra well hidden away in the pit, and sung by artists who are suitably *au fait* with the idiom but are not shackled to the microphone.

In the short term, rock musicals might entice more young people into the theatre, though I believe this to be a wishful fallacy. Of more immediate importance is the fact that the rock idiom has already found its way into more allegedly 'non-rock' musicals than many think. The short-lived *Jack Sheppard* at the Round House had a 'soft rock' feel in many of its numbers, and there is a surprising amount of 'heavy rock' in the accompaniment of the longest-running London musical, *Canterbury Tales*.

As for the future, I think we should prepare ourselves for a theatrical invasion from many artists in the pop side of the business. One cannot imagine David Bowie, for example, with his keenly developed interest in all kinds of theatre, being forever content to make concert appearances in mammoth halls, even when these are well-enough equipped to enable him to put some of his ideas into practice. The Who, also, are poised to make a step and doubtless would dearly love to present a full version of their rock opera, *Tommy*. There could well be some exciting, if noisy, times ahead.

LUNCHTIME THEATRE

Douglas Blake

A little culture at lunchtime is no new idea, for music and talks are usually available, but going to a play at that time of day is a comparatively recent phenomenon, which has already firmly established itself as a form of theatre providing a particular liveliness and intimate communication between players and audience. In view of the amount of lunchtime theatre in the London area alone, it seems inconceivable that this creative activity was unknown a few years ago. But the live theatre is, in any case, a minority art and 'fringe' events such as lunchtime performances and experimental work of various kinds, appeal to but a small percentage of that minority. So what is it all about?

In the first place, the vital source of energy for these activities comes from the actors and directors themselves. For most of the year,

the majority of them are out of work and, even if working in television, they have no contact with the theatre. Lunchtime plays give them all – from well-known players to drama school graduates – a chance to work before an audience and be seen by agents, managers and casting directors who might put some lucrative work their way. Although very important to the artists involved, this 'shop-window' aspect is merely an ancillary bonus to the idea of lunchtime theatre as such, and its real value comes from working on new scripts and in front of hard-to-woo audiences whose numbers can range from as many as fifty to as few as one. These same audiences, who can sit through a play without any noticeable reaction and leave at the end with no more than desultory applause, can also be

warmly responsive if both play and acting are good, however experimental, or even conventional the presentation.

The initiative, therefore, comes from within the creative side of the profession, sparked off by a desire to keep working, even though the financial rewards are small or non-existent. At the most, the cast may be paid a nominal sum for expenses, so their contribution as artists is a valuable subsidy readily available to lunchtime theatre. At first, companies existed on a threadbare shoe-string of a budget, perhaps getting back a few pounds per play from the box-office, and quite often subsidized by the generosity of a member actor who might have recently earned some money in a television series, and wished to show his faith in lunchtime theatre in practical terms. As this form of activity developed and spread, the Arts Council of Great Britain came to accept the value of the work being done by certain companies and gave them assistance in the form of modest grants. Other less securely organized groups were able to cover some of their working costs with the help of Arts Council New Play grants, which are given if a new work is deemed worthy of assistance.

All this has happened well within the last decade and springs from the activities of Theatrescope, a small management formed by a young man, Brian King, and his girl-friend, whose enthusiasm helped to get lunchtime theatre accepted. Their productions were at the Little Theatre Club, an attic in premises at Garrick Yard off

St Martin's Lane, which were at one time
Chippendale's workshops.

Every weekday, a small but loyal audience
would climb the stairs to the top of this
building, pay the modest sum of half a
crown for a picnic lunch consisting of a
filled roll, a banana and a cup of coffee, and
an entertainment to follow. Even in those
comparatively early days, the standard of
performance was often high, but the
presentations themselves were necessarily
simple. Brian King helped to finance the
productions with money he earned through
making garments for a boutique.

Shortly after Theatrescope had established
itself at the Little, a new group appeared on
the scene, this time at the Arts Theatre
Club. Calling themselves Quipu, they set a
new standard of performance during their
short stay there, and one of their plays, *The
Audition*, was eventually taken up by a
management and presented in the West End
as part of a double-bill.

Quipu still exists today and, by a quirk of
fate, now operates at the Little Theatre
Club. Theatrescope, unhappily, had to
retire from the scene when their lease
expired, but I, for one, will always be
grateful for the pioneering work of this
enthusiastic little enterprise.

David Halliwell, author of *Little Malcolm*,
is very much in evidence in the present
Quipu set-up, though the actual productions
are under the direct control of David
Beaumont, a professional actor/director who
devotes all his time to this group. Working
with the assistance of an Arts Council grant,
Quipu's unswerving policy is to present new
plays, and during the 1972–73 season
presented twenty-six of them at the rate of
one a fortnight. Obviously the quality of
writing is bound to vary considerably with
such a large output, but the average standard
over the year was remarkably high, and
Quipu discovered one or two new
playwrights, such as Tony Connor and Peter
King, whose talents they considered worth
nurturing.

The majority of these plays are
straightforward in style, neither severely
conventional nor wildly experimental, but
they are all presented efficiently with seldom
less than competent acting and direction.
Halliwell's own theory of what he terms
'Multiviewpoint Drama' is not imposed on
Quipu writers, though a few have clearly
been influenced by it. In fact, *Muck from
Three Angles*, one of his own one-act plays
and a prototype of the style, has been
presented by two different groups, but not
by Quipu. The Multiviewpoint policy is
pursued occasionally with evening
performances or a visit to the regions, but
wisely the lunchtime activities are open to all
ideas, regardless of form.

Since moving into the Little, David
Beaumont has torn out the old platform
stage, fitted raked seating and installed
lighting which is equal to the demands of
most productions. No bridge rolls and a
banana these days, but there is a bar which
satisfies most customers and also helps to
finance the organization. But despite the
comparative comfort and technical facilities
of this theatre club, it is a place that critics

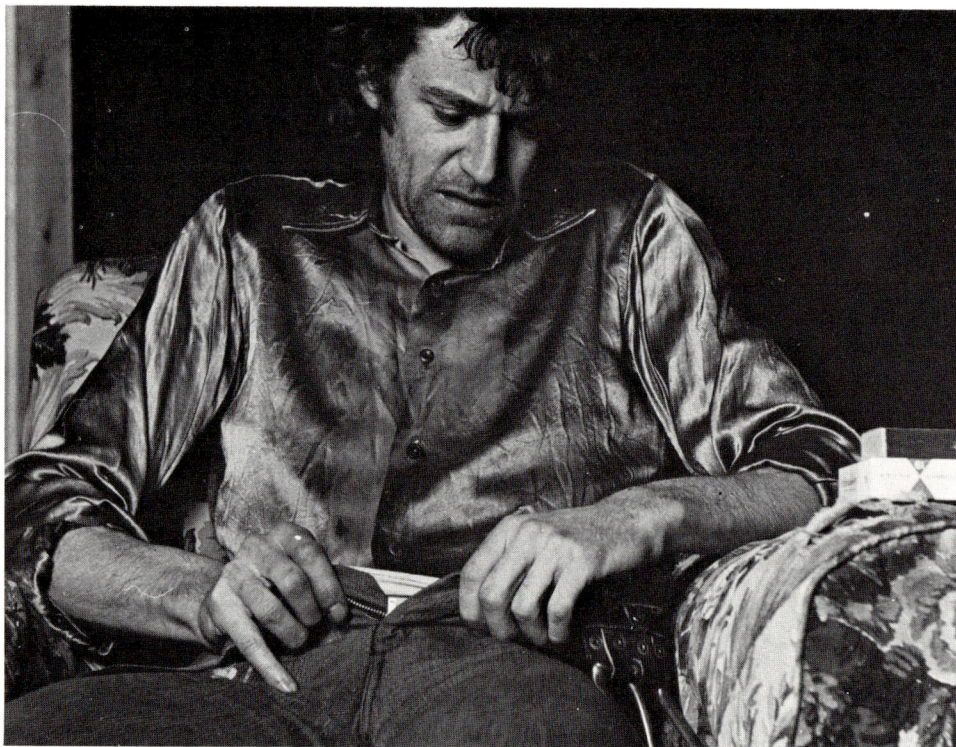

from the main newspapers seem reluctant to visit, a matter of concern for Quipu, whose writers need to have their work reviewed if they are to get at least the feel of critical opinion.

Some other companies are more fortunate in this respect, notably the Soho Theatre Company whose every production gets reasonable press coverage. Perhaps this is due to good public relations, for Verity Bargate has worked hard on this aspect from the very beginning, there being little difference otherwise in standards between the two companies. Frederick Proud, who started Soho Theatre in the basement of a small Chinese restaurant in New Compton Street, is in some ways the uncrowned king of lunchtime theatre. He and Verity Bargate are the personification of the 'fringe' outlook, yet they have a thoroughly professional approach to their work and an ease of manner which endears them to patrons and press alike.

Their Chinese restaurant venture ended with the termination of the lease, but while there they mounted several plays of value both as writing and as experimental productions. After a period of searching in vain for fresh West End premises, they moved temporarily to the King's Head, a pub in Upper Street, Islington, which had recently been taken over by a theatre-minded manager with the object in mind of presenting dinner and a play each evening. This policy was already successful and some lunchtime performances had prepared the ground for Soho Theatre, who soon built up audiences in their new surroundings, where a hot meal could be eaten at a table while watching the play. The aim, however, was still to get back into the West End and a stroke of good luck gave them their present premises – the basement of a building in Riding House Street owned by the Polytechnic. Moving-in was a lengthy process, necessitating another long period without performances, but the basement was transformed into a small, comfortable theatre with a cork-walled stage, raked seating, a foyer and a food-and-drink bar. Here, the company was truly at home and named the new theatre the Soho Poly, a title preserving their own name as well as acknowledging their landlord's. With a measure of physical and financial security behind them, Soho Poly embarked on a new policy of short seasons devoted to a single theme. Towards the end of 1972 this took the form of a season of neglected classics, one-act plays by famous authors –

all of them unperformed for many years. The opening production was a Chekhov rarity, his first play *On the Road*, and was of sufficient interest to entice David Warner and John Turner to play leads. Shaw, Molnar and others followed, each play presented with a sense of style and played by first-rate artists, and reviewed by many of the critics.

Then came the final play, an unfamiliar Sheridan comedy, the costumes for which more than exhausted all the funds left from the current Arts Council grant. So the theatre was 'dark' again for a few weeks until a fresh grant enabled them to open in February 1973 with David Edgar's *Gangsters*, first in a season of new plays. Another, and most important company on the fringe is the Ambiance, so called because their first season a few years ago was held in the basement of the Ambiance restaurant in Queensway. The power behind this virile and financially successful company is Ed Berman, an American whose direction has stamped a recognizable trademark on their work. While at the Ambiance, his deep concern for racial relationships was soon apparent and there, as well as later at the ICA where his company had a temporary home, he presented plays by coloured writers, introducing a fair amount of vigorous new work to the theatrical scene.

Ambiance Lunch-hour Theatre is only one

Patrick Waldron and Michael Scholes in the Quipu production of *The Fight* by Peter King at the Little Theatre Club. *Photograph by David Beaumont*

aspect of the activities of 'Inter-Action', a charitable trust founded in 1968, whose work covers both theatre and community work. They now have their own theatre premises in Rupert Street, a stone's-throw from Piccadilly Circus, which they have named the Almost Free, as members may determine their own membership fee and ticket price from a minimum of one new penny upwards. The success of this policy, shown by the large houses, has inspired Soho Poly to follow their example by suggesting 'Pay what you can afford'.

One of the Inter-Action groups is known as Dogg's Troupe and the playwright Tom Stoppard wrote a play *Dogg's our Pet* especially for the theatre's opening in December 1971. There is, however, no permanent company of actors, even at Ambiance, and as with the other lunchtime groups, casts are newly acquired for each play.

Five minutes' walk from the Almost Free is the Act Inn, a large, well-equipped room over the Duke of Argyle pub in Brewer Street; a room which for many years was the home of the Gallery First Nighters' Club. Run by a young director, Amos Mokardi, Act Inn's policy has so far been a little obscure, with widely variable standards of writing, acting and production. At their best they have been very good indeed, and in early 1973 a season of one-man shows set a new high standard, but at the time of writing their future hangs in the balance through lack of money.

Other groups with a record of success in presenting new plays include the Richmond Fringe, who play at the Orange Tree pub in Richmond; Basement Theatre who, after a long period in a Greek Street basement are temporarily homeless; and the enterprising Recreation Ground who present new plays in the Dryden Room of the tiny Lamb and Flag pub just by Moss Bros in Covent Garden. There are also less successful ventures at other pubs, but all display the need of artists to play before the public. The future of the established groups seems reasonably assured, although they all exist on an economical razor's-edge, and the recently formed Association of Lunchtime Theatres is a collective activity which will give the weaker individual members strength when they need weight behind their frequent negotiations with the Arts Council and Equity, the actor's trade union. Even this Association is not to the liking of one or two groups who still prefer their individual freedom, but as money is the cause of most of their troubles, working closely together and sharing basic facilities will increasingly become a factor to consider, if the sicklier members are to survive and the movement as a whole continue to flourish.

THE MOUSETRAP MAN

Peter Saunders has had the unique experience of celebrating two highly memorable twenty-first birthdays. The first was his own personal twenty-first, but what turned out to be far more exciting was the twenty-first birthday of *The Mousetrap*, Agatha Christie's thriller which he presents at the Ambassadors Theatre. On November 25, 1973, this production of the longest-running play in the history of the British theatre came of age, with a whole string of other record-breaking figures to its credit.

For many years *Chu Chin Chow*, the First War musical, held sway as the longest London run, with 2,238 performances. Once *The Mousetrap* exceeded those figures, way back in 1958, and gained the distinction of being the longest-running production in the history of the British stage, it became a unique phenomenon in the annals of the theatre and developed into an institution which seems to have been with us always. Other shows have beaten the *Chu Chin Chow* record since 1958 – notably *Oliver!*, *Salad Days*, *My Fair Lady*, *The Sound of Music* and *The Black and White Minstrel Show*, but *The Mousetrap* has run well over twice as long as its nearest rival.

In 1970 *The Mousetrap* set a new world record for the greatest number of performances during a continuous run of a play at one theatre, with a total of 7,511. The previous holder of the record was *The Drunkard* by W H Smith and A Gentleman, which ran at the Theatre Mart, Los Angeles, starting in 1933.

Agatha Christie wrote the play originally for the radio, to mark the occasion of Queen Mary's eightieth birthday and it was called *Three Blind Mice*. When Dame Agatha turned it into a full-length stage play it became *The Mousetrap* because the earlier title had already been used for a stage play.

More than 3,000,000 people have seen the show at the Ambassadors and some who went in the early days have since taken their grandchildren. So great is its reputation with overseas visitors, it goes down on their list of the sights of London together with such 'musts' as the Tower and St Paul's Cathedral. A play which has run continuously at one theatre for twenty-one years is surely something not to be missed. What is more, the end of the run is nowhere is sight.

Some might think a production which has run so long would have become a bit jaded by this time. But not with Peter Saunders at the helm! Being a perfectionist, as well as an astute businessman, he is not content to leave even a cast-iron success to chance. The maintenance of this stubborn success is something of a full-time job. It must be kept as fresh as the traditional daisy if it is to pack the house night after night for years on end. In the past, certain players such as Mysie Monte and David Raven stayed in *The Mousetrap* year after year and proudly created their own personal records concerning the number of times an individual artist had played the same part. Mr Saunders has now adopted a different policy and he recasts the play every year, thereby avoiding any risk of artists walking through performances

as a result of endless repetition.

Another clever touch is to engage a new producer every year to prevent the production getting stale or stereotyped as the result of receiving the same direction every year. These different directors bring new ideas to *The Mousetrap*, but Peter Saunders insists upon the play retaining a timeless flavour. There are no arty-crafty changes. Extremes of fashion, such as shoulder-length hair for the men and mini-skirts for the ladies, are avoided. It smacks neither of 1952 – the first year of the run – nor of 1973, but it is the result of a sensible compromise. Slight changes have been made in the script, such as the deletion of references to rationing and identity cards, wartime measures which have long been discontinued. This is a reminder that in the early days of the run, though the War had been over six years, meat, sugar, butter, margarine, bacon and cheese were still rationed. Churchill was Prime Minister, Harry S Truman was President of the United States and Stalin ruled Russia. On the opening night at the Ambassadors, strange as it may seem today, the television programmes listed in *The Times* took up no more than three lines.

Not every artist has the ability to sustain a performance at the same high level for twelve months at a stretch, but that is a risk the actor and the manager has to take at the annual recasting of *The Mousetrap*. The actors know the show will run a year when they sign the contract. If they so wish, they can leave the cast after six months;

Martin Miller as Mr Paravicini and Sheila Sim as
Mollie Ralston in the original cast of *The Mousetrap*,
which opened at the Ambassadors Theatre on
November 25, 1952

otherwise they are obliged to stay for the
full year. They also realize their names will
not be billed. Agatha Christie is the star
name which attracts the public.

Agatha Christie relied upon collaborators
for her earlier plays. Frank Vosper, for
instance, wrote *Love From a Stranger* from
an Agatha Christie story and *Murder at the
Vicarage* was by Moie Charles and Barbara
Toy from a Christie novel, but now Dame
Agatha adapts her stories herself. According
to Peter Saunders, she can condense a novel
into a play with an amazing theatre sense.
She has an instinct for writing lines which
sound natural and actors find them easy to
learn.

Without being disloyal to *The Mousetrap*,
Peter Saunders regards *Witness for the
Prosecution* to be Agatha Christie's finest
piece of theatrecraft, which he staged a year
later in 1953 at the now demolished Winter
Garden Theatre in Drury Lane. Dame
Agatha is of the same opinion. The two
productions are quite different, one being a
trial play, the other a whodunnit.

Witness for the Prosecution had a far from easy
start. It was a dramatization of a short story
without a trial scene, but when it came to the
stage, all the excitement and suspense
stemmed from the written-in courtroom
sequence.

Then came casting troubles. Sir Wilfred
Robarts, QC, the leading part, did not appeal
to actors. Peter Saunders made a list of
thirty-six star and semi-star names as being
suitable for the part. Each one in turn
refused it, convinced it would not work.
Eventually David Horne, who was not on
the original list, agreed to play it. The
production scored a sensational success and
put the then unfashionable Winter Garden
back on the West End theatre map.

There was a two-year run on Broadway and
the film rights were sold for £116,000. The
show was a money-maker from the start, but
Peter Saunders has never been tempted to
revive it because he hesitates to destroy
memories of the ideal casting of the London
and New York stage productions in which
Patricia Jessel was unforgettable and
irreplaceable as Romaine.

But to return to *The Mousetrap* – Peter
Saunders, having studied birth-rate statistics
observes half a million people are born in
Britain every year, which means that some
150,000 come of what he calls *Mousetrap*
age. In other words, that extra number is
available as a potential *Mousetrap* audience.
There are some who sneer and claim the
phenomenal run depends upon the fact that
the play occupies one of London's smallest
theatres, one that seats only 453. Mr
Saunders points out that so small a theatre
has disadvantages. If there are bad houses,
as a result of snow, fog or industrial strife,
it takes so much longer to make up box-
office setbacks.

Others rather disparagingly suggest *The
Mousetrap* owes its success to coach parties.
Once again Mr Saunders disagrees.
Thousands of coach party play-goers have
seen the show in the past, but it has run so
long it is now very difficult to find large
numbers of people living within coach party
radius of the Ambassadors Theatre who have
not seen the play. That particular section of
the population has been exhausted.

Richard Attenborough as Det.-Sgt. Trotter and Sheila Sim as Mollie Ralston in the original 1952 production of *The Mousetrap* at the Ambassadors Theatre

The Mousetrap has been presented in forty-one different countries and has been translated into twenty-two different languages. Peter Saunders guards the English-speaking rights of the play very closely and will continue to do so until the end of the London run. The play cannot be presented on Broadway because American tourists are such good customers at the Ambassadors. It was seen in South Africa in 1954, but it cannot be revived there until after the London run. The theatre in Guernsey is eager to perform it during the summer season. They point out their theatre is not on the touring circuit, but Mr Saunders replies that people who live in Guernsey visit London and are welcome at the Ambassadors box-office.

Back in 1956 the film rights were bought by Romulus Films, on the understanding that the picture could not be seen in London until six months after the last performance at the Ambassadors. As this date is so uncertain, Mr Saunders has twice offered to buy back the film rights, but Romulus prefer to await their opportunity to produce the film themselves when the time eventually comes.

How will Mr Saunders feel when *The Mousetrap* is finally withdrawn? 'It will not be quite like the severing of an artery,' he says, 'because there will be applications from repertory theatres in this country and from countless theatres abroad; later still the amateur rights will become available.' So *The Mousetrap* will not be forgotten overnight after it has been performed for the last time in London.

Since the beginning of *The Mousetrap* Peter Saunders has changed his attitude towards long runs. At one time he wondered whether the runs of West End successes ought to be curtailed to make room for prior-to-London plays on the road, which often have to fold because of the inability to find an empty West End theatre. After much consideration and examination of the large number of new plays which fail to come up to expectations on reaching London, he has decided managements should milk their successes dry and not withdraw a play while it is still making money and keeping people in work. It is bad for the live theatre to have a succession of flops, which so often results in certain papers going out of their way to exaggerate the losses and the disaster involved. Far better to cherish a success when one comes along and make enough money to be able to gamble on future productions which will be needed to replace money-making successes which have run their full course.

Gershwin's music is often heard in Peter Saunders's Hampstead home – called Monkswell, after Monkswell Manor in which the action of *The Mousetrap* takes place. He finds Gershwin scores most relaxing when he gets away from theatre business. At one time he toyed with the idea of presenting *Girl Crazy*, the 1930 Gershwin Broadway hit, in which Ethel Merman made her first appearance on the regular stage, as distinct from vaudeville and cabaret, to sing 'I Got Rhythm'. Ginger Rogers was also in the cast, with her dazzling Hollywood career still before her.

An amateur production was staged at Blackpool at the time Peter Saunders was thinking about presenting the show over here. With Pat Kirkwood he went up to see it, but the book creaked so badly he decided against doing it. He feels *Show Boat* is about the only survivor of that Golden Age of American musicals when Cole Porter, Jerome Kern and George Gershwin were in their heyday.

As owner of the freehold of the Vaudeville Theatre in the Strand and the lessee of the Ambassadors and the St Martin's Theatres, Peter Saunders is convinced that the theatre is healthier now than at any time since the War. That is the final answer to the defeatists who revel in prophesying the early death of live entertainment.

ARCHITECTURAL AWARDS

Three new theatres in England were among the twelve buildings featured in the 1972 Royal Institute of British Architect's Architectural Awards. They were the Crucible Theatre at Sheffield, the Wyvern at Swindon and the Birmingham Repertory Theatre.

Reporting on the Sheffield Crucible, the jury said, 'The architects and their consultants, the clients, their advisers and technical staff, were able to work together from an early date. This collaboration has helped much in the success of the theatre building as a whole, in its detailed function, and in permitting it to be used for a greater variety of types of production than had been envisaged at the conception.

'The design ideas and general aesthetic extend right through the theatre from the large elements down to the cutlery in the excellent restaurant area.'

Concerning the Wyvern Theatre at Swindon, the jury were impressed by the consistency of detail, quality of finish, the restraint, choice of colour, control of scale and the pleasant way that one space leads into another.

The Birmingham Repertory Theatre found favour for being 'lively and exciting internally', but the jury were unhappy about the external wall surfaces, which they considered to be inconsistently handled, resulting in the feeling that externally the building was somewhat uncontrolled. Their conclusion, however, was that the theatre epitomizes the optimism, energy and liveliness of post-war Birmingham.

A bronze plaque was awarded to each theatre, suitable for fixing to the fabric of the building.

A DECADE OF WORLD THEATRE SEASONS

Peter Daubeny

Having presented his tenth and last World Theatre Season at the Aldwych Theatre, with the Governors of the Royal Shakespeare Company, Peter Daubeny looks back on this unique achievement in the history of the London theatre.

The first World Theatre Season was launched at the Aldwych Theatre in 1964, presented by the Governors of the Royal Shakespeare Company and myself to mark the 400th anniversary of Shakespeare's birth. Over the past ten years the Season has become a sort of crash-course in theatrical education, which shakes London's long-conditioned stock responses. As Alan Brien wrote in the *Sunday Telegraph*, it makes us 'better equipped to judge the triumphs, as well as the failures, of our own native companies'. This in my mind summarizes its purpose and fulfilment.

The presentation of foreign theatre in London was not a completely new invention, because ever since the end of the War, in my years as an independent impresario, I had had the opportunity of bringing many foreign companies over to London. But the establishment of an annual Season was new. We, in England, were aware of the best in foreign films, for we had recourse to sub-titles and were thus able to understand them; we were able to judge for ourselves major and minor novels which were translated for us to read; we knew what was going on in the world of music, which is a universal language. Now we had the opportunity of regularly seeing, in the context of these

Seasons, the very best in world theatre. All the world is hearsay until one confronts it face to face; and now we were able to do this. The language-barrier between stage and audience was overcome very successfully with the introduction of a system of simultaneous translation through a portable earphone.

Gradually it came about that all the great companies of the world wanted to come and show their work in the world's theatrical capital, the theatre's own Common Market, and many companies have made return visits. Ingmar Bergman, for example, presented his fourth London production in the 1973 Season. The first was before the Seasons began and there were subsequent visits with the Royal Dramatic Theatre of Stockholm in 1968 and 1971. During the 1973 Season, too, the Comédie Française made their fourth World Theatre Season visit. Italian, German, Russian, Spanish, Polish, Czech and Greek companies have also returned to London to take part in World Theatre Seasons.

Every visiting company presents its own special problem. Generally speaking accommodation for the companies has never been one of the major problems, except in certain cases when national diets and temperamental demands have had to be catered to. Accommodation has been helped greatly by the close association that we have built up over the years with specific London hotels.

With Negro companies, of which I have brought over several, the accommodation

can be very difficult and deeply embarrassing, because one realizes that the apartheid situation has not been solved. In my book, *My World of Theatre*, I recalled the terrible incident experienced by Rosalind Cash when she appeared in *Lusitanian Bogey* with the Negro Ensemble Company from the United States. From the gallery of the Aldwych there were shouts of 'If you were white, you'd be thrown off that stage, you bastards!' 'Portugal is our Atlantic ally!' 'Go home, niggers!'

As well as the individual problems posed by each participating company, there are general problems which are perennial. One of these is finance. With the limited funds the World Theatre Season has at its disposal, it has invariably been a great struggle to keep within our budget.

In all negotiations one has to be economist as well as ambassador, Minister without portfolio, editor, director, cutter and, above all, diplomat. For example, even to persuade a director to have one interval instead of two, not to mention cutting the text itself, will often take all one's diplomacy and powers of persuasion.

Of course, the Seasons are often politically fraught as well. One tries to be apolitical, but realizes that in the process one is in fact being political because one is bringing together countries which, sadly, have no contact except on this level of theatre. It is good that all forms of art are now usually seen as ambassadors of understanding. The theatre is especially powerful in this; the union of actor and audience can achieve a

104

flashpoint of communication which penetrates every barrier.

Although I now work in close association with the Royal Shakespeare Company, and with their full help, the pressures of the Seasons have been far greater than the pressures involved when I was presenting foreign companies independently at theatres such as the Stoll and the Palace. These pressures are mainly caused by the fact that one is working all the time to meet deadlines. The planning for any one Season has to begin while the previous Season is in progress and one is constantly faced with the threat of being criticized if it is not only not as good as, but not better than the last. Despite this problem of pressure and a year constantly interrupted by frequent visits abroad, I feel sure the Season has succeeded in establishing and sustaining its own vitality and appeal. It is certainly respected and admired all over the world, proved by the fact that my book, *My World of Theatre*, already published in England, is now being published in five other countries.

Without doubt, the most successful companies, both critically and in terms of box-office, have been the Noh Theatre of Japan and the Zulu Theatre Workshop Company from Natal. Both in turn broke all box-office records at the Aldwych, in and out of Season, and in both instances we saw longer queues than we had ever seen before. The Noh is the most illusive and esoteric form of theatre. The performers' art lies in their perfected sense of timing. Many of the most dramatic points of Noh Theatre seem to be moments of silence and immobility, which in a curious magical way reinforce the effect of each individual element of the drama. Either one is hypnotized by their exotic brilliance, as I am, or one is bored stiff. The influence of the Noh on both film and theatre directors has been immense. The energy and excited rhythms of the Zulu Company were totally different from the quiet grace of the Noh. When with my wife, Molly, I had seen the company performing in their native country in the open air, I had never envisaged the tumultuous enthusiasm with which they were greeted on their first night at the Aldwych and which was maintained right to the last minute of their stay. Overnight, this London appearance shot them to world fame and led to the planning of a world tour. I was very proud to welcome them back to the Aldwych with *Umabatha* for the tenth World Theatre Season. But I have been very proud of every company I have presented.

Other companies, too, had their international 'break' at the World Theatre Season and went on to conquer the world. One of the most successful was the Nuria Espert Company in Lorca's *Yerma*, directed by Victor Garcia, which also returned during the 1973 Season.

Artistic bonds are among the strongest between nations, and witnessing these productions at the World Theatre Season, it is hoped both young and old will learn to understand other nations and cultures, to be less critical and more sympathetic.

We must remember, also, how invaluable it is that young artists – actors and others – should have an opportunity of witnessing a new approach, with new techniques and new ideals. I am convinced, by my own experience, that art is the most direct method of exchanging mutual affections, which breed friendship in a sad world.

In my summation of these Seasons, I would like to quote the last paragraph of my book: 'I have been twenty-nine years in the theatre, and I have just presented my two hundredth production in London, Montherlant's *La Ville Dont Le Prince Est Un Enfant*. I have been stage-struck since a boy, and throughout the drift and debris of a million events flashing by like a single heart-beat, I have touched hands with death, held hands with love and beheld the touchstone of magic – the theatre.'

Peter Daubeny accompanied Princess Margaret
backstage at the Aldwych to meet the Natal
Theatre Workshop Company after a performance
of *Umabatha* by Welcome Msomi, who wrote the
play and acted the leading part.
Photograph by the Press Association Ltd

WORLD THEATRE SEASON AT THE ALDWYCH THEATRE

Productions for the 10th Season – the last in
the present series under the artistic direction
of Peter Daubeny

March 26–31. **Germany:** Bochum
Schauspielhaus presented *Kleiner Mann –
Was Nun?*, a revue about Berlin in the
twenties and thirties, by Hans Fallada,
adapted by Tankred Dorst and directed
by Peter Zadek.

April 2–7. **Spain:** Nuria Espert Company
presented Victor Garcia's production of
Yerma by Lorca.

April 9–14. **Austria:** Burgtheater of Vienna
presented Gerhard Klingenberg's
production of *Liebelei* by Schnitzler.

April 16–21. **France:** The Comédie
Française presented *Le Médecin Volant* by
Molière, with Jean-Laurent Cochet's
production of *Le Malade Imaginaire* by
Molière.

April 23–28. **France:** The Comédie
Française presented Shakespeare's
Richard III, directed by Terry Hands.

April 30–May 5. **Italy:** Peppino De
Filippo's Italian Theatre Company
presented *The Metamorphoses of a
Wandering Minstrel* by Peppino De Filippo.

May 14–19. **Belgium:** The Rideau de
Bruxelles presented *L'Enchanteur
Pourrissant* by Guillaume Apollinaire,
adapted by Pierre Laroche.

May 21–26. **Poland:** Cracow Stary Theatre
presented Andrzej Wajda's adaptation and
production of *The Possessed* by
Dostoyevsky.

May 28–June 2. **Sweden:** Royal Dramatic
Theatre of Stockholm presented Ingmar
Bergman's production of *The Wild Duck*
by Ibsen.

June 4–16. **Japan:** The Umewaka Noh
Theatre presented three programmes of
of eight different Noh dramas.

June 18–30. **South Africa:** The Natal
Theatre Workshop Company presented
Umabatha, Welcome Msomi's Zulu drama
on the theme of *Macbeth*.

PLAYS OF THE YEAR

ABSURD PERSON SINGULAR

Alan Ayckbourn directed the world première of his own comedy, *Absurd Person Singular*, presented in-the-round at Scarborough's Library Theatre. Audiences of holiday-makers were highly amused by the three acts, each set in a different kitchen. The author presented three married couples and their lunatic happenings at three Christmas Eve parties.

A play by Alan Ayckbourn. Presented by the Theatre-in-the-Round at the Library Theatre, Scarborough, on June 26, 1972.

Cast included:

Jane Hopcroft	*Philippa Urquart*
Sidney Hopcroft	*Piers Rogers*
Ronald Brewster-Wright	
	Christopher Godwin
Marion Brewster-Wright	
	Matyelok Gibbs
Eva Jackson	*Jennifer Piercy*
Geoffrey Jackson	*Ray Jewers*

Directed by the Author

ALL SET FOR MURDER

The Actress Beatrix Carter played a leading part in her own thriller, *All Set for Murder*, seen at the Northampton Repertory Theatre, under the direction of Willard Stoker.

A keen admirer of Agatha Christie, Miss Carter set her play in the lounge of a West Country hotel, where the staff and guests all harbour secrets which are brought to light by a suave blackmailer, played by Michael Reeves. With admirable craftsmanship, Miss Carter makes it obvious who is to be killed before the curtain falls on the first act.

A play by Beatrix Carter. Presented at Northampton Repertory Theatre on August 22, 1972. Designed by Alan Miller Bunford.

Cast included:

Gwen Harvey	*Jill Johnson*
Bunny Harvey	*David Brierley*
Professor Khan	*Leader Hawkins*
Frank Charterhouse	*Michael Reeves*
Miss Fellows	*Gabrielle Blunt*
Mrs Downs	*Beatrix Carter*
Sgt Purdy	*Michael Stock*
Det.-Insp. Tanner	*Henry Knowles*

Directed by Willard Stoker

ALPHA ALPHA

Howard Barker's *Alpha Alpha*, presented at the Open Space Theatre, was a comic-strip satire on a pair of East End criminal twins who are quite ruthless in their violence. It also includes face-slashing and murder.

David Schofield and Anthony Milner were most convincing as the evil twins and Miriam Karlin gave one of her superlative performances as the doting mother, proud of her offspring's achievements without understanding anything about the nature of them.

A play by Howard Barker. Presented at the Open Space Theatre on September 18, 1972.

Cast included:

Morris	*David Schofield*
Mickey	*Anthony Milner*
Nora Scrubs	*Miriam Karlin*
Lord Gadsby	*Dallas Cavell*
Bernadette	*Carol Hazell*
Other parts	*Malcolm Storry*

Directed by Peter Watson

AN INSPECTOR CALLS

Christopher Denys was responsible for the powerfully directed revival of *An Inspector Calls* by J B Priestley at the Pitlochry Festival. It is one of Priestley's most gripping plays, this drama of a society in need of purging which reveals the individual and collective guilt of the leading characters for the death of the poor girl victim.

Victor Lucas dominated the production as the mysterious Inspector, with accurately observed performances by Peter Ducrow and Sheila Brownrigg as the man and wife and Lois Hantz and Christopher Saul as their children.

Revival of play by J B Priestley. Presented at the Pitlochry Festival Theatre on June 12, 1972. Designed by Helen Wilkinson.

Cast included:

Arthur Birling	*Peter Ducrow*
Sybil Birling	*Sheila Brownrigg*
Sheila Birling	*Lois Hantz*
Eric Birling	*Christopher Saul*
Gerald Croft	*Donald MacIver*
Edna	*Colette Kelly*
Inspector Goole	*Victor Lucas*

Directed by Christopher Denys

AN OTHELLO

An Othello was a play by Charles Marowitz, after Shakespeare, and staged at the Open Space Theatre. It draws attention to the status of the House and the Field Negroes in the days of slavery.

Shakespeare's words remain as the core, but Marowitz wrote interruptions and speeches which showed Othello as the tool of his white superiors and the enemy of the Field Negro, symbolized by Iago. The white man's attitude – 'Do you think we want a coon trailing round these islands with a white pussy in tow?' – implements Iago's actions, yet ultimately both classes of Negro are the losers.

Rudolph Walker and Anton Phillips gave strong performances as Othello and Iago.

A play by Charles Marowitz, after Shakespeare. Presented at the Open Space Theatre on June 8, 1972. Designed by Robin Don.

Cast included:

Desdemona	*Judy Geeson*
Othello	*Rudolph Walker*
Iago	*Anton Phillips*
Cassio	*David Schofield*
Brabantio	*Edward Phillips*
Duke	*Malcolm Storry*
Lodovico	*Richard Monette*

Directed by Charles Marowitz

AND WAS JERUSALEM BUILT HERE?

The setting of Barry Collins's new play seen at Leeds Playhouse, *And Was Jerusalem Built Here?* was a cloth-manufacturing area of the West Riding of Yorkshire at the time of the Luddite Riots about 1812, when the workers fiercely resented the introduction of machinery, which they smashed, at the same time burning the mills.

The agony and misery of the Industrial Revolution was stressed in this grim and gripping play, in which Terrence Hardiman, Frances Cuka, Patrick O'Connell and Howard Rawlinson played the leading parts, under the brilliant direction of Bill Hays.

A play by Barry Collins. Presented at Leeds Playhouse on May 24, 1972.

Cast included:

Carwright	*Howard Rawlinson*
Booth	*Terrence Hardiman*
Anna	*Frances Cuka*
Mellor	*Patrick O'Connell*
Father	*Alan Hockey*

Directed by Bill Hays

APPLAUSE

Lauren Bacall's blazing star quality swept London off its feet when she stepped on to the stage of Her Majesty's Theatre in *Applause*, the Broadway musical based on the film, *All About Eve*. She is no song-bird, but puts over her numbers with that same expertise which Rex Harrison demonstrated when he plunged into a musical without possessing a traditional musical comedy voice.

Not since Mary Martin played here in *South Pacific* has an American star made such a powerful impact as Lauren Bacall, who knows how to project personality and characterization across the footlights with an aim that never fails to hit the bull's eye. She was ideally cast in the Bette Davis role of the ageing star whose reputation is undermined by the young adoring fan who worms herself into her entourage and eventually threatens to eclipse her.

Angela Richards was superb as this treacherous youngster who gave the impression that butter would not melt in her mouth. Sheila O'Neill led the dancing sequences with the Gypsies with enormous gusto.

A musical based on the film *All About Eve* and the original story by Mary Orr. Presented by Bernard Delfont and Alexander H Cohen at Her Majesty's Theatre on November 16, 1972. Book by Betty Comden and Adolph Green; music by Charles Strouse; lyrics by Lee Adams; scenery by Robert Randolph; costumes by Ray Agha-yan; orchestrations by Philip J Lang; dance and incidental music arranged by Mel Marvin; musical director – Robert Lowe; choreography by Ron Field.

Cast included:

Margo Channing	*Lauren Bacall*
Eve Harrington	*Angela Richards*
Howard Benedict	*Basil Hoskins*
Bill Sampson	*Eric Flynn*
Buzz Richards	*Rod McLennan*
Karen Richards	*Sarah Marshall*
Duane Fox	*Ken Walsh*
Sheila	*Sheila O'Neill*

Directed by Ron Field

Left: Edward Woodward as Robin Hood and Adrienne Posta as Maid Marian in the London Palladium Pantomime, *Babes in the Wood.* *Photograph by Dezo Hoffmann*

Right: Freddie Jones and Belinda Low in *The Baker, The Baker's Wife and the Baker's Boy* at the Newcastle University Theatre

BABES IN THE WOOD

After seeing *Babes in the Wood* at the London Palladium, Milton Shulman suggested that if audience participation went any further it would be only fair to pay the customers Equity rates.

The comedy was in the hands of Derek Nimmo and Bill Maynard, with Julian Orchard, revelling in female impersonation, but Rod Hull and his fantastic Emu won the comedy laurels of the evening.

Edward Woodward, with an agreeable singing voice and a flair for duelling, made a most acceptable Robin Hood with captivating Adrienne Posta as his Maid Marian.

For more than three hours the audience was treated to glimpses of fluorescent butterflies, a medieval fair, living toys, ballet-dancers, flying actors and a villainous Sheriff in the person of Alan Curtis, who threatened to poison the children's ice cream in the interval.

A pantomime presented by Louis Benjamin and Leslie Grade at the London Palladium on December 19, 1972. Book by Phil Park, with comedy scenes and additional dialogue by Eric Merriman and Austin Steele. Décor by Tod Kingman, costume designs by Cynthia Tingey and choreography by Pamela Devis. Musical director: Gordon Rose.

Cast included:

Robin Hood	*Edward Woodward*
Rodney Willoughby Fortescue	*Derek Nimmo*
Nurse Bunty Biddle	*Julian Orchard*
Jasper Snatchem	*Bill Maynard*
Sheriff of Nottingham	*Alan Curtis*
Lady Marian Fitzwalter	*Adrienne Posta*

With *David Bexon, John Wyman, Jack Francois, Bill Tasker, Alan Turvey, Georgia Jee, Tom Chatto, Bertie Hare, Jilly Coram, Steve Emerson, Tim Condren, Nicky Benton, Rod Hull* and *Emu, the Pamela Devis Dancers, the Bel Canto Singers* and *the Peggy O'Farrell Children*

Directed by Albert J. Knight

THE BAKER, THE BAKER'S WIFE AND THE BAKER'S BOY

The Tyneside Theatre Company, as part of the Newcastle-on-Tyne 1972 Festival, presented *The Baker, the Baker's Wife and the Baker's Boy*, an Anouilh play as recent as 1968, translated by Lucienne Hill. Touched with fantasy, the play concerns the squabbling of a once-happy couple who have growing children on their hands. Yvonne Mitchell and Freddie Jones played the parents in a Gareth Morgan production which suffered from the vast darkened stage, upon which each set was wheeled into place. Anouilh was obviously influenced by the French student unrest of 1968 and it was not all that easy for English audiences to appreciate this particular work.

The British première of play by Jean Anouilh, translated by Lucienne Hill. Presented by the Tyneside Theatre Company at Newcastle University Theatre on September 26, 1972. Designed by William Dudley. Music by Iwan Williams.

Cast included:

Adolphe	
Louis XVI	*Freddie Jones*
The Pioneer	
Elodie	
Marie Antoinette	*Yvonne Mitchell*
The Pioneer's Wife	
Toto	*Stephen James*
Marie Christine	*Tessa Carley*
Adèle	
Elvira	*Vicky Ireland*
Fessard Lebouze	
Municipal Guard	*Peter Carlisle*
Cattle Rustler	
Edouard	
Hubert de la Prebende	*Michael Attwell*
The Lieutenant	
The Butler	*Tim Barlow*
The Maid	
The Waitress	*Gillian Hanna*
The German Girl	
Josyane	*Belinda Low*
Mlle Tromphe	*Robin Soans*
Red Indians	*David Rintoul*
	Chris Driscoll
	Robin Soans

Directed by Gareth Morgan

Millicent Martin as Polly and
Harold Innocent as Peachum in the
Chichester Festival Theatre
production of *The Beggar's Opera*.
Photograph by John Timbers

BAKKE'S NIGHT OF FAME

Bakke's Night of Fame, presented
at the Shaw Theatre, was a tough
uncompromising play, set in the
death-cell of an American prison.
Far from being a tract on capital
punishment, it is the story of the
condemned man in tragic–comic
confrontation with authority on
his last night on earth. Hywel
Bennett as the man condemned
for murder, David Healy as a
jailer and Nikolas Simmonds as
a priest gave outstanding performances.

A play by John McGrath. Pre-
sented by the Dolphin Theatre
Company at the Shaw Theatre,
Euston, on October 2, 1972. The
play was based on *A Danish
Gambit*, the novel by William
Butler. Designed by Johanna
Bryant.

*Cast included: Bill Bailey, Hywel
Bennett, Ray Edwards, David
Healy, Nikolas Simmonds, Gordon
Sterne, Nik Zaran* and *Marc
Zuber*

Directed by Peter James

THE BEGGAR'S OPERA

The 1971 Chichester Festival Season opened with an inventive
production of *The Beggar's Opera*,
directed by Robin Phillips who
used a listening chorus, seated on
the rim of the stage, to assist with
business and to join in the songs
from time to time.

As Wendy Monk remarked in
her observant commentary of the
production, it was impossible to
forget the teeming slums that
surrounded Peachum's den, so
cleverly suggested by Daphne
Dare's inventive setting. The entire production pulsated with life.

Millicent Martin was a pretty
Polly, with a commonsense head
on her shoulders; Angela Richards
sang Lucy's songs with rare
understanding of their significance;
Harold Innocent and Maggie Fitz-
gibbon were strangely contrasted
as the murderous Peachums and
John Neville was the irresistible
charmer as Macheath.

A revival of the opera by John
Gay. Presented at Chichester Fes-
tival Theatre on May 3, 1972.
Designed by Daphne Dare. Music
arranged and directed by Martin
Best; choreography by Sheila
O'Neill.

Cast included:

Peachum	*Harold Innocent*
Lockit	*Michael Aldridge*
Macheath	*John Neville*
Mrs Peachum	*Maggie Fitzgibbon*
Polly Peachum	*Millicent Martin*
Lucy Lockit	*Angela Richards*
Diana Trapes	*June Jago*
Jenny Diver	*Sarah Atkinson*

Directed by Robin Phillips

Dudley Moore and Peter Cook in
their own revue, *Behind the Fridge*.
Photograph by Sophie Baker

BEHIND THE FRIDGE

In their two-man show, *Behind the Fridge* at the Cambridge Theatre, Peter Cook and Dudley Moore provided ample proof that the art of intimate revue is far from extinct, by presenting one of the most amusing and witty shows seen in the West End for a long time.

Of the four members of the epoch-making *Beyond the Fringe*, Alan Bennett and Jonathan Miller have gone their own ways, one to write successful plays, the other to direct. Peter Cook and Dudley Moore remain on the stage as comedians who have mellowed and have a gentle touch, even in their hilariously funny sketch about the young film-star who visits his working-class father, following the death of the mother. The audience found the show much to their liking and the critic Frank Marcus 'left the theatre feeling a happier and healthier man', after having missed the first night on account of a depressing bout of influenza.

A revue written and performed by Peter Cook and Dudley Moore. Presented by Donald Langdon for Hemdale at the Cambridge Theatre on November 21, 1972. Staged by Peter Cook and Dudley Moore, in association with Joseph McGrath, who also directed the film sequences. Designed by Voytek.

THE BIG ROCK CANDY MOUNTAIN

Avis Bunnage went back to Stratford's Theatre Royal in East London to direct an off-the-beaten-track Theatre Workshop panto-mime called *The Big Rock Candy Mountain*, a folk-song entertainment by Alan Lomax and Yola Miller.

The show proved an enormous success with those who have grown a little tired of Jack and the Beanstalk, Aladdin and Cinderella. Toni Palmer was seen as the Princess, Maxwell Shaw was an old codger and Long John Baldry the ballad-singing cowboy.

The story was set in the Big Rock Candy Mountain:

> Where the doughnuts grow on
> bushes
> And you sleep out every night
> Where Saturday stays all the week
> And you never change your
> socks
> And the little streams of lemon
> squash
> Come trickling down the rocks.

A folk-song pantomime by Alan Lomax and Yola Miller, with songs by Woodie Guthrie, Alan Lomax and others from the past. Presented by Theatre Workshop at the Theatre Royal, Stratford, East 15, on December 21, 1972. Costumes by Willie Burt and settings by Guy Hodkinson and Mark Pritchard.

Cast included: Long John Baldry, Philip Davis, Yvonne Edgell, Ken Hill, Johnny Lyons, Brian Murphy, Toni Palmer, Judith Paris, Peter Rankin and *Maxwell Shaw*

Directed by Avis Bunnage

THE BRASS HAT

Thomas Muschamp in his play *The Brass Hat*, seen at the Yvonne Arnaud Theatre, Guildford, explored, with masterly understanding, the closed society of Army life. By birth, marriage or adoption all the characters are members of modern military society, an organization riddled with rules and ferocious taboos. The moral question of the man sacrificing a few for the many was neatly exploited in Mr Muschamp's play.

A play by Thomas Muschamp. Presented at the Yvonne Arnaud Theatre, Guildford, on July 4, 1972. Designed by Pamela Ingram.

Cast included:

Brigadier John Brown   *Ian Bannen*
Clarissa Holden   *Toby Robins*
Major George Bradley
    Donald Douglas
Lt.-Col. Guy Holden
    Michael Gambon
Maj.-Gen. Charles
    Arbuthnot-Green *Wensley Pithey*
Directed by Clifford Williams

Alec McCowen took over the name-part in *Butley* at the Criterion Theatre from August 7, 1972 for a ten-week season. The part was created by Alan Bates and later played by Richard Briers before the Alec McCowen engagement

BRUSSELS

Jonathan Hales, author of *Brussels*, seen at the Royal Court Theatre Upstairs and later at Greenwich Theatre on October 10, considers the Boy Scouts are an amazing institution – unquestionably British and quite unlike the Hitler Youth or the Young Pioneers.

In a superbly realistic outdoor set by Roger Butlin, the young cast gave some convincing and compelling performances in Mr Hales's nostalgic look back to his wolf-cub days.

A play by Jonathan Hales. Presented in association with the Royal Court Theatre Upstairs at Greenwich Theatre on October 10, 1972. Designed by Roger Butlin with costumes by Harriet Geddes.

Cast included:
Skipper   *John Ringham*
Ken   *Peter Armitage*
Sir William   *Geoffrey Wearing*
Irene   *Sylvia Carson*
Brenda   *Lorraine Hill*

Directed by Jonathan Hales assisted by Joan Mills

BUNNY

Back in a straight play, Eartha Kitt played a captivating New York call-girl in Norman Krasna's *Bunny*, first seen in this country at the Coventry Belgrade Theatre. She becomes involved in a platonic affair with a wealthy widower and store-owner, played by David Kossoff. Much of the comedy sprang from the fact that his family, who hoped to inherit his fortune, were worried that Bunny would try to marry the old man and so cut them out of his will.

A play by Norman Krasna. Presented by Paul Elliott and Duncan C Weldon for Triumph Theatre Productions, at the Criterion Theatre on December 8, 1972. Setting by Terry Parsons.

Cast included:
Morris Fine   *Barry Martin*
Bunny Novak   *Eartha Kitt*
Howard Wheeler   *Robert Beatty*
Doctor Jane Wheeler   *Judith Arthy*
Doctor Carl Benson   *Burnell Tucker*
Aaron Bromberg   *David Kossoff*
Ruth Goldman   *Mary Preston*
Saul Bromberg   *Jon Croft*
Stuart Goldman   *Peter Miles*

Directed by Alexander Doré

Rosemary McHale as Luciana, Chris Harris as Dromio of Ephesus and Judy Cornwell as Adriana in *A Comedy of Errors* presented by the Royal Shakespeare Company. *Photograph by Douglas H. Jeffrey*

CASTE

That milestone in stage naturalism, T W Robertson's *Caste* was directed at Greenwich Theatre by Robert Cushman. In staging this story of the little ballet-dancer who married a soldier who belonged to the upper classes, Mr Cushman permitted the actors playing aristocratic parts to overact to the point of provoking laughter where it was out of place.

He was much more successful with the members of the working class and there were memorable performances from Ann Penfold as Polly Eccles, Peter Gordon as her plumber-admirer and Alfie Bass as the drunken father.

A revival of play by T W Robertson. Presented at Greenwich Theatre on September 14, 1972. Designed by David Cockayne.

Cast included:
Marquise de St Maur
　　　　　　Yvonne Coulette
Hon. George D'Alroy
　　　　　　Geoffrey Beevers
Captain Hawtree　*Tim Preece*
Dixon　　　　　*Owen Jones*
Esther Eccles　*Barbara Ewing*
Polly Eccles　　*Ann Penfold*
Sam Gerridge　*Peter Gordon*
Eccles　　　　　*Alfie Bass*

Directed by Robert Cushman

CATHERINE HOWARD

Beverley Cross, that well-established dramatist who wrote the Catherine Howard episode for the television serial, *The Six Wives of Henry VIII,* later adapted the television script to the stage in a play called *Catherine Howard,* seen at Bournemouth and later at York Theatre Royal, directed by Richard Digby Day.

The stage version hardly touched the mind or stirred the emotions despite talented performances from John Humphry and Elizabeth Bennett as Henry and his fifth wife. The writing was taut and the action swift, one of the highlights of the play being when Catherine is told by Norfolk she will never see her lover, Thomas Culpeper, again.

A play by Beverley Cross. Presented at York Theatre Royal on May 23, 1972, after a première at Bournemouth Playhouse on May 9. Scenery by Hugh Durrant and costumes by Kit Surrey.

Cast included:
Catherine Howard
　　　　　　Elizabeth Bennett
Duke of Norfolk　*Michael Cadman*
King Henry VIII　*John Humphry*
Thomas Culpeper　*Martin Potter*

Directed by Richard Digby Day

A COMEDY OF ERRORS

Clifford Williams's highly successful Royal Shakespeare Company production of *A Comedy of Errors* returned to Stratford-upon-Avon as the only comedy in the Roman Season. The production proved as magical as ever, in spite of being the fourth time round at Stratford, after being played in London, West Berlin, Leningrad, Moscow, Washington, New York and other major cities.

It bubbled with ingenious farcical touches and proved to be a cast-iron success in the RSC repertoire. It sparkled brightly, played by a new cast who obviously enjoyed themselves as enormously as the audience relished their antics.

A revival of the play by Shakespeare. Presented by the Royal Shakespeare Company at the Royal Shakespeare Theatre, Stratford-upon-Avon, on June 20, 1972. Setting by John Wyckham and Clifford Williams, with costumes by Anthony Powell. Music by Peter Wishart.

Cast included:
Antipholus of Ephesus
　　　　　　Corin Redgrave
Antipholus of Syracuse　*John Wood*
Dromio of Ephesus　*Chris Harris*
Dromio of Syracuse
　　　　　　Geoffrey Hutchings
Angelo　　　　*Gerald James*
Solinus　　*Clement McCallin*
Aegeon　　*Raymond Westwell*
Adriana　　　*Judy Cornwell*
Luciana　　*Rosemary McHale*

Directed by Clifford Williams

COSTA PACKET

Described as a candy-floss entertainment, *Costa Packet* was a musical directed by Joan Littlewood at Stratford East's Theatre Royal, concerning people on a package holiday in Spain. Highly amusing were the performances of Avis Bunnage and Ken Hill as a snobbish couple from Birmingham and Maureen Sweeney and Suzan Cameron as a couple of giggling bikini girls. It was a pleasant enough evening.

Entertainment by Frank Norman, Lionel Bart and Alan Klein. Presented by Gerry Raffles for Theatre Workshop at the Theatre Royal, Stratford, East 15, on October 5, 1972. Choreography by Judith Paris; setting by Guy Hodgkinson and Mark Pritchard; costumes by Willie Burt; musical direction by David Gould.

Cast included: J Aitken, Gaye Brown, Avis Bunnage, Suzan Cameron, Larry Dann, Griffith Davies, Philip Davis, Ken Hill, John Lyons, Judith Paris, Maxwell Shaw, Maureen Sweeney, Valerie Walsh, Peter Rankin and David Grigg

Directed by Joan Littlewood

COWARDY CUSTARD

At a time when old-time revue is out of fashion, *Cowardy Custard*, a lavish collection of Noël Coward's theatre songs, sketches and snatches from the pages of his autobiography, won a standing ovation at the Mermaid Theatre, in a richly satisfying show, directed by Wendy Toye.

The young players – Patricia Routledge, Una Stubbs, Elaine Delmar, Derek Waring, Jonathan Cecil and John Moffatt possessed a flair for putting over the Coward numbers of yesteryear with intense feeling for their humour, content and verbal dexterity.

It was an unforgettable tribute to the work of the Master, the sort of occasion which is normally staged for one-night only at a midnight matinee organized to raise funds for a deserving theatre charity. It reminded the audience what they had been missing since intimate revue had been shelved and it was proof that Coward's work could still fill the house, even without such idols as Gertrude Lawrence, Yvonne Printemps, Beatrice Lillie and Maisie Gay to put over the numbers.

An entertainment devised by Gerald Frow, Alan Strachan and Wendy Toye featuring the words and music of Noël Coward. Presented at the Mermaid Theatre on July 10, 1972. Designs by Tim Goodchild and lighting by Charles Bristow. Orchestrations by Keith Amos. Musical director John Burrows.

Cast included: Olivia Breeze, Geoffrey Burridge, Jonathan Cecil, Tudor Davis, Elaine Delmar, Laurel Ford, Peter Gale, John Moffatt, Patricia Routledge, Anna Sharkey, Una Stubbs and Derek Waring

Directed by Wendy Toye and the cast

CRETE AND SERGEANT PEPPER

John Antrobus wrote a new comedy for the Royal Court Theatre, *Crete and Sergeant Pepper*, which turned out to be little more than a succession of Goonish sketches, concerning a mad Major, who organizes an elaborate escape from a prisoner-of-war camp in Crete in 1941.

Bill Maynard gave an endearing performance as Sergeant Pepper and Raymond Francis matched his achievement with an effective interpretation as the deranged Major. The critic Peter Lewis confessed that many a chuckle escaped him watching the rich assortment of strictly logical idiots following the rule book like a sacred text.

A play by John Antrobus. Presented at the Royal Court Theatre on May 24, 1972. Designed by Douglas Heap with costumes by Deirdre Clancy.

Cast included:

Sergeant Pepper	*Bill Maynard*
Private Milligan	*James Hazeldine*
An Officer	*Raymond Francis*
Gunner Jackson	*Stephen Rea*
Corporal Jones	*Bernard Gallagher*

Directed by Peter Gill

A CRISIS OF CONSCIENCE

Prospect Theatre Company presented under the title of *A Crisis of Conscience* at Edinburgh King's Theatre a new version of *Ivanov* by Chekhov, translated by Ariadne Nicolaeff and adapted by Toby Robertson, who was also responsible for the direction.

Derek Jacobi gave an impressive performance as the young man who fell out of love after encouraging a Jewish girl to become his wife. His awareness of her continuing love and need of him punishes this man with a conscience to a drastic degree.

Marilyn Taylerson gave a poignant performance as the dejected young woman who did everything within her power to save the marriage. Richard Briers and Willoughby Goddard supplied light relief in their scenes.

A new version of Chekhov's *Ivanov*, translated by Ariadne Nicolaeff and adapted for this production by Toby Robertson. Presented by the Prospect Theatre Company at the King's Theatre, Edinburgh, on November 3, 1972. Designed by Robin Archer. Music by Carl Davis.

Cast included:

Nicholas Ivanov	*Derek Jacobi*
Anna	*Marilyn Taylerson*
Count Simon Shabelsky	*Willoughby Goddard*
Paul Lebedev	*Michael Goodliffe*
Zia	*Antonia Pemberton*
Sasha	*Sharon Gurney*
Doctor Lvov	*Christopher Burgess*
Martha Babakina	*Frances Cuka*
Nicholas Kassuth	*Richard Briers*
Michael Borkin	*Simon Gough*
Mrs Nazarovna	*Anne Dyson*
Yegorushko	*Bob Hornery*

Directed by Toby Robertson

Amanda Reiss as the Duchess of York, the present Queen Mother, and Andrew Ray as the Duke of York, later George VI, in *Crown Matrimonial*. *Photograph by Anthony Buckley*

CROSS ROAD

Cross Road, staged at the Westminster Theatre, was an attempt by Ailsa Hamilton, Juliet Boobbyer and Ronald Mann to put the story of Frank Buchman and Moral Re-armament on the stage with the help of slides, film music and recordings. It was the work of many people and it was played by a cast from five continents.

The stage documentary made excellent entertainment, with arresting visual images, fused with the contribution of multi-racial singers, actors and musicians. The narration was delivered by Garard Green and Paul Campbell simulated the voice of Frank Buchman quite convincingly.

A multi-media experiment to tell the Frank Buchman story. Presented at the Westminster Theatre on May 4, 1972, created by Ailsa Hamilton, Juliet Boobbyer and Ronald Mann, with visual and set designs by W Cameron Johnson.

Cast included: Chris Gill, Christine Butler, Gérard Gigand, Sandile Makhwelo, Sylvia Haller, Dick Ruffin, Bob Corcoran and *Rob Lancaster.* The narrator was *Garard Green* and the voice of Frank Buchman was impersonated by *Paul Campbell*

CROWN MATRIMONIAL

Wendy Hiller gave the crowning performance of her long and distinguished career as Queen Mary in *Crown Matrimonial*, Royce Ryton's documentary play about the Abdication, directed by Peter Dews at the Haymarket Theatre. Miss Hiller's deeply moving interpretation showed Queen Mary as the mother who found it difficult to talk to her son, whom she could never forgive for putting personal happiness before duty to the Throne and the Monarchy.

As the unprepared Duchess of York, Amanda Reiss made a deep impression, resenting the colossal burden being placed upon the shoulders of her stuttering husband. Set in Queen Mary's sitting-room at Marlborough House, the play, unbiased in its viewpoint, was written with deep sincerity, revealing how Edward VIII's decision to abdicate in order to marry Mrs Simpson must have affected members of the Royal Family. Peter Barkworth as Edward and Andrew Ray as his brother-heir, were very well cast and convincing in their performances.

A play by Royce Ryton. Presented by Michael Codron, by arrangement with the Frederick Harrison Trust Ltd, at the Haymarket Theatre on October 19, 1972. Designed by Finlay James.

Cast included:

Queen Mary	*Wendy Hiller*
King Edward VIII	*Peter Barkworth*
Duke of York	*Andrew Ray*
Duchess of York	*Amanda Reiss*
Princess Royal	*Jane Wenham*
Countess of Airlie	*Joan Haythorne*
The Hon. Margaret Wyndham	*Barbara Atkinson*
Mr Monckton	*Noel Johnson*
Duchess of Gloucester	*Heather Kyd*
Footman	*Leonard Cracknell*

Directed by Peter Dews

Wendy Hiller as Queen Mary in
Crown Matrimonial.   *Photograph by*
Anthony Buckley

DAMES AT SEA

The Hampstead Theatre Club cleverly revamped *Dames at Sea*, that delightful pastiche of Hollywood musicals, originally seen at the Duchess Theatre, and presented it as a late-night show. The cast was well chosen, sparkled delightfully, and provided an enjoyable night out. One critic called it a genuine diamond, another a gem to treasure and a third a small pearl. It was polished to perfection and much appreciated by all who saw it.

A revival of the musical spoof of Hollywood in the 1930s, in a revised form. Presented at the Hampstead Theatre Club on November 15, 1972. Book and lyrics by George Haimsohn and Robin Miller and music by Jim Wise. Designed by Saul Radomsky; choreographed by Gillian Gregory. Musical directed Tommy Gilhooly.

Cast included:

Mona Kent	*Pip Hinton*
Joan	*Barbara Young*
Hennesy	*Richard Owens*
Ruby	*Debbie Bowen*
Dick	*Nicholas Bennett*
Lucky	*Freddie Eldrett*
Captain	*Richard Owens*

Directed by Paul Ciani

117

Julia Foster and Deborah Kerr in *The Day After the Fair*. *Photograph by Mark Gudgeon*

THE DARK RIVER

The women seemed to have the best parts in Rodney Ackland's Second World War success, *The Dark River*, revived at the Gardner Centre for the Arts at the University of Sussex, and they were ably played by Katherine Barker in the Peggy Ashcroft part, Ann Firbank as her close friend and Elspeth March as a retired headmistress and owner of the house on the Thames – the Dark River – where the action takes place.

Frank Marcus neatly commented upon this play, when he said, [Mr Ackland] 'has something to say, his intentions are deeply honourable, and he gives us a glimpse of how people behaved at a specific and important point in history'. The play was written during the Spanish Civil war, but not seen in London until 1943.

A revival of the play by Rodney Ackland. Presented at the Gardner Centre at the University of Sussex, Brighton, on September 12, 1972. Designed by Saul Radomsky.

Cast included:

Ella Merriman	*Elspeth March*
Mervyn Webb	*Nicholas Battershill*
	Anthony Burton
Mr Veness	*Clive Elliott*
Stanley Maltby	*Peter Baldwin*
Catherine Lisle	*Katherine Barker*
Gwendolin Mulville	*Ann Firbank*
Alan Crocker	*Michael Johnson*
Edmund Lester Reade	
	Robert MacLeod
Christopher Lisle	*Michael Burrell*
Nurse	*Helen Kluger*

Directed by Gordon McDougall

THE DAY AFTER THE FAIR

After a nineteen-year-long absence from the stage Deborah Kerr returned to London at the Lyric Theatre to play a highly rewarding acting role in *The Day After the Fair*, a gripping dramatization of a Thomas Hardy story set in 1900.

This conventional-type play with a strong story-line, dealt with real people faced with emotional situations which made good theatre and the entire cast played with deep feeling and genuine sincerity.

Deborah Kerr was seen as the frustrated wife of a rich brewer in Salisbury, acting as a go-between and writing love-letters to a young man in London on behalf of her illiterate servant-girl who could neither read nor write. The brewer's wife and the London correspondent, who turned out to be a young barrister, fell in love with each other through their letters.

The reception following the strange wedding of the barrister and the peasant girl had a shattering sequel when the bridegroom discovered by chance he had been deceived and not married the girl to whom he lost his heart on paper. Julia Foster and Paul Hastings played these parts with rare understanding of the plight of young lovers in distress.

A play by Frank Harvey, based on a Thomas Hardy story called *On the Western Circuit*. Presented by Frith Banbury and Jimmy Wax, by arrangement with Arthur Cantor, at the Lyric Theatre on October 4, 1972. Décor by Reece Pemberton and costumes by Robin Fraser Paye.

Cast included:

Arthur Harnham	*Duncan Lamont*
Letty	*Avice Landon*
Edith	*Deborah Kerr*
Sarah	*Jiggy Bhore*
Anna	*Julia Foster*
Charles Bradford	*Paul Hastings*

Directed by Frith Banbury

Sheila Brownrigg, Ian Lindsay,
Sarah Stephenson, Lois Hantz,
Alice Fraser and Pamela Pitchford
in J M Barrie's *Dear Brutus*.
Photograph by Viking Studios Ltd

DEAD EASY

A nine-week comedy season opened at the Coventry Belgrade Theatre with considerable flourish when Irene Handl appeared in a new comedy-thriller by Jack Popplewell called *Dead Easy*. Miss Handl played a caretaker char-woman who shows considerable flair as a detective when murder occurs on her own doorstep, and her superb theatrical craftsmanship made a highly entertaining evening. Her outstanding supporting colleagues were the attractive Janet Mahoney, and Robert Cawdron as the detective who is outwitted by his charlady rival.

A play by Jack Popplewell. Presented by Paul Elliott and Duncan C Weldon for Triumph Theatre Productions, in association with the Belgrade Theatre, at the Belgrade Theatre, Coventry, on January 23, 1973. Designed by Martin Johns.

Cast included:

Andrews	*Nicholas Evans*
Lily Piper	*Irene Handl*
Det.-Supt. Harry Baxter	
	Robert Cawdron
George Hamilton	*Alan White*
Brewster	*Dennis Clinton*
Collins	*Joseph Wise*
Det.-Con. Goddard	*Peter Wilkins*
Aimé Watson	*Janet Mahoney*

Directed by John Downing

DEAR BRUTUS

Kenneth Ireland, Artistic Director of the Pitlochry Festival Theatre, is a keen Barrie enthusiast and *Dear Brutus* has a special place in his affections. In consequence, this was the second revival of *Dear Brutus* at Pitlochry in just over ten years and was played to mark the Festival Theatre's twenty-first anniversary gala.

It came up to the highest expectations, with Clive Perry's skilful direction capturing all the magic moments in this world of might-have-beens. Helen Wilkinson created all the necessary beauty and mystery of the wood, an ideal setting for the fey Lob of Robert Aldous. Ian Lindsay and Alice Fraser reached memorable heights as Matey and Lady Caroline in the wood scene.

A revival of the play by J M Barrie. Presented at the Pitlochry Festival Theatre on May 19, 1972. Designed by Helen Wilkinson.

Cast included:

Mr Dearth	*Victor Lucas*
Mr Purdie	*Alec Heggie*
Mr Coade	*Peter Ducrow*
Matey	*Ian Lindsay*
Lob	*Robert Aldous*
Mrs Dearth	*Sheila Brownrigg*
Mrs Purdie	*Lois Hantz*
Mrs Coade	*Pamela Pitchford*
Joanna Trout	*Sarah Stephenson*
Lady Caroline Laney	*Alice Fraser*
Margaret	*Colette Kelly*

Directed by Clive Perry

THE DOCTOR'S DILEMMA

John Clements was responsible for the best revival of *The Doctor's Dilemma* by Bernard Shaw for many a year when it was presented at the Chichester Festival Theatre in the summer of 1972.

Milton Shulman remarked upon the topicality of this play, first seen in 1906: 'Shaw's jibes at the profession's ignorance, callousness and high fees still provoke gusts of laughter among audiences only too familiar with the foibles and fallacies of fashionable medical treatment.'

Joan Plowright, alluringly costumed in pre-Raphaelite style, stole most of the reviews, being all the audience would expect of a painter's wife and model. Her plea for medical help for the man she loved was deeply moving and enhanced this fine actress's already well-established reputation.

The Harley Street figures were convincingly played by John Clements, John Neville, Michael Aldridge and William Mervyn, with Robin Phillips as the exasperating young artist. The casting was flawless.

A revival of the play by Bernard Shaw. Presented at the Chichester Festival Theatre on May 17, 1972. Settings by Michael Warre and costumes by Beatrice Dawson.

Cast included:

Redpenny	*Richard Cornish*
Emmy	*Bee Duffell*
Sir Colenso Ridgeon	*John Neville*
Leo Schutzmacher	*Harold Kasket*
Sir Patrick Cullen	*William Mervyn*

Cutler Walpole — *Michael Aldridge*
Sir Ralph Bloomfield Bonington
— *John Clements*
Dr Blenkinsop — *Eric Dodson*
Jennifer Dubedat — *Joan Plowright*
Minnie Tinwell — *Angela Richards*
Louis Dubedat — *Robin Phillips*
A Waiter — *Kenneth McClellan*
Newspaper Man — *Brian Poyser*
Mr Danby — *Alan Brown*
Directed by John Clements

DON'T PINCH THE TEASPOONS

The actor Terence Edmond wrote his second comedy, *Don't Pinch the Teaspoons*, which was directed by Robin Midgley at the Leicester Phoenix Theatre. The story concerned a Queen's Counsel in his fifties who has a young mistress suffering from kleptomania. Her father is also a QC and both lawyers are in line for a High Court seat.

The girl is caught shop-lifting and her father is on the verge of discovering both her guilty secrets. The parts were well played by Ronan O'Casey, Liza Goddard and John Robinson.

A play by Terence Edmond. Presented by Leicester Theatre Trust at the Phoenix Theatre, Leicester, on October 4, 1972, by arrangement with Thurlow Enterprises. Designed by Paul Wright.

Cast included:
Annabelle Dyson — *Liza Goddard*
Roland Chilvers — *Ronan O'Casey*
Elwyn Dyson — *John Robinson*
Lee — *Darryl Kavann*
Suzanne Chivers — *Louie Ramsay*
Witherspoon — *David Bird*
Murdoch — *Roy Macready*
Directed by Robin Midgley

DOWNRIGHT HOOLIGAN

C G Bond, former resident dramatist at the Victoria Theatre, Stoke-on-Trent, was author of *Downright Hooligan*, presented at the same theatre under the direction of Bob Eaton. A young man boots to death an old-age pensioner in a London betting-shop on the slightest of pretexts and the author sets out to try and discover the reason for such brutality. There were sensitive and powerful performances by Polly Warren, Terry Malloy and Graham Watkins.

A play by C G Bond. Presented at the Victoria Theatre, Stoke-on-Trent, on October 3, 1972. Designed by Graham Marsden.

Cast included:
Sid
Johnnie — *Peter Clough*
Marjery
Aunt — *Mandy Jenner*
Peter
Uncle Edward — *Nick Darke*
Pathologist
George Marsden — *Terry Molloy*
Ian Rigby — *Graham Watkins*
Mrs Jones
Mrs Rigby — *Polly Warren*
Mrs Mason
Gran — *Romy Saunders*
Shirts
Policeman — *Alan David*
Raincoat
Mr Rigby — *Brian Gwaspari*
Man with Dog
Harris — *Peter Walshe*
Directed by Bob Eaton

THE DRAGON VARIATION

Dulcie Gray, Michael Denison and Alfred Lynch played the three characters in *The Dragon Variation*, a compelling piece of theatre by Robert King, seen at Billingham Forum Theatre before embarking on a regional tour.

The play concerns a lonely widow living in a remote country cottage, who peoples her private world with her ideal man in the guise of several different ones. Her nephew arrives with a breath of the real world, and complicates the widow's solitary game, which she plays by her own rules.

A play by Robert King. Presented at Billingham Forum Theatre on September 6, 1972, and later toured under the auspices of Paul Elliott and Duncan C Weldon for Triumph Theatre Productions and John Gale for Volcano Productions, in association with Billingham Forum. Designed by Brian Currah.

Cast included:
The Woman — *Dulcie Gray*
The Man — *Michael Denison*
The Writer — *Alfred Lynch*
Directed by Tony Sharp

DREAMS OF MRS FRASER

Gabriel Josipovici's fragmentary play for two characters, *Dreams of Mrs Fraser*, staged at the Royal Court Theatre Upstairs, was based on fact. Mrs Fraser was wife of a sea captain whose ship was wrecked off the coast of Australia in 1836. She was captured by aboriginal natives, who gave her hospitality and tattooed her in the most spectacular fashion during her three-year stay with them.

She escaped to civilization, surviving a seven-month walk through the forests and she ended up by becoming a circus freak. Rosemary Martin played Mrs Fraser, with Mark McManus as a circus compère and the convict with whom she escaped, but the author failed to make any positive comment on this highly dramatic story. He failed to get under their skins.

A play by Gabriel Josipovici. Presented at the Royal Court Theatre Upstairs on August 4, 1972. Designed by Harriet Geddes. Music by John Dalby.

Cast included:

Mrs Fraser	*Rosemary Martin*
John Redbold	*Mark McManus*

Directed by Roger Croucher

EDEN END

Priestley's *Eden End* was well worth reviving and enjoyed a successful tour during the autumn of 1972, after opening at Billingham Forum Theatre. Renée Asherson riveted attention as Lilian Kirby, left at home to look after her parents when her sister left their remote North of England village to go on the stage at the turn of the century.

How well Priestley understands stage people and how convincingly he puts them into plays and novels. Joan Greenwood and Anthony Bate as the man-and-wife players were ideally cast in the parts created by Beatrix Lehmann and Ralph Richardson almost forty years ago. Their stage creations were tinged with the tawdry glitter associated with actors eternally condemned to the touring circuit. Behind it all one was constantly aware of cheap digs and slow Sunday trains in which actors of that era spent so much of their time. Mr Bate's panache stirred memories of Donald Wolfit, who was always larger than life and never failed to command attention, even off-stage.

A revival of play by J B Priestley. Presented by Henry Sherwood Productions Ltd at Billingham Forum Theatre on September 25, 1972. Designed by Geoffrey Scott, with costumes by Anthony Holland.

Cast included:

Wilfred Kirby	*Michael Fleming*
Sarah	*Eileen Beldon*
Lilian Kirby	*Renée Asherson*
Dr Kirby	*Sebastian Shaw*
Stella Kirby	*Joan Greenwood*
Geoffrey Farrant	*David Crosse*
Charles Appleby	*Anthony Bate*

Directed by William Chappell

THE EFFECT OF GAMMA RAYS ON MAN-IN-THE-MOON MARIGOLDS

Sheila Hancock dominated *The Effect of Gamma Rays on Man-in-the-Moon Marigolds* at the Yvonne Arnaud Theatre in Guildford, as the widowed mother of two daughters. Her poignant performance gripped the attention of the audience, who marvelled at the range and depth of her playing. Yvonne Antrobus played the plain daughter, with Pamela Moiseiwitsch as the pretty one.

A play by Paul Zindel. Presented by the Yvonne Arnaud Theatre, Guildford, on October, 17, 1972. Designed by Daphne Dare.

Cast included:

Tillie	*Yvonne Antrobus*
Beatrice	*Sheila Hancock*
Ruth	*Pamela Moiseiwitsch*
Nanny	*Rosalind Atkinson*
Janice Vickery	*Pamela Denton*

Directed by Melvin Bernhardt

Agatha Christie visited the Yvonne Arnaud Theatre in Guildford in the summer of 1972 to meet the cast of her new play, *Fiddlers Three*. This picture shows Julia Knight, Doris Hare, Allan Davis, who directed the production, Mark Wing-Davey, Dame Agatha, George Lacy, Arthur Howard, Raymond Francis, Gabor Baraker, Suzanne Barrett, Daphne Newton, Bruce Montague and John Boswall.
Photograph by Stuart Robinson

A FART FOR EUROPE

Howard Brenton and David Edgar collaborated to write *A Fart for Europe*, staged at the Royal Court Theatre Upstairs as a means of letting off steam for those exasperated by the endless Fanfares for Europe staged in the West End since this country joined the Common Market.

The script was on the dull side, with its variations on *King Lear*, but Hugh Hastings, Jeremy Child and Alun Armstrong gave highly imaginative performances that deserved better collaboration from the authors.

A play by Howard Brenton and David Edgar. Presented at the Royal Court Theatre Upstairs on January 9, 1973. Designed by Di Seymour.

Cast included:

King Lear	*Hugh Hastings*
Kent	*Jeremy Child*
Edgar	*Alun Armstrong*

Directed by Chris Parr

Donald MacIver, Sarah
Stephenson, Christopher Saul,
Alice Fraser, Alec Heggie, Robert
Aldous and Victor Lucas in *A
Footstool for God*.   *Photograph by
Viking Studios Ltd*

FINEST FAMILY IN THE LAND

The action of Henry Livings's ironic comedy, *Finest Family in the Land*, given a Theatre Workshop production at the Theatre Royal, Stratford East, was set on the sixteenth floor of a towering block of working-class flats, rather like those on the doorstep of the theatre itself.

The combination of a lost key and the family's meeting with a psychopath named Ponce Weatherby, superbly played by Maxwell Shaw, unmasked this very ordinary family in such a way that the play-goer's attention was held throughout the evening, as he visualized this typical Lancashire family living their typical day-to-day lives.

A play by Henry Livings. Presented by Gerry Raffles for Theatre Workshop at the Theatre Royal, Stratford East, London, on July 27, 1972. Setting and lighting by Mark Pritchard and Guy Hodgkinson and costumes by Willie Burt.

Cast included:

Milton Harris	*Brian Murphy*
Dora Harris	*Eileen Kennally*
Enoch Harris	*Griffith Davies*
Corrie	*Clare Sutcliffe*
Ponce Weatherby	*Maxwell Shaw*

Directed by the Author

A FISH IN THE SEA

A new rock play, *A Fish in the Sea* by John McGrath, was presented at Liverpool Everyman Theatre, as a follow-up to his earlier play, *Soft or a Girl?*, which was well received by audiences who admired Mr McGrath's eye and ear for the Liverpool idiom.

The later play gave Jonathan Pryce a splendid opportunity to play a wild rebellious Scot, who joins the UDA in Belfast and later returns to England a hunted man, seeking solace in the emotional relationship with a Liverpool girl, played with remarkable sensitivity by Angela Phillips. Hard rock music heightened the dramatic situation.

A play by John McGrath, with music by Norman Smeddles and lyrics by John McGrath. Presented at the Everyman Theatre, Liverpool, on December 26, 1972. Designed by Peter Ling. Music arranged and directed by Antony Hayes and performed by Petticoat and Vine.

Cast included:

Mr Maconochie	*Brian Young*
Mrs Maconochie	*Jean Hastings*
Willy	*Terence Durrant*
Yorry	*Antony Sher*
Andy	*Jonathan Pryce*
Sandra	*Allison Steadman*
Fiona	*Pauline Moran*
Mary	*Angela Phillips*
Dafydd	*Robert Putt*
Derek	*Phillip Joseph*
Rev. Griffiths	*Barry Woolgar*
Roman Candle	*Robert Putt*
Mr Hackett	*Barry Woolgar*

Directed by Alan Dossor

A FOOTSTOOL FOR GOD

Bill Watson, Scottish author of *A Footstool for God*, given its world première at the Pitlochry Festival Theatre, describes it as the story of a nobleman who becomes obsessed with the desire to build a church so splendid that it will astonish God, at a time when the world about him is laid waste by ceaseless wars. It is set in fifteenth-century Scotland. Victor Lucas played the leading part, with all the authority of a great prince and a man of high intellect and fine feelings in the squalor of medieval Scotland.

The world première of a play by Bill Watson. Presented at th Pitlochry Festival Theatre on May 4, 1972. Designed by Helen Wilkinson.

Cast included:

William St Clair	*Victor Lucas*
Meg	*Alice Fraser*
William	*Ian Lindsay*
Countess of Douglas	
	Sarah Stephenson
Courland	*Peter Ducrow*
Aytoun	*Alec Heggie*
Sir Patrick Grey	*Donald MacIver*
Father Miles	*Robert Aldous*
Alain Chartier	*Christopher Saul*
Roubakin	*Jenny Galloway*
Jendella	*Colette Kelly*

Directed by Joan Knight

FRIENDS, ROMANS AND LOVERS

The delightfully non-sensical comedy by Samuel Taylor, *Friends, Romans and Lovers*, seen at the Yvonne Arnaud Theatre at Guildford, grows out of the macabre incident of the father of a young American businessman being killed in a car crash in Italy. The daughter-in-law is about to go home for a family wedding at the opening of the play, leaving her husband to cope with red-tape complications concerning the collection of his father's body.

The plot thickens with the appearance of a young English actress, also trying to claim the dead body of her mother, a victim of the same crash. Richard Easton, Felicity Kendal and Joanna McCallum provided amusing performances as members of the macabre triangle.

A play by Samuel Taylor. Presented at the Yvonne Arnaud Theatre, Guildford, on May 16, 1972. Designed by Pamela Ingram, with costumes by Margaret Graham.

Cast included:
Alexander Ben Claiborne
    Richard Easton
Diana Claiborne *Joanna McCallum*
John Wesley   *Richard Pendrey*
Waiter   *Ernst Ulman*
Assistant Hotel Manager
    Hubert Willis
Porter   *Lionel Guyett*
Baldassare Pantaleone *Leigh Lawson*
Alison Ames   *Felicity Kendal*
Vittorio Spina   *Anthony Morton*
Directed by Allan Davis

THE FRONT PAGE

The National Theatre scored a triumph when they staged *The Front Page* by Ben Hecht and Charles MacArthur, in a splendid Michael Blakemore production which stressed the laughter and the nostalgia of this grim Chicago story of the late 1920s.

It is set in the newsroom of a Chicago courthouse just before the dawn hanging of a prisoner who has shot a Negro cop. Corruption is in the air, and there were memorable performances by Alan MacNaughton as the editor determined to get a scoop, Denis Quilley as the ace reporter, Maureen Lipman as the tart who loves the convict, so realistically played by Clive Merrison.

Most of the critics agreed that no company of seasoned American players, imported from Broadway, could have played with greater authenticity of feeling or deeper sincerity.

A revival of the play by Ben Hecht and Charles MacArthur. Presented by the National Theatre Company at the Old Vic on July 6, 1972. Designed by Michael Annals.

Cast included:
Walter Burns   *Alan MacNaughton*
Hildy Johnson   *Denis Quilley*
Besinger   *Benjamin Whitrow*
McCue   *Gawn Grainger*
Kruger   *David Ryall*
Murphy   *James Hayes*
Wilson   *Allan Mitchell*
Endicott   *John Shrapnel*
Schwartz   *David Bradley*
The Mayor   *Paul Curran*
Sheriff Hartman   *David Bauer*
Earl Williams   *Clive Merrison*
Diamond Louie   *Stephen Grief*
Peggy Grant   *Anna Carteret*
Mrs Grant   *Mary Griffiths*
Molly Malloy   *Maureen Lipman*
Directed by Michael Blakemore

FROM THIS DAY FOREVER

The Castle Theatre at Farnham staged an intriguing thriller by Martin Worth called *From This Day Forever*, with an ingenious plot and entertaining, amusing dialogue.

A young man and woman walk into a deserted house in the country. There are signs of recent occupation, but the pair stay on and the tension mounts until the owner returns. The couple was played in lively fashion by Julie Neubert and Granville Saxton.

A play by Martin Worth. Presented by Farnham Repertory Company at the Castle Theatre, Farnham, on May 23, 1972. Designed by Paul Mayo.

Cast included:
A Girl   *Julie Neubert*
A Young Man   *Granville Saxton*
A Youth   *Hessel Saks*
A Neighbour   *Dorothy Edwards*
An Estate Agent   *Alan Partington*
A Woman   *Angela Barlow*
A Policeman   *Roger Ostime*
Directed by John Link

THE GARDEN

In *The Garden*, seen at the Hampstead Theatre Club, Julia Jones sets three characters – a middle-age bachelor, played by John Paul; his housekeeper, played by Diana Coupland; and her son who has a homosexual relationship with the bachelor. There are two intruders, former occupants of the house – a drunken failure and his son, played with compelling effect by Edward Judd and Brian Deacon.

It was a play of sensitive human relationships which held the audience firmly after the first act when the author seemed to be feeling her way. It made an enthralling evening.

A play by Julia Jones. Presented at the Hampstead Theatre Club on September 4, 1972. Designed by Douglas Heap.

Cast included:

Will	*Brian Deacon*
Lettice	*Diana Coupland*
Henry	*Stephen Temperley*
Norman	*John Paul*
Jack	*Edward Judd*

Directed by Vivian Matalon

GATHERING OF THE CLAN

Staged at the Everyman Theatre in Cheltenham, the British première of *Gathering of the Clan* by Andrew Rosenthal suggested a New England version of *Dear Octopus*, though it was rather more dramatic than the Dodie Smith play.

Rosamond Burne dominated the plot as the family matriarch, confined to a wheel-chair, following a stroke. She has used power and wealth to enable her family to organize their lives to the best of their ability. Helen Christie gave a memorable performance as the youngest daughter returning to the family fold after twenty years in Europe.

A play by Andrew Rosenthal. Presented at the Everyman Theatre, Cheltenham, on September 19, 1972. Designed by Donald Patel.

Cast included:

Louise	*Nancy Gower*
Burt Gurnee	*Robert Robertson*
'M' (Emmie) Gurnee	
	Dorothy Primrose
'C'(Catherine) Waldo	
	Kathleen Byron
Wynn Bonnard	*Helen Christie*
Minnie Fallon	*Rosamond Burne*
Hank Waldo	*Brian Badcoe*
Angie Waldo	*Anne Pearson*

Directed by Malcolm Farquhar

GIVE A DOG A BONE

Peter Howard's play for children, *Give a Dog a Bone*, was presented for its ninth season at the Westminster Theatre during the 1972 Christmas season. It seems to have a universal appeal, judging by the energetic audience participation it inspires. Apart from having been performed in America, Africa, Holland, India and Switzerland, it has been filmed and subtitled in a number of languages, including Chinese, Swedish, Norwegian, Arabic and Danish.

A play with book and lyrics by Peter Howard and music by George Fraser. Presented by Westminster Productions Ltd, in association with Moral Re-armament at the Westminster Theatre for its ninth Christmas season on December 7, 1972. Settings by W Cameron Johnson, costumes by Dorothy Phillips and lighting by Louis Fleming. Musical direction by Louis Mordish.

Cast included:

Ringo	*Gordon Reid*
Mr Space	*Donald Scott*
Mickey Merry	*Liz Edmiston*
Rat King	*Richard Warner*
Ma Merry	*Betty Emery*
Pa Merry	*Malcolm Williams*
Mrs Cat	*Linda James*
Mr Mouse	*Roy Heymann*
Pearly King	*John Green*
Lord Swill	*Philip Newman*
Mrs Cow	*Helena Leahy*
Miss Sheep	*Elaine Pearce*
Miss Duck	*Carolyn James*
Mr Horse	*John Fleming*
Mr Fox	*Steve Lane*
Mr Cockerel	*Ian Sharp*
Major Domo	*Susan Claire*
Rat Dancers	*Rosemary Stacey*
	Susan Nye

Directed by Henry Cass and Bridget Espinosa

THE GOOD OLD BAD OLD DAYS

Anthony Newley and Leslie Bricusse collaborated to create what might be called a philosophical musical in *The Good Old Bad Old Days* at the Prince of Wales Theatre – a spectacular musical drama concerning God, the Devil and Mankind, played against ever-changing backgrounds which include Ancient Rome, the discovery of America, the French Revolution and Broadway.

Anthony Newley played the Devil, with Paul Bacon as God, about to destroy the modern world for its wicked ways. The book was a bit old fashioned, but Disley Jones designed magnificently effective settings to heighten the amazing vigour of Mr Newley's direction and the vitality of Paddy Stone's choreography. The visual side of the production was its brightest feature, with brilliantly contrived scenes of shimmering and glowing beauty.

A musical with book, music and lyrics by Leslie Bricusse and Anthony Newley. Presented by Bernard Delfont and Richard M Mills for the Bernard Delfont Organization Ltd at the Prince of Wales Theatre on December 20, 1972. Settings by Disley Jones, costumes by Anthony Mendleson and choreography by Paddy Stone. Musical director – Robert Mandell.

Cast included:

Bubba	*Anthony Newley*
Gramps	*Paul Bacon*
Simon	*Bill Kerr*
Biggs	*Robb Stuart*
Small Person	*George Claydon*
William	*Fred Evans*
Grace	*Julia Sutton*
Beloved	*Caroline Villiers*
John	*Terry Mitchell*
Girl	*Lesley Roach*
Boy	*Keith Chegwin*

Directed by Anthony Newley assisted by Paddy Stone

GONE WITH THE WIND

Harold Fielding presented Drury Lane with an instant smash-hit in Joe Layton's £150,000 production of a spectacular musical based on Margaret Mitchell's American Civil War epic, *Gone With the Wind*.

The crowded stage pictures recalled those famous melodramas that were all the vogue at the Lane at the turn of the century. *Gone With the Wind* showed us Atlanta Railway Station, where an engine belching smoke and steam earned its own round of applause, and later the entire city is engulfed by realistic flames of terrifying ferocity.

The show appealed to the public because the leading characters are convincingly real and their conflict makes good theatre. Though the score by Harold Rome is without a haunting lilt, it is pleasant enough on the ear and serves to heighten the melodramatic situations of the plot.

As Scarlett O'Hara, who is rarely off-stage during the three-hour show, June Ritchie demonstrated an abundance of star quality and in her first West End musical, she expertly projected her numbers with a remarkable degree of realism. The American star, Harve Presnell, making his London début as Rhett Butler, had a powerful enough physique, but as an actor his impact did not come up to expectations. Patricia Michael and Robert Swann were ideally and sympathetically cast as Melanie and Ashley Wilkes.

A musical version of the novel by Margaret Mitchell. Joe Layton's production, presented by Harold Fielding at Drury Lane on May 3, 1972.

Music and lyrics by Harold Rome; book by Horton Foote; scene designs by David Hays and Tim Goodchild; costume designs by Patton Campbell; lighting by Richard Pilbrow and musical direction by Ray Cook.

Cast included:

Scarlett O'Hara	*June Ritchie*
Rhett Butler	*Harve Presnell*
Melanie Hamilton	*Patricia Michael*
Ashley Wilkes	*Robert Swann*
Mammy	*Isabelle Lucas*
Prissy	*Marion Ramsey*
Aunt Pittypat	*Bessie Love*
Frank Kennedy	*Brian Davies*
Belle Watling	*Doreen Hermitage*
Doctor Meade	*Ronald Adam*

Directed and choreographed by Joe Layton

THE GREAT NORTHERN WELLY-BOOT SHOW

The Offshore Theatre Company, a profit-sharing co-operative in which all the members, writers, musicians and actors work on an equal basis, brought their Edinburgh Festival success, *The Great Northern Welly-boot Show* to the Young Vic on November 7 for a three-week season.

It was a political–satirical musical based on the Upper Clyde Shipbuilders, written by Tom Buchan with lyrics and music by Billy Connolly, the folk-singer who was also in the cast. When the shipyard was threatened with closure and was liquidated by order of the Government, the workers took over the yard and ran it for six months before it was rescued by foreign private enterprise. This show was a musical spoof based on that situation, set in a Wellington-boot factory.

A musical by Tom Buchan, with lyrics and music by Billy Connolly. Presented by the Offshore Theatre Company at the Young Vic on November 7, 1972.

Cast included: John Bett, John Buick, Juliet Cadzow, Doreen Cameron, Billy Connolly, Brandy di Franck, Roy Hanlon, Lesley Mackie, Patrick Malahide, John Mulvaney, Roy Sampson, Kate Stark, Gavin Sutherland and John Yule

Directed by Robin Lefevre

GYMNASIUM

Written by Robin Chapman, *Gymnasium* at the Greenwich Theatre turned out to be a play of conflict between two cultures, physical versus mental.

Three members of the staff of a South London secondary modern school discover the multi-purpose hall where they hold their madrigal rehearsals has been taken over by a gymnastic group who insist upon their physical superiority. They refuse to give way and during a violent scene the female member of the staff is raped, and the two men are knocked out.

A play by Robin Chapman. Presented at the Greenwich Theatre on August 17, 1972. Designed by Roger Butlin.

Cast included:

Thomas Gibson	*Charles West*
Lucy Thwaite	*Barbara Ewing*
James Roskill	*John Golightly*
Percy Briggs	*Peter Gordon*
Terry	*Andrew Bradford*
Gymnasts	*John York,*
	Paul Alexander, Peter Attard
	and *Louis Cabot*

Directed by John Cox

HAMLET

Peter Coe directed an entirely new production of *Hamlet* for the final summer season presentation at the temporary Southwark Globe Playhouse on Bankside.

It was a modern-dress version, some of the characters giving the impression of gangsters in a Fascist state and Donald Houston's Claudius, wearing sinister steel-rimmed sun-glasses, favoured a Nazi-inspired salute.

Keith Michell gave a vital flashing performance as the Prince of Denmark, a highly intelligent reading of the part in this strange environment, where the women and the men wore trouser-suits.

The other productions in this windswept almost open-air playhouse were imported from elsewhere. The Sheffield Crucible Theatre provided *The Shoemaker's Holiday* and *A Man For All Seasons* and the Northcott Theatre of Exeter brought their *Cornish Passion Play* for a week.

A revival of the Shakespeare play. Presented by the Globe Playhouse Trust Ltd as the final production of the John Player Season at the Bankside Globe Playhouse, Southwark, on August 10, 1972. Set designed by Robert Bahl, with costumes by Ingeborg and music by Joe Griffiths.

Cast included:

Hamlet	*Keith Michell*
Horatio	*Gary Raymond*
Rosencrantz	*David Gwillim*
Guildenstern	*Peter Ellis*
Leading Actor	*Ralph Nossek*
Claudius	*Donald Houston*
Polonius	*Ron Moody*
Laertes	*Peter Harlow*
Osric	*Peter Greene*
Gertrude	*Helen Cherry*
Ophelia	*Carolyn Seymour*
Fortinbras	*Tony Gilby Garner*
First Gravedigger	*Ron Moody*
Ghost	*Ralph Nossek*

Directed by Peter Coe

Denholm Elliott as Brack and Jill
Bennett as Hedda in John
Osborne's adaptation of Ibsen's
Hedda Gabler

HARD TIMES

Frank Hatherley's dramatization of
Dickens's sprawling novel, *Hard
Times*, made a most enjoyable
evening at the Octagon Theatre,
Bolton, because the author had
condensed the material with loving
care and had an eye for stage highlights. A vivid impression is
obtained of work people seething
with discontent in the knowledge
that they are in dead-end jobs
which offer no hope of a better
life. Roger Hume and John Pickles
gave memorable performances as
the MP and the rich industrialist
who are the pillars of the story.

A play by Frank Hatherley from
the novel by Charles Dickens. Presented at the Octagon Theatre,
Bolton, on September 5, 1972.
Designed by Edward Furby.

Cast included:

Josiah Bounderby	*Roger Hume*
Thomas Gradgrind	*John Pickles*
Tom Gradgrind	*Ken Binge*
Louisa Gradgrind	*Linda Beckett*
Mrs Gradgrind	*Dione Ewin*
Sissy Jupe	*Angela Cheyne*
Mrs Sparsit	*Rosemary Towler*
James Harthouse	*Michael St John*
Stephen Blackpool	
	Richard Wardale
The Old Lady	*Eileen Davies*

Directed by Geoffrey Ost

HEDDA GABLER

Jill Bennett played Hedda Gabler
as a cool, ruthless, detached, bitchy
destroyer in John Osborne's new
adaptation of Ibsen's play, *Hedda
Gabler*, at the Royal Court. This
Hedda chooses to be bored,
married to her bookworm husband and incarcerated in the vast
gloomy villa with the musty smell
of lavender and rose petals in the
air. Alan Tagg's design evoked
the atmosphere down to the last
detail.

John Osborne's adaptation,
without offending ardent Ibsenites,
presented an unstilted and natural
version of the text by using such
phrases as 'Good chums', 'nosing
around' and 'Don't yell so!'.

Mary Merrall gave a moving
performance as Aunt Juliana;
Ronald Hines made an acceptable
dull dog of Tesman and Denholm
Elliott's smirking Judge Brack
was an untraditional, but attractive
reading of the part.

In a programme note, John
Osborne wrote, 'As I see it,
Hedda Gabler has her fun at the
expense of others. . . . Like many
frigid people, her only true feelings
are expressed in jealousy, posses-
siveness and acquisitive yearnings.'

Revival of play by Henrik Ibsen
in a new adaptation by John
Osborne. Presented at the Royal
Court Theatre on June 28, 1972.
Designed by Alan Tagg, with
costumes by Deirdre Clancy.

Cast included:

George Tesman	*Ronald Hines*
Hedda Tesman	*Jill Bennett*
Juliana Tesman	*Mary Merrall*
Mrs Elvsted	*Barbara Ferris*
Judge Brack	*Denholm Elliott*
Eilert Lovborg	*Brian Cox*
Berthe	*Anne Dyson*

Directed by Anthony Page

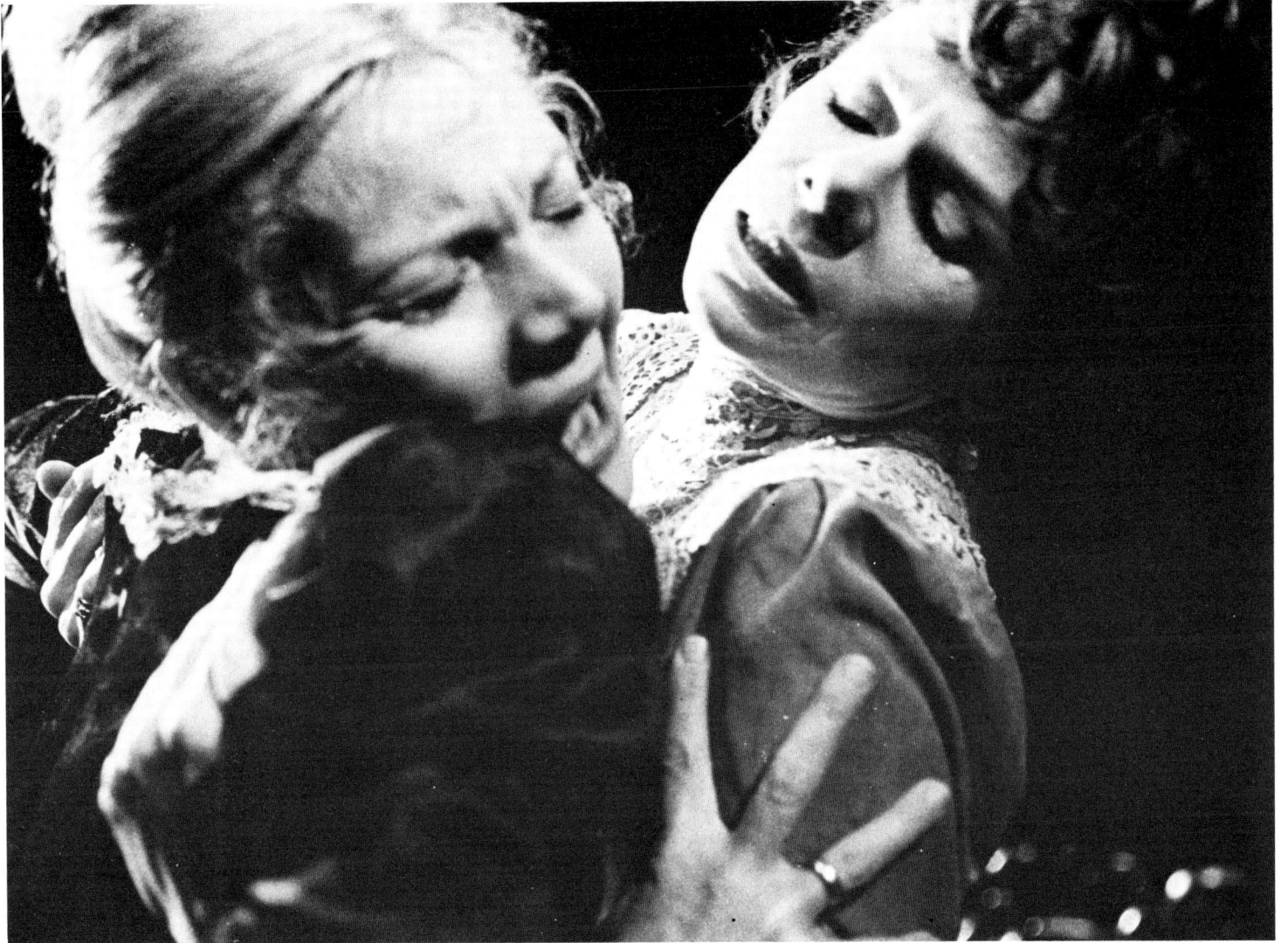

Barbara Ferris as Mrs Elvsted and
Jill Bennett as Hedda in *Hedda
Gabler*

Anne Stallybrass as Maggie
Hobson and Andrew Robertson as
Willie Mossop in the Young Vic's
revival of *Hobson's Choice*.
Photograph by Reg Wilson

HELEN

At Leicester Phoenix Theatre Robin Midgley directed the Euripides comedy, *Helen*, with a delicacy which enhanced the richness of the humour. He had the good fortune to obtain Fenella Fielding to play the name-part and she enjoyed over-playing in a tasteful manner which underlined the comedy without throwing the production out of balance. David Dodimead, as the shipwrecked Spartan king, aided and abetted Miss Fielding in the most skilful manner to get full value from the amusing dialogue. Excellent support was forthcoming from Betty Hardy, Darryl Kavann and Charles Hyatt.

A play by Euripides. Presented by the Leicester Theatre Trust Ltd at the Leicester Phoenix Theatre on November 25, 1972. Designed by Paul Wright. Music composed by Bernard Keeffe.

Cast included:

Helen	*Fenella Fielding*
Teukeros	*Martin Friend*
Aphrodite	*Gwen Taylor*
Hera	*Christine Welch*
Athene	*Catherine Crutchley*
Menelaos	*David Dodimead*
Old Woman	*Betty Hardy*
Greek Slave	*Charles Hyatt*
Theoclymenos	*Darryl Kavann*
Castor	*Tim Meats*
Pollux	*Hugh Coleridge*

Directed by Robin Midgley

HIGH INFIDELITY

Jack Popplewell exploited the old saying that behind every successful man there is a clever woman in *High Infidelity*, seen at Richmond Theatre, under the neat direction of Hugh Goldie. Mr Popplewell, after seeing his work in performance, with Anthony Booth and June Barry in the leading parts, doubtless gained by the audience reaction and proceeded to start rewriting certain scenes. There was considerable promise in this story of a man's rise to fame because his wife knew how to play her cards cunningly with those in a position to advance her husband's career.

A play by Jack Popplewell. Presented by Richmond Theatre Productions Ltd at Richmond Theatre on October 2, 1972. Designed by Mary Pickard.

Cast included:

Herbert Henry Talmadge	
	Anthony Booth
Jane Fenwick	*Janet Mahoney*
Susan Jones	*June Barry*
Arthur George Renton	
	Brendan Barry
Lord Harry Doncaster	
	Terence Skelton
Duchess of Summerdale	
	Vicki Woolf
Robert de Courville	*Rodney Diak*

Directed by Hugh Goldie

HOBSON'S CHOICE

For well over half a century *Hobson's Choice*, Harold Brighouse's comedy of life in Salford in the 1880s, has never failed to fill a theatre whenever the part of Maggie Hobson has been sincerely and realistically cast.

Anne Stallybrass scored a memorable personal success in the Young Vic revival, neatly directed by Bernard Goss. John Barber gave a vivid impression of her achievement when he said she made herself look as plain as Salford Town Hall, while giving a performance of great subtlety. Peter Bayliss played her father on broader, almost music-hall comedy lines, but Andrew Robertson as her young man, chose a realistic approach to harmonize with that of Miss Stallybrass.

Play by Harold Brighouse. Presented at the Young Vic on January 29, 1973. Designed by Alan Barlow.

Cast included:

Ada Figgins	*Ursula Mohan*
Alice Hobson	*Lois Daine*
Vickey Hobson	*Mel Martin*
Freddy Beenstock	*Ian Charleson*
Maggie Hobson	*Anne Stallybrass*
Albert Prosser	*Alun Lewis*
Henry Horatio Hobson	*Peter Bayliss*
Mrs Hepworth	*Julia McCarthy*
Tubby Wadlow	*Alan Foss*
Willie Mossop	*Andrew Robertson*
Jim Heeler	*Ian Taylor*
Doctor MacFarlane	*Michael Byrne*

Directed by Bernard Goss

Maxwell Shaw, Philip Davis, Mary Larkin, Ron Hackett, Jean Boht, Patience Collier, Brian Murphy, Dudley Sutton, Griffith Davies and Clive Barker in Joan Littlewood's Theatre Workshop revival of

Brendan Behan's *The Hostage*.
Photograph by Donald Cooper

THE HOSTAGE

After a lapse of fourteen years Joan Littlewood decided to revive one of her resounding Theatre Workshop successes, *The Hostage*, by Brendan Behan at the Theatre Royal, Stratford East. She managed to secure a number of players from the original cast – Dudley Sutton, Brian Murphy, Celia Salkeld and Clive Barker.

The Censor has disappeared since the original production, so Joan Littlewood restored some of the religious cuts and introduced some new material. The rousing songs were put over with tremendous gusto and Maxwell Shaw, as the keeper of the boarding-house, setting for the events, Patience Collier as the 'sociable worker' and the poignantly-spoken Teresa of Mary Larkin made a deep impression in this revival which just fell short of expectations.

A revival of the play by Brendan Behan. Presented by Gerry Raffles for Theatre Workshop at the Theatre Royal, Stratford, East 15, on May 30, 1972. Set and lighting by Guy Hodgkinson and Mark Pritchard.

Cast included:

Patrick	*Maxwell Shaw*
Colette	*Celia Salkeld*
Mr Mulleady	*Brian Murphy*
Miss Gilchrist	*Patience Collier*
Leslie Williams	*Philip Davis*
Teresa	*Mary Larkin*
A Volunteer	*Clive Barker*

Directed by Joan Littlewood

HULLABALOO

The underground Criterion Theatre was transformed into a palatial underground lavatory by the stage designer, Ralph Koltai, when Harold Fielding presented 'a sort of revue' called *Hullabaloo*.

The popular female impersonators, Roy Starr and Michael Rogers, appeared on a West End stage for the first time in their career, which had previously been devoted to highly successful seasons in cabaret and at Hampstead Theatre Club late-night revues.

The individual style of the wit and humour of Rogers and Starr was ideally suited to the show. Jimmy Edwards made some excellent contributions to the programme, without his all-too-familiar musical instrument and the American singer and dancer, Chelsea Brown, was a distinct asset to the show.

'A sort of revue', presented by Harold Fielding at the Criterion Theatre on October 31, 1972. Costumes by Rob Ringwood and Michael Southgate; designs by Ralph Koltai; choreography by Irving Davies and musical direction by Peter L Collins.

Cast included: Rogers and Starr, Jimmy Edwards, Chelsea Brown, Marcia Ashton, Ted Merwood and Roy North

Directed by Frank Dunlop

I AND ALBERT

Lewis Fiander rather stole the show when he appeared in the musical *I and Albert* in the scene in which Disraeli performs a few conjuring tricks to amuse the ageing Victoria.

Polly James had ample scope to transform Victoria from the youthful princess to the sombre widow and Taube made a convincing Prince Consort. John Schlesinger directed the show at a tremendous tempo, which did not give the leading characters a chance to be developed.

As the critic John Barber remarked, Laurence Houseman's *Victoria Regina* did it all so much better away back in the 1930s.

A musical with book by Jay Allen, music by Charles Strouse and lyrics by Lee Adams. Sets and projections by Luciana Arrighi, costumes designed by Alan Barrett; musical direction by Gareth Davies, orchestrations by Gordon Langford and musical staging by Brian Macdonald. Presented by Lewis M Allen and Si Litvinoff, in association with Theatre Projects and Richard Lukins, by arrangement with Donald Albery at the Piccadilly Theatre on November 6, 1972.

Cast included:

Victoria	*Polly James*
Baroness Lehzen	*Silvia Beamish*
Lord Melbourne	
Disraeli	*Lewis Fiander*
Lord Palmerston	
Gladstone	*Aubrey Woods*
Prince Albert	*Sven-Bertil Taube*
Prince Ernest	*Christopher Guard*

Directed by John Schlesinger

132

Polly James as Queen Victoria,
with Martin Dell and
George Raistrick in *I and Albert*.
Photograph by Michael Childers

I CLAUDIUS

Expectation ran high when John Mortimer wrote a play based on those two famous Robert Graves books, *I Claudius* and *Claudius the God*, with David Warner in the name-part.

Mr Warner's fascinating performance as the lame, persecuted Claudius was a great achievement, but the play was too episodic and never really left the ground, despite well-played scenes with Charles Lloyd Pack, John Turner, Warren Clarke and Sara Kestelman. Freda Jackson's Livia made one long to see her dominating the cast of a thrilling play about the Borgias.

The setting by William Dudley seemed designed expressly to exterminate any suggestion of atmosphere. It consisted of a tier of wooden planks stretching the entire width of the stage, rather like the section of a stand at a football stadium. The entire action was played on these open steps, upon which the actors, stood, sat and rolled. Above them the complicated lighting equipment was visible in all its stark ugliness, which hardly contributed to one's enjoyment. Once upon a time the designer contributed towards the make-believe which was part of theatre-going.

A play by John Mortimer, based on *I Claudius* and *Claudius the God* by Robert Graves. Presented by Michael White in association with Woodfall Ltd at the Queen's Theatre on July 11, 1972. Settings by William Dudley, costumes by Sue Plummer, movement by Eleanor Fazan and music by John Addison.

Cast included:

Claudius	*David Warner*
Augustus	*Charles Lloyd Pack*
Livia	*Freda Jackson*
Cassius	*John Turner*
Calpurnia	*Rosalind Ayres*
Caligula	*Warren Clarke*
Messalina	*Sara Kestelman*
Narcissus	*Desmond Gill*

Directed by Tony Richardson

Edgar Wreford who played the monk in *The Inferno*. *Photograph by Mark Gudgeon*

THE INFERNO

In *The Inferno* by Ian Curteis, directed by Peter Dews at the Greenwich Theatre, Michele Dotrice played Elizabeth Barton, a sixteenth-century Kentish farm girl who developed religious mania, resulting in visions and prophecies. When prepared to denounce the forthcoming marriage of Henry VIII and Anne Boleyn, the girl is arrested, tortured, tried in Star Chamber and executed at Tyburn.

Edgar Wreford played Edward Bocking, a monk who exerted his influence over Elizabeth to expound his own religious and political beliefs. In performance the highly promising dramatic story, told in modern colloquial dialogue, fell flat and did not provide the players with particularly inspiring material.

A play by Ian Curteis. Presented at the Greenwich Theatre on November 30, 1972. Set and costumes designed by David Cockayne.

Cast included:

Fr Richard Masters	*John Baddeley*
Thomas Cobb	*George Selway*
Ann Barton	*Ann Tirard*
Elizabeth Barton	*Michele Dotrice*
Archbishop Warham	*John Gill*
Alice Bagot	*Jean Leppard*
Mary Hughes	*Marion Fiddick*
Dr Edward Bocking	
	Edgar Wreford
Fr William Hadleigh	*Keith Drinkel*
Fermor	*Stuart Knee*
Peasant Woman ⎫	*Daphne*
Prioress ⎭	*Odin-Pearse*

Prior Goldwell	*Peter Dews*
Gentlewoman	*Jean Leppard*
Henry	*Hugh Sullivan*
Clerk	*David Sands*
Chancellor	*Antony Brown*
Preacher	*Stuart Knee*

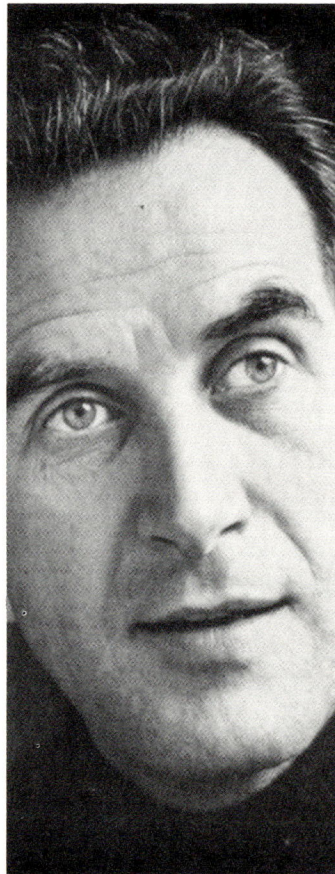

Directed by Peter Dews

THE ISLAND OF THE MIGHTY

John Arden and Margaretta D'Arcy in their play *The Island of the Mighty*, which the Royal Shakespeare Company presented at the Aldwych Theatre, were not concerned with King Arthur as the romantic figure who sat with his knights at the Round Table. They gave a far more realistic picture of Ancient Britain.

Their King Arthur had the grim task of trying to keep Britain together after the withdrawal of the Romans and faced a constant struggle against treachery and the poverty of existence. The settings by Timothy O'Brien and Tazeena Firth gave a vivid picture of a desolate country, dotted with bleak towns, dominated by the inevitable castle. Patrick Allen gave the impression that Arthur was a man of remarkable personality, and he was well supported by Estelle Kohler, Emrys James, Richard Pasco and Lila Kaye.

A play by John Arden with Margaretta D'Arcy. Presented by the Royal Shakespeare Company at the Aldwych Theatre on December 5, 1972. Designed by Timothy O'Brien and Tazeena Firth. Choreography by David Toguri and music by Carl Davis.

Cast included:

Merlin	*Emrys James*
Arthur	*Patrick Allen*
Medraut	*Richard Pasco*
Bedwyr	*Morgan Sheppard*
Balin	*Roger Rees*
Balan	*David Calder*

Prince of Strathclyde	
	Anthony Pedley
Taliesin	*Richard Mayes*
Queen of the Wild Cat Picts	
	Lila Kaye
Pictish Ambassador	
	Heather Canning
Pictish Princess	*Lisa Harrow*
Pictish Poet	*Tony Church*
Pictish War-Leader	
	Michael Shannon
Sacred King	*Lloyd McGuire*
Garlon	*Mike Pratt*
King Pellam	*Denis Holmes*
Aneurin	*Bernard Lloyd*
The Prince of Gododdin	
	Gordon Gostelow
Gwenhwyvar	*Estelle Kohler*
Caradoc	*Ted Valentine*
Dylan	*Peter Machin*
Morgan	*Beatrix Lehmann*

Directed by David Jones

Patrick Allen as Arthur and Richard
Pasco as Medraut in the Royal
Shakespeare Company's
production of *The Island of the
Mighty.* *Photograph by Reg Wilson*

Alan David as Pangloss, Nick Darke as Candide, Romy Saunders as Earthquake Victim in *It's All For The Best*

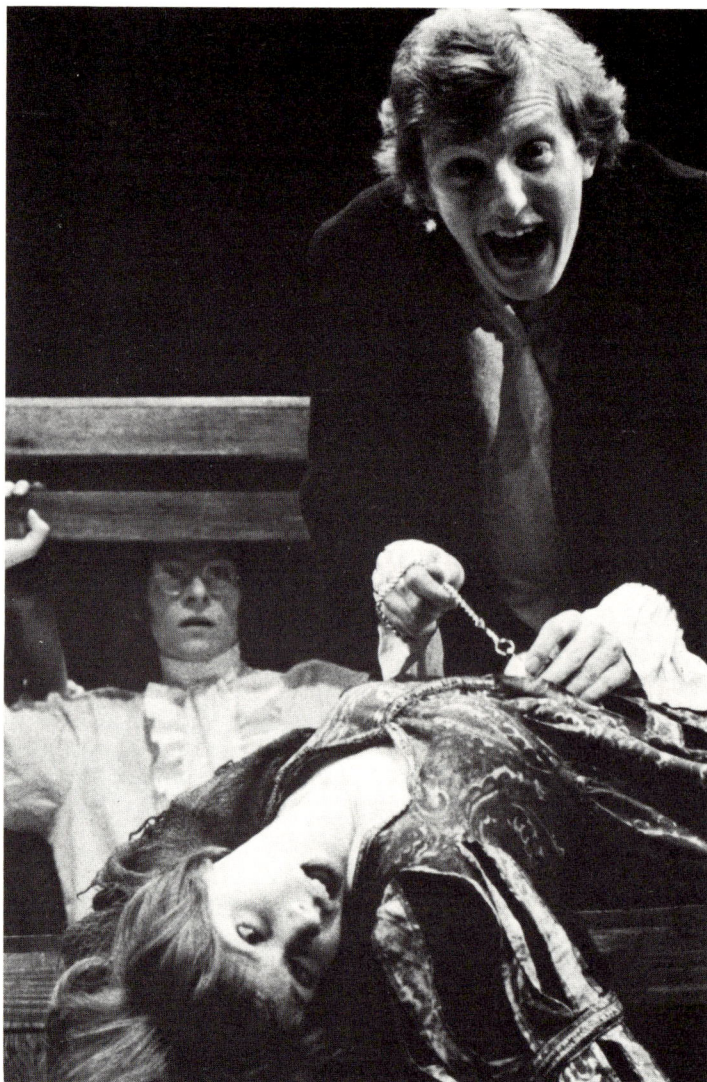

IT'S ALL FOR THE BEST

Steve Gooch's adaptation of Voltaire's *Candide*, at the Victoria Theatre, Stoke-on-Trent, under the title of *It's All for the Best* proved a racy interpretation of the famous novel, with wars, shipwrecks, floggings, hangings, rapings, murder and other disasters. The outstanding performances were given by Nick Darke as Candide, Alan David as Pangloss and Graham Watkins as an old woman with one buttock. By playing many parts between them, the company gave an admirable display of versatility.

An adaptation by Steve Gooch of Voltaire's *Candide*. Presented at the Victoria Theatre, Stoke-on-Trent, on May 16, 1972. Designed by Graham Marsden, with music composed and directed by Stuart Johnson.

Cast included:

Paquette	*Mandy Jenner*
Pangloss	*Alan David*
Cunnigunda	*Polly Warren*
Candide	*Nick Darke*
Monsieur le Baron	*Peter Walshe*
Brother Giroflée	*Brian Gwaspari*
Cacambo	*Martin Wimbush*
King of Burglars	*John Darrell*
Protestant Vicar	*Terry Molloy*
Don Issachar	*David Miller*
Old Woman	*Graham Watkins*
Monsieur Jacques	*Peter Clough*
Miss Clarion	*Romy Saunders*

Directed by Peter Cheeseman

JESUS CHRIST SUPERSTAR

Following a tremendous publicity fanfare, *Jesus Christ Superstar*, the Rock Opera concerning the last seven days of Jesus at Nazareth, opened at the Palace Theatre to a mixed critical reception in the Press.

It certainly rocked the theatre as far as sheer volume of sound was concerned, every member of the large cast having a hand-microphone, apart from other amplifying equipment which must have been installed around and above the stage. Frequently leading members of the cast screamed into their microphones with such intensity one expected them to break a blood vessel or ruin their vocal cords for ever.

The story was played without traditional scenery, on a glass stage illuminated from below, a stage equipped with lifts to change the contour from scene to scene. The actors were blinded by dazzling beams of light directed at them from various points above the stage.

There was no spoken dialogue and the players were not really called upon to act; they wore costume, and sang their numbers with deafening volume of sound and that was about all that happened. The production was a miracle of mechanical efficiency, but devoid of any real emotion or genuine feeling.

A musical with lyrics by Tim Rice and music by Andrew Lloyd Webber. Presented by Robert Stigwood, in association with

136

MCA Inc, by arrangement with David Land, at the Palace Theatre on August 9, 1972.

Scenic designs by Brian Thomson, costume designs by Gabriella Falk and musical direction by Anthony Bowles.

Cast included:

Jesus	*Paul Nicholas*
Judas	*Stephen Tate*
Peter	*Richard Barnes*
Simon	*Derek James*
Mary	*Dana Gillespie*
Pilate	*John Parker*
Herod	*Paul Jabara*

Directed by Jim Sharman

JOCK

Russell Hunter appeared in a new one-man play, *Jock*, by W Gordon Smith, at the King's Theatre, Glasgow, on June 12, 1972, for the Clyde Fair International. Scottish history, folklore and customs were seen through the eyes of a down-to-earth serving soldier and the script was neatly laced with humour. A native of Glasgow and a product of the Perth and Glasgow Citizens' repertory companies, Mr Hunter was ideally cast in this symbolic role. Jimmy Goddard directed.

A one-man play by W Gordon Smith. Presented by Clyde Fair International at King's Theatre, Glasgow, on June 12, 1972.

Jock   *Russell Hunter*

Designed and directed by James Goddard

JOSEPH AND THE AMAZING TECHNICOLOR DREAMCOAT

It was inevitable that *Joseph and the Amazing Technicolor Dreamcoat* by Andrew Lloyd Webber and Tim Rice, who were responsible for *Jesus Christ Superstar*, should find its way to the West End. It opened at the Albery Theatre in Frank Dunlop's Young Vic production which had been such a success at the 1972 Edinburgh Festival.

This enchanting creation which first started life as a musical piece for the schoolboy choir of Colet Court School, became a resounding musical hit on the professional stage; tuneful, witty, colourful, uplifting and exciting. Gary Bond dominated the production as the good-humoured and handsome Joseph, supported by Joan Heal's delightful Potiphar's wife, and Peter Reeves as the slick Narrator. Frank Dunlop's direction was flawlessly fluid.

The Prologue with which the evening opens, to expand the programme to a two-hour entertainment, was not on the same high level as *Joseph*, with God and tinsel-waving angels, who might have been imported from the Folies Bergère, in the cast list.

A Pop Oratorio with music by Andrew Lloyd Webber and lyrics by Tim Rice. Designed by Nadine Baylis, with choreography by Christopher Bruce, orchestrations by David Cullen, and musical direction by Anthony Bowles. Executive producer – Bob Swash and production supervisor – Joe Aveline.

A Young Vic production presented by Robert Stigwood, by arrangement with Donald Albery, in association with Qwertyuiop Productions, Michael White and Granada, by arrangement with David Land at the Albery Theatre on February 13, 1973.

An earlier version was performed as part of the 1972 Edinburgh International Festival at the Edinburgh Haymarket Ice Rink on August 21, 1972.

Cast included:

Narrators	*Pete Reeves*
	Peter Blake
	Maynard Williams
Jacob	*Alex McAvoy*
Leah	*Joan Heal*
Rachel	*Joanna Wake*
Zilpah	*Alison Groves*
Bilhah	*Frances Sinclair*
Joseph	*Gary Bond*
Reuben	*Paul Brooke*
Simeon	*Maynard Williams*
Levi	*Mason Taylor*
Napthali	*Dudley Rogers*
Isaachar	*Frank Vincent*
Asher	*Sam Cox*
Dan	*Ian Trigger*
Zebulun	*David Wynn*
Gad	*Kevin Williams*
Benjamin	*Roy North*
Judah	*Peter Blake*
Potiphar	*Ian Trigger*
Potiphar's Wife	*Joan Heal*
Baker	*Roy North*
Butler	*Kevin Williams*
Pharaoh	*Gordon*

Directed by Frank Dunlop

JOURNEY'S END

Journey's End still remains a masterpiece. It is the finest war play that came out of the 1914–18 conflict because the author, R C Sherriff, proved to be a keen observer with a rare flair for documenting his facts in a highly theatrical fashion which still convinces the audience as a piece of real life. In consequence it is the most moving plea for peace which has ever been written.

The Mermaid invited the 69 Theatre Company from the University of Manchester to present their revival, so sensitively directed by Eric Thompson, for a London season and the production later transferred to the Cambridge Theatre. The cast gave the right impression of the ages of Sherriff's characters. Peter Egan gave a powerful impression of Stanhope, the vicar's son drinking far too heavily to retain his sanity after three years in the trenches; Christopher Good conveyed the boyish enthusiasm of Raleigh; James Maxwell had the required maturity for Osborne, the Uncle of the Mess, and the rest of the cast did full justice to Sherriff's play, so well worth reviving.

Revival of play by R C Sherriff. A 69 Theatre Production from the University Theatre in Manchester, presented at the Mermaid Theatre in London on May 18, 1972, by arrangement with Eddie Kulukundis and Richard Pilbrow. Designed by Alan Pickford.

Cast included:

Lieutenant Osborne *James Maxwell*

2nd Lieutenant Raleigh   *Christopher Good*
Captain Stanhope   *Peter Egan*
2nd Lieutenant Trotter   *Colin Prockter*
2nd Lieutenant Hibbert   *Bruce Robinson*
Private Mason   *Harry Landis*
Directed by Eric Thompson

JULIUS CAESAR

Peter James directed a most effective production of *Julius Caesar* for the Young Vic Company, using a small number of players, recorded crowd noises and a simple set with a few Fascist symbols to suggest the 1930s. The emphasis was on political hypocrisy and it worked extremely well.

Peter McEnery as Cassius and Nigel Hawthorne as Brutus gave dominating and vividly contrasting performances, equalled by Hywel Bennett's vital Anthony. The simplified approach to the play enabled the audience to concentrate more easily on the central issues of those troubled times.

A revival of the play by Shakespeare. Presented by the Young Vic at their own theatre on August 21, 1972. Designed by John Napier.

Cast included:
Mark Anthony   *Hywel Bennett*
Marcus Brutus   *Nigel Hawthorne*
Cassius   *Peter McEnery*
Julius Caesar   *Richard Beale*
Casca   *Roy Marsden*
Calpurnia   *Susan Sheers*
Portia   *June Watson*

Directed by Peter James

JUST PLAIN MURDER

The first thriller to be written by Roy Plomley, one of the most famous names on BBC radio, was *Just Plain Murder*, tried out at Bexhill-on-Sea.

It concerned three sons who learned from their dying father's will they were to lose their inheritance to a young floosey. They decided the only solution was for her to die first. But murder was not as easy as they imagined and Mr Plomley wrote an amusing comedy-thriller in which everyone other than the intended victim fell foul of the sons' scheming.

A play by Roy Plomley. Presented by Theatre South East at the De La Warr Pavilion, Bexhill-on-Sea, on July 27, 1972. Designed by Merope Mills.

Cast included:
Alan Braggart   *Robert Kingswell*
Nigel Braggart   *David Chant*
David Braggart   *David Masterman*
'Wolfie'   *Peggy Paige*
Det.-Sgt Wilby   *Roger Davis*
Veronica Holt   *Virginia Moore*
Det.-Insp. Jarrold   *Richard Burnett*

Directed by Richard Burnett

The Kabuki Theatre of Japan appeared in London for the first time at Sadler's Wells Theatre on June 5, 1972. This all-male company from Tokyo presented abbreviated versions of two of the most popular items in the Kabuki repertoire. Given in full, the entertainment would have lasted best part of the night.

Kabuki is an acquired taste for the baffled Western play-goer. The movement of the players is slow and ritualistic; the facial expression is extraordinarily restrained and the faces are painted an expressionless white; plucked-string sounds and curious human-voice sounds are heard off-stage. The costumes were sumptuous and elaborate, but considerable concentration was required on the part of the audience to keep boredom at bay while trying to appreciate this form of Japanese theatre which originated in Shakespeare's day. The magic is not instantly obvious to Western theatre-goers.

Left: David King as Lear and Susan Glanville as Cordelia in the Ludlow Festival production of *King Lear*

Right: Timothy Dalton as Edgar, Trevor Martin as Kent and Timothy West as Lear in the Prospect Theatre Company's production of *King Lear*. Photograph by Mark Gudgeon

KIDNAPPED

The Edinburgh Lyceum presented an ingenious and imaginative stage adaptation of Robert Louis Stevenson's *Kidnapped* which emerged as a hit folk-opera.

Bill Bryden staged the production against a skeleton setting which housed Steeleye Span, a modern pop group who sometimes provided background music, sometimes punctuated the action and dominated the finale when the cast were rocking and rolling about the stage with considerable brio.

In some strange manner Keith Dewhurst's adaptation of the famous novel lived very happily, and was even enhanced by the pop music element of the production.

Paul Young played David Balfour with youthful sincerity, Rikki Fulton gave a strong study of the Duke of Argyll, and much of the comedy was provided by John Grieve as Cluny MacPherson.

Stage version by Keith Dewhurst of the novel by Robert Louis Stevenson, with music by Steeleye Span. Presented at the Edinburgh Lyceum on August 3, 1972. Designed by Geoffrey Scott, with costumes by Lorraine McKee.

Cast included:

David Balfour	*Paul Young*
Alan Breck Stewart	*James Grant*
Cluny MacPherson	*John Grieve*
Duke of Argyll	*Rikki Fulton*

and James More MacGregor
Lord Advocate Prestongrange
Leonard Macquire
Robin Oig MacGregor *Bill McCabe*
Directed by Bill Bryden

KING LEAR

The Ludlow Festival Shakespeare productions by Nicolas Young have become something of a tradition and his direction of *King Lear* in the open air, backed by the mighty walls of Ludlow Castle, made the tragedy more impressive than ever.

The Lear of David King took on operatic proportions in the opening scenes of senile ranting. It was matched by the flashingly sexy Edmund of Nicholas Willatt and the Fool of Paul Arlington, superbly played as a huddled, venerable figure. The Regan and Goneril of Shirley Stelfox and Jill Tanner were well tuned to the interpretations of Lear and Edmund, but the Cordelia of Susan Glanville did not get to the heart of Lear's favourite daughter.

A revival of the play by Shakespeare. Presented as part of the Ludlow Festival in the open air at Ludlow Castle on June 27, 1972.

Cast included:

King Lear	*David King*
Regan	*Shirley Stelfox*
Goneril	*Jill Tanner*
Cordelia	*Susan Glanville*
Edmund	*Nicholas Willatt*
Kent	*Robert Cartland*
The Fool	*Paul Arlington*

Directed by Nicolas Young

KING LEAR

Unlike the Prospect Theatre production of *Love's Labour's Lost* at the Aldwych Theatre, *King Lear*, which was also directed by Toby Robertson, was entirely free of gimmicks. It was played by actors in off-white woollen costumes, working under intense lighting against black drapes. It was a highly concentrated production, intent upon bringing Lear's tragedy close to everyday experience.

Timothy West's Lear was driven out of his mind through shattering events and not through senility. He brought great humanity to his interpretation. The timelessness of Shakespeare's tragedy was stressed by the black evil of Mark Jones's Edmund and the splendid Edgar of Timothy Dalton.

140

A revival of the play by Shakespeare. Presented by Prospect Theatre Company at the Aldwych Theatre on June 7, 1972. Designed by Robin Archer. Music by Carl Davis.

Cast included:

King Lear	*Timothy West*
Goneril	*Sheila Ballantine*
Regan	*Vivienne Martin*
Cordelia	*Jill Dixon*
Earl of Kent	*Trevor Martin*
Earl of Gloucester	*John Bailey*
Edmund	*Mark Jones*
Duke of Albany	*Christopher Burgess*
Duke of Cornwall	*Ralph Watson*
Edgar	*Timothy Dalton*
Lear's Fool	*Ronnie Stevens*

Directed by Toby Robertson

Albert Finney in *Krapp's Last Tape*.
Photograph by John Haynes

KRAPP'S LAST TAPE

Preludes to death is how John Barber described Beckett's two short plays, *Krapp's Last Tape* and *Not I*, performed as a double-bill at the Royal Court Theatre, under the direction of Anthony Page. Albert Finney gave a strong performance as the old has-been, awakening highlights of his past, playing tapes he had made on many past birthdays. The voice was much more significant than action in this familiar Beckett monologue.

A play by Samuel Beckett. Presented by the English Stage Company at the Royal Court Theatre on January 16, 1973, together with the first performance of *Not I* by the same author. Designed by Jocelyn Herbert.

Cast included:
Krapp   *Albert Finney*
Directed by Anthony Page

Top: Richard Chamberlain as Thomas Mendip and Anna Calder-Marshall as Jennet Jourdemayne in *The Lady's Not For Burning.*   Photograph by John Timbers

Bottom: Kim Braden, June Jago, David McKail, Richard Chamberlain, Harold Innocent, Paul Hastings, Brian Hayes and Richard Cornish in *The Lady's Not For Burning.*   Photograph by John Timbers

THE LADY'S NOT FOR BURNING

Richard Chamberlain drew the town to the Chichester Festival Theatre when he appeared in the John Gielgud part of Thomas Mendip in *The Lady's Not for Burning.* He spoke the lines well and had an impressive stage presence. He was partnered by Anna Calder-Marshall in Pamela Brown's old part of Jennet Jour-demayne, but she lacked the mysterious quality to suggest she might have been a witch. They played well together, but they lacked the strength of personality to carry the memory of their separate predicaments through the scenes from which they were absent.

There were fine supporting performances from Richard Cornish, Michael Aldridge, Harold Innocent, June Jago and Leslie French. Robin Phillips made a sound job of the direction which was not easy on the open stage. One should be conscious in this Christopher Fry play of enclosure in a house, protected from the mundane world and the witch-hunters outside.

A revival of the play by Christopher Fry. Presented at the Chichester Festival Theatre on July 19, 1972. Designed by Daphne Dare. Music by Richard Kayne.

Cast included:

Alizon Eliot	*Kim Braden*
Nicholas Devize	*Richard Cornish*
Margaret Devize	*June Jago*
Humphrey Devize	*David McKail*
Hebbie Tyson	*Michael Aldridge*
Jennet Jourdemayne	
	Anna Calder-Marshall
The Chaplain	*Leslie French*
Edward Tappercoom	
	Harold Innocent
Matthew Skipps	*Brian Hayes*
Directed by Robin Phillips	

Richard	*Paul Hastings*
Thomas Mendip	
	Richard Chamberlain

LET'S MURDER VIVALDI!

David Mercer translated his short television play, *Let's Murder Vivaldi!* to the stage with conspicuous success, when it was presented at the King's Head Theatre Club in Islington.

It concerned two couples. Ben, a young architect, is living in squalor and disharmony with Julie; Gerald, a middle-aged civil servant on the executive grade, solves the problem of living with his wife Monica in a more ingenious fashion. The two pairs are linked through Ben and Julie working together and forming a strange liaison. With lively and realistic dialogue Mr Mercer penetrates the lives of these four people and carried the play along at a breathlessly exciting pace. The performances of Tom Conti, Diane Mercer, Diana Fairfax and Kevin Stoney were memorable and well worth seeing.

A play by David Mercer. Presented at the King's Head Theatre Club in Islington on October 25, 1972. Setting by John Scully.

Cast included:

Ben	*Tom Conti*
Julie	*Diane Mercer*
Monica	*Diana Fairfax*
Gerald	*Kevin Stoney*

Directed by Robert Gillespie

LIBERTY RANCH

Caryl Brahms and Ned Sherrin, as an idea for a new musical, thought about Westernizing *She Stoops to Conquer*. The resulting *Liberty Ranch* provided an amusing evening at the Greenwich Theatre.

Derek Griffiths was the best thing in the fast-moving show as Tony Lumpkin, who is transfigured into a half-caste Red Indian named Tommy Hawke and Elizabeth Seal, as vital as ever, played Kate Hardcastle who impersonates Miss Ruby in a flurry of red skirts. Gillian Lynne's direction and choreography kept the show energetically on the move, with lots of comic detail.

Musical based on Oliver Goldsmith's *She Stoops to Conquer*. Concept and lyrics by Caryl Brahms and Ned Sherrin; book by Dick Vosburgh and music by John Cameron. Presented at the Greenwich Theatre on July 18, 1972, by arrangement with the Stigwood Organization.

Designs by Roger Butlin, with costume designs by Richard Berkeley Sutcliffe. Musical director – Barry Booth.

Cast included:

Tommy Hawke	*Derek Griffiths*
Mrs Culpepper	*Margaret Courtenay*
Colonel Culpepper	*Bill Kerr*
Connie Kate Culpepper	*Elizabeth Seal*
George F Hastings	*Bob Sherman*
Charles Marlow II	*David Kernan*

Choreographed and directed by Gillian Lynne

LLOYD GEORGE KNEW MY FATHER

William Douglas Home wrote no more than an after-dinner trifle in *Lloyd George Knew My Father* at the Savoy Theatre, but the script offered Peggy Ashcroft and Ralph Richardson an opportunity to transform mediocre lines into something that sounded like high comedy. They used the vehicle with the utmost skill and completely captivated the audience.

Dame Peggy played a General-Knight's wife who threatened to take her life as a protest against a by-pass being built across the parkland of their stately home that dated back three centuries. Sir Ralph was never in better form as the bumbling, hard-of-hearing old soldier who exasperated the other characters in the play as surely as he delighted the audience. His flair for polished comedy, never missed an opportunity to get a laugh. Without their highly-skilled professional fooling, it might have been a sorry evening. With it, it was a joy.

A play by William Douglas Home. Presented by Ray Cooney for Ray Cooney Productions Ltd and John Gale for Volcano Productions Ltd, by arrangement with Hugh Wontner, at the Savoy Theatre on July 4, 1972. Setting by Anthony Holland.

Cast included:

Lady Boothroyd	*Peggy Ashcroft*
Robertson	*Allan Barnes*
General Sir William Boothroyd	*Ralph Richardson*
Hubert Boothroyd, MP	*James Grout*
Maud Boothroyd	*Janet Henfrey*
Sally Boothroyd	*Suzan Farmer*
Simon Green	*Simon Cadell*
Rev. Trevor Simmonds	*David Stoll*

Directed by Robin Midgley

Left: Dinsdale Landen, Sydney Bromley, Sinead Cusack, Elizabeth Spriggs and Michael Williams in the Royal Shakespeare Company's production of Dion Boucicault's comedy, *London Assurance*, at the New Theatre. Judi Dench created the part of Grace Harkaway when the Royal Shakespeare Company presented this production at the Aldwych Theatre in 1970 and she played it again at the New. She left the cast to have a baby and Miss Cusack took over in June 1972. *Photograph by John Timbers*

Right: Laurence Olivier as James Tyrone in the National Theatre production of *Long Day's Journey into Night* which was added to the 1972 autumn season at the Old Vic, after opening to a rave press at the New Theatre in the Spring

Left: Vivienne Martin as Jaquenetta, Michael Graham Cox as Costard and Ian Sharp as Moth in the Prospect Theatre Company's production of *Love's Labour's Lost.* Photograph by Mark Gudgeon

Right: Peter Woodthorpe as the actor and Mike Pratt as Pepel in the Royal Shakespeare Company's production of *The Lower Depths*

LOVE'S LABOUR'S LOST

Prospect Theatre Company slipped into the Aldwych for a short season between the end of the World Theatre Season and the return of the Royal Shakespeare Company to present *Love's Labour's Lost* and *King Lear.*

Toby Robertson favoured a Pop Art approach and in the words of Irving Wardle turned it into an Elizabethan *Salad Days.* It introduced the strumming of guitars, microphones disguised as flowers, the puffing of marijuana and young men dressed as elegant drop-outs and even astronauts. Milton Shulman considered the most felicitous moments to be when Shakespeare's lines accompanied some pleasing songs by Carl Davis, and the production took on the air of a charming pop festival.

The comics came best out of this attempt to relate Shakespeare's earliest play to modern times. Michael Graham Cox as Costard, Ronnie Stevens as Sir Nathaniel, and Timothy West as Holofernes were a delight and in the Shakespeare way Timothy Dalton as Berowne, John Bailey as Armado and Prunella Scales as the Princess of France were ideal.

A revival of the play by Shakespeare. Presented by Prospect Theatre Company at the Aldwych Theatre on June 5, 1972. Designed by Robin Archer. Music by Carl Davis.

Cast included:

Ferdinand	*Mark Jones*
Longaville	*Christopher Burgess*
Dumaine	*Michael Percival*
Berowne	*Timothy Dalton*
Costard	*Michael Graham Cox*
Don Adriano de Armado	
	John Bailey
Princess of France	*Prunella Scales*
Katherine	*Jill Dixon*
Maria	*Sheila Ballantine*
Rosaline	*Delia Lindsay*
Sir Nathaniel	*Ronnie Stevens*
Holofernes	*Timothy West*

Directed by Toby Robertson

THE LOWER DEPTHS

During the rehearsals of *The Lower Depths* when Maxim Gorky's doss-house drama was first presented at the Moscow Art Theatre, the author advised the actors to shout the lines. 'To hell with naturalism!,' he cried.

David Jones, director of the Royal Shakespeare Company's revival at the Aldwych, seemed to take the same line of approach. In consequence, this plotless play was presented with an excess of dramatic projection, which was too powerful for what is essentially an intimate, shared unravelling of souls. To avoid the play becoming overwhelmingly depressing, Mr Jones stressed the humour to the point of raucousness.

This revival was a collection of acting studies, rather than a tightly integrated ensemble presentation, but there was impressive playing by Peter Woodthorpe as the drink-sodden actor; Gordon Gostelow as the old traveller who offers the dregs of humanity the comfort of illusory happiness; Morgan Sheppard as the man who loses his lock-making tools and Alison Fiske as the pathetic prostitute.

A revival of the play by Maxim Gorky, in a new translation by Kitty Hunter Blair and Jeremy Brooks. Presented by the Royal Shakespeare Company at the Aldwych Theatre on June 29, 1972. Setting designed by Timothy O'Brien, with costumes by Timothy O'Brien and Tazeena Firth.

Cast included:

Mikhail	*Tony Church*
Andrey Kleshch	*Morgan Sheppard*
Nastya	*Alison Fiske*
The Baron	*Richard Pasco*
The Actor	*Peter Woodthorpe*
Vasska Pepel	*Mike Pratt*
Luka	*Gordon Gostelow*
Vassilissa	*Heather Canning*

Directed by David Jones

MACBETH

Michael Blakemore's National Theatre production of *Macbeth* at the Old Vic was a compelling domestic drama set in a bleak granite castle and peopled with Elizabethan courtiers rather than one of the great tragedies of dramatic literature.

Anthony Hopkins presented a Macbeth wetting his lips and sweating with conscience and Diana Rigg made a moving Lady Macbeth, who spat on her crucifix and used it as an imaginary dagger. But one expected Lady Macbeth to be more awesome and more impressive. Miss Rigg would be quite capable of giving such a reading of the part, but it would not have fitted into Michael Blakemore's conception of the play. Alan MacNaughtan made a majestic monarch, with Denis Quilley playing Banquo with decided authority.

A revival of the play by Shakespeare. Presented by the National Theatre Company at the Old Vic on November 9, 1972. Designed by Michael Annals, with music and sound by Marc Wilkinson.

Cast included:

First Witch	*Sheila Burrell*
Second Witch	*Mary Griffiths*
Third Witch	*Maureen Lipman*
Duncan	*Alan MacNaughtan*
Malcolm	*Ronald Pickup*
Macbeth	*Anthony Hopkins*
Banquo	*Denis Quilley*
Lady Macbeth	*Diana Rigg*
Fleance	*Roger Monk*
Porter	*Harry Lomax*
Macduff	*Gawn Grainger*
Lady Macduff	*Louise Purnell*
Macduff's son	*David Parfitt*
Doctor	*Kenneth Macintosh*
Gentlewoman	*Jeanne Watts*

Directed by Michael Blakemore

MAID OF THE MOUNTAINS

When Emile Littler presented and directed the revival of *Maid of the Mountains* at the Palace, there were drastic differences from Daly's 1917 production which made the alluring José Collins an evergreen legend.

In the first place, Mr Littler billed Jimmy Edwards, grossly miscast incidentally, in the comedy role of General Malona, above the other artists in the company – even above Lyn Kennington, who gave a highly professional and tuneful rendering of the José Collins part of the Maid.

Mr Littler also decided to make Baldasarre, the Chief Brigand impressively played by Gordon Clyde, a singing part in this revival. Originally Baldasarre was played by Arthur Wontner, as José Collins decided not to have a singing hero.

Strange tricks were played with the locale. During the first interval the story travelled from the Dolomites to the South Seas, for no discernible reason, except that Mr Littler may have had a fine selection of sarongs in the theatre wardrobe.

It would seem Mr Littler lacked complete faith in the appeal of the melodious Fraser-Simson score. Otherwise why did he interpolate two popular numbers from other hit shows – 'The Song of the Vagabonds', with revised lyric, from *The Vagabond King* and 'Pedro the Fisherman' from *Lisbon Story*?

A revival of the musical comedy, directed and presented by Emile Littler at the Palace Theatre on April 29, 1972.

Book by Frederick Lonsdale and Emile Littler. Music by Harold Fraser-Simson, with additional numbers by James W Tate, Rudolph Friml and Harry Parr Davies. Lyrics by Harry Graham, Brian Hooker, E Clifford Harris and Valentine, and Harold Purcell. Choreography by Malcolm Goddard; scenery and costumes designed by Alec Shanks and lighting by Michael Northen. Musical director – Derek Taverner.

Cast included:

Teresa	*Lyn Kennington*
Baldasarre	*Gordon Clyde*
Tonio	*Jimmy Thompson*
General Malona	*Jimmy Edwards*
Beppo	*Neville Jason*
Victoria	*Janey Mahoney*
Angela	*Susan Maudsley*
Lieutenant Rugini	*Richard Manuel*
The Jailer	*Martin Dell*

Directed by Emile Littler

Oliver Ford-Davies and Mia
Farrow in a revival of J M Barrie's
Mary Rose

After a five-year absence from London, Marcel Marceau opened a four-week Sadler's Wells season on July 24, 1972. Even though twenty years have passed since Marceau first conquered London, the great French mime was at the very peak of his career. He has mellowed and never cast so sure a spell over his audience.

He has held sway for so long because apart from being a master craftsman in the art of mime, he is a keen observer of humanity and creates on stage familiar figures in situations we have either experienced ourselves or can easily appreciate in others.

So superbly are Marceau's mimodramas conceived and constructed, they never become stale or weary through being seen again and again, season after season.

'Falling in Love Again' is Marlene Dietrich's signature tune. The title is also a reliable forecast of what happens to us whenever she returns to London, as she did on May 29 at the Queen's Theatre. We all fell in love again.

Dietrich is the past-mistress of showmanship – a superb perfectionist who never ceases to work on her programme and the art of projecting her seductive personality, with the result that she is hailed as a living legend with a timeless appeal.

She strolls nonchalantly on stage, the most theatrically glamorous creature imaginable, sparkling with jewels, trailing arctic white furs and attired in a sultry clinging gown which is a masterpiece of the *haut couturier*'s inspiration.

The magic never fails because nothing is left to chance. Even her cleverly playful manipulation of the curtain at the end of the show, rehearsed to perfection, has the air of an impromptu idea and further delights an already bewitched audience.

She never attempts a song beyond her range, and not since Chaliapin's day has there been any other artist with the secret of casting a spell by the cunning use of silence.

MARY ROSE

Just as Alicia Markova was born to dance Giselle, Mia Farrow was singled out to appear as Barrie's Mary Rose. The American actress, with her haunting face and those enormous eyes was so right for the part, and the 69 Theatre Company of Manchester are to be congratulated upon casting her for the name-part in their production of *Mary Rose* which later came to the Shaw Theatre in London.

She breathed new life into Barrie's melodramatic mystery of the girl who disappeared on a lonely island, only to return a quarter of a century later, untouched by time. Mia Farrow made us believe in the possibility of it all, which suggests she may be earmarked for a future Peter Pan. Few other American actresses have perfected the gift of speaking English so purely without a trace of any transatlantic burr.

A revival of the play by J M Barrie. Presented by the 69 Theatre Company, by arrangement with the Dolphin Theatre Company, at the Shaw Theatre, on July 13, 1972. Designed by Johanna Bryant. Music composed by John Taverner.

Cast included:

Mrs Otery	*Carmel McSharry*
Mr Morland	*Oliver Ford-Davies*
Mrs Morland	*Ann Way*
Mr Amy	*Lee Fox*
Mary Rose	*Mia Farrow*
Harry	
Simon Blake }	*Ralph Bates*
Cameron	*Roy Sampson*

Directed by Braham Murray

THE MATING GAME

Julia Lockwood and Clive Francis played two incongruous and un-expected virgins in the highly sophisticated setting of a luxurious Park Lane penthouse flat in *The Mating Game*, a farce by Robin Hawdon, racily directed by Ray Cooney at the Apollo. Terry Scott and Aimi Macdonald provided hilarious contrast as a couple more conversant with the ways of the world. Avril Angers, as the porter's wife who 'does' for the penthouse tenants, brought the character to life in the most convincing and amusing manner.

The designer, Hutchinson Scott, constructed a bed which appeared and vanished at the touch of a button, a property to delight any pantomime Dame. This gimmick helped Mr Cooney to extract the last ounce of laughter from the dialogue.

A play by Robin Hawdon. Presented by John Gale (for Volcano Productions Ltd) and Ray Cooney (for Ray Cooney Productions Ltd) at the Apollo Theatre on June 14, 1972. Setting by Hutchinson Scott.

Cast included:

Draycott Harris	*Clive Francis*
Honey Tooks	*Aimi Macdonald*
James Harris	*Terry Scott*
Julia Carrington	*Julia Lockwood*
Mrs Finney	*Avril Angers*

Directed by Ray Cooney

ME

Al Mancini played the leading part in *Me*, an autobiographical play by the Glasgow writer, C P Taylor, staged at the Glasgow Citizens' Theatre for the opening of the Clyde Fair International. In some quarters the incessant use of four-letter words was considered unnecessary, as their repetition reached the point of boredom. Some members of the audience took offence at the giant-size replica of a sex organ which formed part of the setting. Al Mancini, Thelma Ruby and Peter Frye captured the sentimental humour of the Jewish race in a memorable scene.

A play by C P Taylor, subtitled *A Letter to Scotland*. Presented by Clyde Fair International at the Glasgow Citizens' Theatre on June 15, 1972. Designed by John Halle.

Cast included: Al Mancini, Michael McKevitt, John Croft, Robert Walker, Frank Jarvis, Colin Stepney, Katherine Barker, Thelma Ruby and *Peter Frye*

Directed by Kevin Billington

Emrys James as Shylock and Tony Church as Antonio in the Royal Shakespeare Company's production of *The Merchant of Venice*. Photograph by Donald Cooper

MEASURE FOR MEASURE

The enterprising National Youth Theatre presented *Measure for Measure* at the Shaw Theatre in Euston Road, as a straightforward narrative, under the direction of Paul Hill. There were some fine individual performances, such as Jonathan Coy as Angelo, Albert Welling as the Duke and Irene Richard as Isabella.

Measure for Measure is one of Shakespeare's most complex plays and its interpretation has led to endless discussion. The National Youth Theatre oversimplified their production and in consequence the text lost some of its significance. But it was a splendid attempt.

A revival of the play by Shakespeare. Presented by the National Youth Theatre at the Shaw Theatre, Euston Road, on September 6, 1972. Designed by Christopher Lawrence.

Cast included:
The Duke	*Albert Welling*
Angelo	*Jonathan Coy*
Escalus	*Shaun Austin-Olsen*
Claudio	*Len Preston*
Isabella	*Irene Richard*

Directed by Paul Hill

THE MERCHANT OF VENICE

The Royal Shakespeare Company opened their summer season at the Aldwych Theatre with the Terry Hands production of *The Merchant of Venice*, first seen at Stratford-upon-Avon the previous year.

Terry Hands's direction was remarkable for its gaiety and well-knitted ensemble playing and for humour which he discovered in parts of the text not previously considered amusing. Susan Fleetwood's Portia was youthful, innocent and natural; Bernard Lloyd's Bassanio was a real charmer; Emrys James's Shylock was a genuine human being with a sense of humour and dignity he maintained even to his last exit from the courtroom with his robes covering his head.

Roger Rees played Gratiano as an extrovert; Peter Woodthorpe's Spanish grandee Arragon was most impressive and the allure of Jessica's voice, played by Alison Fiske, was something to remember.

Timothy O'Brien's sombre set came as a shock to anyone who recalls Venice as a city of light – with vast expanses of water and sky.

A revival of the play by Shakespeare. Presented by the Royal Shakespeare Company – a recast version of their 1971 Stratford-upon-Avon production – at the Aldwych Theatre on June 22, 1972. Designed by Timothy O'Brien, with costumes by Timothy O'Brien and Tazeena Firth. Music by Guy Woolfenden.

Cast included:
Antonio	*Tony Church*
Bassanio	*Bernard Lloyd*
Gratiano	*Roger Rees*
Lorenzo	*David Calder*
Shylock	*Emrys James*
Jessica	*Alison Fiske*
Launcelot Gobbo	*Peter Geddis*
Old Gobbo	*Gordon Gostelow*
Portia	*Susan Fleetwood*
Nerissa	*Lynn Dearth*
Prince of Morocco	*Robert Ashby*
Prince of Arragon	*Peter Woodthorpe*

Directed by Terry Hands

THE MIDDLE WATCH

That comedy-hit of the 1920s, *The Middle Watch*, revived particularly well at the Pitlochry Festival Theatre, under the direction of Christopher Denys, who had the right touch to present this picture of life aboard HMS *Falcon*, when two attractive young ladies get left behind after an engagement party. The gaiety was unforced and gave Alice Fraser an opportunity to show her skill as a comedienne as Mary Carlton – a delightful performance in light comedy. Alec Heggie, Ian Lindsay, Davis Shackleton and Tony Roper coped amusingly with their nautical roles.

A revival of the play by Ian Hay and Stephen King-Hall. Presented at the Pitlochry Festival Theatre on May 1, 1972. Designed by Alan Stewart.

Cast included:
Marine Ogg	*David Shackleton*
Ah Fong	*Tony Roper*
Captain Randall	*Christopher Saul*
Fay	*Sarah Stephenson*
A Guest	*Colette Kelly*
Flag Lieutenant	*Donald MacIver*
Nancy	*Lois Hantz*
Commander Baddeley	*Ian Lindsay*
Charlotte Hopkinson	*Sheila Brownrigg*
Admiral Hewitt	*Robert Aldous*
Mary Carlton	*Alice Fraser*
Lady Hewitt	*Pamela Pitchford*
Able Seaman	*John Kesl*
Captain Maitland	*Alec Heggie*
Corporal Duckett	*Tony Roper*

Directed by Christopher Denys

John Turner as Alceste and Vickery Turner as Célimène in *The Misanthrope*. *Photograph by Studio Edmark*

A MIDSUMMER NIGHT'S DREAM

Peter Brook's highly imaginative production of *A Midsummer Night's Dream*, which took Stratford-upon-Avon by storm in 1970, was recast in the summer of 1972 and given a few performances at the Aldwych Theatre before embarking upon a twelve-month world tour, covering western and eastern Europe, America and Japan.

Capacity houses acclaimed this production, so very different from the traditional classical treatment of Shakespeare's fairy play. Titania slept upright on a bed of scarlet ostrich feathers suspended in mid-air; Puck wore a lime-green satin track-suit and vied with Oberon to spin plates like Oriental jugglers; Puck and Oberon also indulged in a trapeze act, both hanging from their swings by their feet; the Mechanicals were cloth-capped and delightfully loutish.

The Royal Shakespeare players spoke their lines beautifully and enjoyed every moment of the horseplay and the knockabout comedy.

A revival of the play by Shakespeare. Presented by the Royal Shakespeare Company at the Aldwych Theatre, at the start of a twelve-month world tour, on August 8, 1972. Designed by Sally Jacobs. Music by Richard Peaslee, the Musicians, the Actors and Felix Mendelssohn.

Cast included:

Theseus and Oberon	*Alan Howard*
Hippolyta and Titania	*Gemma Jones*
Philostrate and Puck	*Robert Lloyd*
Egeus and Quince	*Philip Locke*
Bottom	*Barry Stanton*
Flute	*George Sweeney*
Starveling	*Richard Moore*
Snout	*Malcolm Rennie*
Snug	*Hugh Keays Byrne*
Hermia	*Zhivila Roche*
Lysander	*Bruce Myers*
Helena	*Jennie Stoller*
Demetrius	*Glynne Lewis*
Fairies	*David Meyer*
	Anthony Meyer
	Pauline Munro
	Roshan Seth

Directed by Peter Brook

THE MISANTHROPE

Frank Hauser who translated and directed the Oxford Playhouse production of *The Misanthrope* by Molière, says if this particular work is not the greatest comedy in all drama, it has few rivals and no superiors. Most ingeniously, his English version in rhyming couplets, employed for the main part words in common everyday use, which meant the comedy was not too removed from our own time.

The acid verbal duelling of Lynda Marchal's Arsinoé and Vickery Turner's Célimène, provided the humorous highspot of the evening. The entire company spoke their lines with remarkable clarity and precision and Alix Stone's tasteful décor and the muted colours of her costumes were a joy to the eye.

A play by Molière, translated by Frank Hauser. Presented by Meadow Players Ltd at Oxford Playhouse on October 16, 1972. Designed by Alix Stone.

Cast included:

Alceste	*John Turner*
Philinte	*John Rhys-Davies*
Oronte	*Desmond Water-Ellis*
Célimène	*Vickery Turner*
Basque	*Michael Claughton*
Eliante	*Carol Frazer*
Clitandre	*Nicholas Amer*
Acaste	*Christopher Guinee*
Guard of the Court	
	Patrick Monckton
Arsinoé	*Lynda Marchal*
Du Bois	*Patrick Monckton*

Directed by Frank Hauser

151

Barbara Jefford as Mother Marie-Thérèse Vauzou and Margaretta Scott as Mother Josephine Imbert greet Rita Tushingham as Bernadette Soubirous of Lourdes on her first day at the Convent of Nevers in *Mistress of Novices*. *Photograph by Morris Newcombe*

MR SYDNEY SMITH COMING UPSTAIRS

Brian Oulton was author and leading player in *Mr Sydney Smith Coming Upstairs*, which opened the newly restored Harrogate Theatre after a nine-month closure.

The choice was not a happy one, as the play was too long and too wordy to grip the attention of the audience, being based on the life of a nineteenth-century country cleric who was not specially interesting. Peggy Thorpe-Bates played Mrs Smith.

A play by Brian Oulton. Presented at the Harrogate Theatre on October 12, 1972. Designed by Ian Adley, with special costumes by Mary Chambers.

Cast included:

The Rev. Sydney Smith	Brian Oulton
Catherine Smith	Peggy Thorpe-Bates
Saba	Janet Lees Price
Douglas	John McNulty
Emily	Lesley Grayburn
Wyndham	Louis Cabot
Annie Kay	Suzanne Bertish
Bunch	Alison Frazer
Robb	Murray Brown
The Earl	Michael Cotterill
The Countess	Elizabeth Tyrrell
Milestones	Leslie Lawton
The Bishop	Owen Holder

Directed by Brian Howard

MISTRESS OF NOVICES

Rita Tushingham and Barbara Jefford had magnificent acting parts in *Mistress of Novices* by John Kerr, which opened at the Piccadilly Theatre. Miss Tushingham was Bernadette whose vision of Our Lady put Lourdes on the pilgrims' map. Miss Jefford was Mistress of Novices at the Convent of Nevers, which Bernadette entered eight years after seeing the visions, when she wanted to be alone and escape from publicity.

The conflict springs from the older woman's jealousy. 'Why,' she asks, 'should the vision have been vouchsafed to an ignorant peasant girl and not to someone like myself?' This resentment leads the Mistress of Novices to spiritual and mental cruelty, as well as to ill-treatment and causes her to come near to losing her own faith in her anxiety to destroy the validity of Bernadette's vision.

A play by John Kerr. Presented by Triarch Productions Ltd at the Piccadilly Theatre on February 15, 1973, by arrangement with Donald Albery. Designed by Berkeley Sutcliffe.

Cast included:

Mother Josephine Imbert	Margaretta Scott
Sister Marthe Fores	Beau Daniels
Bishop of Nevers	Geoffrey Keen
Mother Marie-Theres Vauzou	Barbara Jefford
Sister Emilienne Duboe	Heather Bell
Sister Vincent Garros	Jill Raymond
Sister Bernard Dalias	Sally Reymond
Sister Stanislas Paschal	Valerie Verdon
Mother Alexandre Roque	Brenda Kempner
Bernadette Soubirous	Rita Tushingham
Father Douce	Joss Clewes
Doctor St Cyr	Brandon Brady
Sister Louise Cartier	Karen Ford
A Nun	Jean Ainslie
A Nun	Pat Brackenbury
First Reader	Linda Gray
Second Reader	Hermione Gregory

Directed by Charles Hickman

Rita Tushingham as Bernadette
Soubirous and Barbara Jefford as
Mother Marie-Thérèse Vauzou in
Mistress of Novices.   *Photograph
by Morris Newcombe*

Cicely Courtneidge, Dinah Sheridan and Diane Hart in *Move Over Mrs Markham*, the successful play by Ray Cooney and John Chapman at the Vaudeville Theatre. Moira Lister created the part of Mrs Markham, but Dinah Sheridan took over in June, 1972, so that Miss Lister could fulfil other commitments. *Photograph by Godfrey Argent*

MOTHER EARTH

A rock musical on the subject of pollution came to the Round House, Chalk Farm, under the title of *Mother Earth*. The songs were of a derivative nature and it was difficult to isolate one from another, but they served to deal with the evils of our time, even though the action was set in 1999. Two artists who had been in *Hair*, Peter Straker and Linda Kendrick, brought their considerable talents to the cast.

A musical revue, with book and lyrics by Ron Thronson and music by Toni Shearer. Presented by Gordon Mills and Harold Davison for MAM with Sidney Terry and John Keam at the Round House, Chalk Farm, on September 20, 1972.

Cast included: Peter Straker, Frank Aeillo, Ziggy Byfield, Sharon Campbell, Helen Chappel, Robert Cotton, Mark Johnson, Linda Kendrick, Jane Lee, Nina McCarthy, Roy North, Pat Scott, Vicky Silva and Mary Tamm

Produced by Douglas Harrison
Directed by Terry Palmer

154

Richard Pasco as Thomas Becket in the Royal Shakespeare Company's production of T S Eliot's *Murder in the Cathedral*

MURDER IN COMPANY

The thriller by Philip King and John Boland, *Murder in Company*, set in a church hall during an amateur dramatic company's rehearsal, was presented by Theatre South East at the De La Warr Pavilion at Bexhill-on-Sea.

The authors succeeded in fooling the audience on several occasions during the action of the play, which had humour and horror neatly laced in its construction. Michael ffoulkes directed a company which included Peggy Paige, David Masterman, Alan Granville and Virginia Moore.

A play by Philip King and John Boland. Presented by Theatre South East at the De La Warr Pavilion, Bexhill-on-Sea, on September 21, 1972.

Cast included:

Alan Wilson	*Alan Buckman*
Margaret Stephens	*Barbara Farrell*
Ted Smith	*David Masterman*
Philip Stephens	*Richard Burnett*
Ronnie Meadows	*Alan Granville*
Phoebe Kershaw	*Peggy Paige*
Patricia Robins	*Virginia Moore*
Doris Stewart	*Janice Hosker*

Directed by Michael ffoulkes

MURDER IN THE CATHEDRAL

The Royal Shakespeare Company revived T S Eliot's *Murder in the Cathedral* at the Aldwych and gave Richard Pasco a chance to reach the peak of his career as Thomas Becket. This sensitive actor gave an impressive performance of great vocal beauty, making us believe in Becket as martyr, saint and statesman. He all but equalled Robert Donat's unforgettable performance in the same part.

Terry Hands directed the drama with a contemporary touch and Farrah's set of Hessian strips and silver foil on a tip-tilted stage conveyed the atmosphere of the period by the simplest means. The simple, haunting music of Ian Kellam suited the mood of the play.

Susan Fleetwood was impressive as the Leader of the Chorus and so was Brewster Mason as the Fourth Tempter and Fourth Knight.

A revival of the play by T S Eliot. Presented by the Royal Shakespeare Company at the Aldwych Theatre on August 31, 1972. Designed by Farrah. Music by Ian Kellam.

Cast included:

Thomas Becket	*Richard Pasco*
First Priest	*Denis Holme*
Second Priest	*Nickolas Grace*
Third Priest	*Morgan Sheppard*
First Tempter First Knight	*Bernard Lloyd*
Second Tempter Second Knight	*Anthony Pedley*
Third Tempter Third Knight	*Tony Church*
Fourth Tempter Fourth Knight	*Brewster Mason*
Chorus Leader	*Susan Fleetwood*

Directed by Terry Hands

John Harding and Kenneth
Williams in the same outsize
trouser suit in *My Fat Friend*

MY FAMILY CAME OVER WITH THE NORMANS

Perth Theatre presented the première of Roger Milner's enjoyable comedy, *My Family Came Over with the Normans*, an unpretentious comment on class distinction. Dorothy Edwards and Martin Heller played Lord and Lady Bredon, with Ron Bain as their young son, who preferred a Scottish orphan girl met on holiday to the ageing little rich girl their parents had lined up as their future daughter-in-law. Janet Michael played the orphan and Carole Snape the heiress.

A play by Roger Milner. Presented at Perth Theatre on December 6, 1972. Designed by Helen Wilkinson.

Cast included:

Lord Bredon	*Martin Heller*
Lady Bredon	*Dorothy Edwards*
Hon. Barry Bredon	*Ron Bain*
Pamela Morris-Parker	*Janet Michael*
Sandra Copeland	*Carol Snape*
Harker	*Bruce Bennett*
Dr James Baker	*Roger Kemp*

Directed by Joan Knight

MY FAT FRIEND

In his first stage play, *My Fat Friend*, Charles Laurence gave Kenneth Williams the opportunity of his life to delight audiences with endless camp babble and to play amusing variations on a cheeky homosexual theme. Mr Williams rolled his eyes, pointed his lines and enjoyed being so generously served by an author skilled in writing hilariously outrageous lines, which were put across with such remarkable expertise.

This trifle of a play concerned a young but decidedly plump young lady who sold books in Hampstead and took in two lodgers, John Harding and Kenneth Williams. A handsome customer, Bernard Holley, falls in love with her at first sight on the eve of departing to the Persian Gulf for four months. While he is away Kenneth Williams takes her in hand and slims her down to sylph-like proportions to surprise the admirer on his return. They are shattered to discover that he loses interest when he comes back because he is only attracted by large ladies.

A play by Charles Laurence. Presented by Michael Codron at the Globe Theatre on December 6, 1972. Designed by Alan Pickford.

Cast included:

James	*John Harding*
Henry	*Kenneth Williams*
Vicky	*Jennie Linden*
Tom	*Bernard Holley*

Directed by Eric Thompson

Robert Powell as the lovesick
Scythrop Glowry and Nerys
Hughes as Marionetta in *Nightmare
Abbey*.   *Photograph by Stuart
Robinson*

NIGHTINGALE

Tribute was paid to Florence Nightingale by Ted Craig and Eilian Wyn in *Nightingale*, seen at the Worthing Connaught Theatre. Their work was based on an earlier play *The Lady With a Lamp* by Reginald Berkeley, in which Edith Evans scored a great success.

As Florence Nightingale, Rosalind Shanks gave a moving performance, epitomizing all the dedication and tenderness of the nursing profession. Everything was sacrificed to duty. Nine other members of the cast played twenty-five parts in Ted Craig's brilliant, swift-moving production, acted against ever-changing token settings. Eilian Wyn and John Cunningham narrated in word and song.

A play based on *The Lady With a Lamp* by Reginald Berkeley and the essay by Lytton Strachey, adapted by Ted Craig and Eilian Wyn. Presented at the Worthing Connaught Theatre on May 9, 1972. Designed by Stuart Stanley, with costumes by Stuart Stanley, Glynnis Ruscoe and Yvonne Simons.

Cast included:
Florence Nightingale
                Rosalind Shanks
Other parts played by: John Dommett, Eilian Wyn, John Cunningham, Peter May, Richard MacKenna, Anthea Holloway, Jane How, Stephen Churchett, Judy Nunn, Guy Siner, David Murch

Directed by Ted Craig

NIGHTMARE ABBEY

John Fernald, directed *Nightmare Abbey*, Anthony Sharp's adaptation of Thomas Love Peacock's Gothik Farce.

In an illuminating programme note Mr Fernald wrote: The Theatre of the Absurd may be thought to be a modern phenomenon, but *Nightmare Abbey* with its outrageous domestics and its cultured crackpots anticipates Ionesco by a century and a half. No one has surpassed Thomas Love Peacock in creating endearing eccentrics.

Robert Powell as the hero in love, Karin Fernald as the intellectual stranger and Nerys Hughes as the 'blooming and accomplished young lady' gave outstanding performances.

A revival of the Gothik Farce by Anthony Sharp, adapted from the novel by Thomas Love Peacock. Presented at the Yvonne Arnaud Theatre, Guildford, on November 7, 1972. Designed by Pamela Ingram, with costumes by Margaret Graham.

Cast included:

Crow	*Harold Goodwin*
Raven	*Peter Madden*
Mr Glowry	*George Benson*
Mr Toobad	*Laurence Hardy*
Scythrop Glowry	*Robert Powell*
Mr Hilary	*William Bond*
Mr Listless	*Richard Carey*
Mr Flosky	*Philip Lowrie*
Fatout	*Peter Dixon*
Marionetta	*Nerys Hughes*
Stella	*Karin Fernald*

Directed by John Fernald

157

NIGHT WATCH

Honor Blackman, past-mistress in the art of playing leading ladies in thrillers, headed the cast of *Night Watch*, a story of terror, mystery and murder by Lucille Fletcher, which opened at York Theatre Royal.

All the action took place at night in winter. Miss Blackman saw a dead man staring at her through the window of a derelict house opposite and that started off a whole chain of events and situations, which baffled the police and the psychiatrist. The finger of suspicion pointed in various directions in turn. George Baker, Elspet Gray and Paul Dawkins lent excellent support under the able direction of Vivian Matalon.

A play by Lucille Fletcher. Presented by Ray Cooney, for Ray Cooney Productions Ltd, by arrangement with George W George and Barnard S Straus, at York Theatre Royal on October 30, 1972. Setting by Brian Currah.

Cast included:

Pamela Wheeler	*Honor Blackman*
John Wheeler	*George Baker*
Edith	*Barbara Laurenson*
Det.-Sgt Walker	*Brian Badcoe*
PC Anderson	*Philip Dunbar*
Curtis Appleby	*Paul Dawkins*
Diana Cooke	*Elspet Gray*
Dr Margaret Lake	
	Georgine Anderson
Sam Hoke	*Kenneth McClellan*

Directed by Vivian Matalon

NORMAN, IS THAT YOU?

Alfred Marks was hardly off-stage in *Norman, Is That You?*, a slick, continuously amusing comedy by Ron Clark and Sam Bobrick, which opened at Brighton Theatre Royal. He played a man with a successful dry-cleaning business in Harrogate. When his wife runs off to Scotland with his brother he rushes to London to confide in his twenty-three-year-old window-dresser son. The father is amazed to discover the boy is a homosexual, sharing a flat with a friend who wears scarlet velvet trousers.

The bewildered and exasperated Mr Marks gave a lively comedy performance, scoring a laugh on every line, at first refusing to accept the situation; after reading books on the subject he comes to realistic terms with it when his wife returns from her adventure. Paul Seed, Paul Freeman and Joy Shelton provided excellent teamwork as the boys and the wife in this play which was highly amusing without being either cheap or vulgar.

A play by Ron Clark and Sam Bobrick. Presented by JCD Theatres Ltd at Brighton Theatre Royal on October 23, 1972. Designed by Hutchinson Scott.

Cast included:

Norman Charlton	*Paul Seed*
Terry Hobart	*Paul Freeman*
Ben Charlton	*Alfred Marks*
Mary	*Valerie Minifie*
Beatrice	*Joy Shelton*

Directed by Robin Phillips

NOT I

To make a Samuel Beckett double-bill at the Royal Court Theatre, the English Stage Company followed a revival of *Krapp's Last Tape*, with a totally unfamiliar novelty called *Not I*.

The author concentrates his attention on speech, to the almost complete exclusion of physical movement. On a darkened stage, the only visible features of the leading character, Mouth, are the lips of Billie Whitelaw. A shrouded, listening figure is played by Brian Miller. The voice of the panic-stricken woman poured out seemingly meaningless phrases, and the speaker would appear to be on the verge of death in this twelve-minute monologue written for the speaking mouth. It was a highly dramatic experience, with its frightening silences, and marked Miss Whitelaw as an actress with remarkable technical control and achievement.

A première of play by Samuel Beckett. Presented by the English Stage Company at the Royal Court Theatre on January 16, 1973, together with *Krapp's Last Tape*. Designed by Jocelyn Herbert.

Cast included:

Mouth	*Billie Whitelaw*
Auditor	*Brian Miller*

Directed by Anthony Page

OEDIPUS NOW

Svetlana Beriosova was granted leave of absence from the Royal Ballet to make her début as a dramatic actress at the Hampstead Theatre Club, playing The Sphinx, Jocasta and Antigone in James Roose-Evans's meditation on the text of Sophocles in a play called *Oedipus Now*.

There were moments when the audience was invited to think in silence on the implications of this tragedy; the idea was somewhat confusing and much of the grandeur associated with Greek tragedy was lost. The finest acting came from David March as Tiresias and the Shepherd.

A meditation on the tragedy by Sophocles, compiled by James Roose-Evans. Presented at the Hampstead Theatre Club on October 9, 1972. Designed by Peter Rice.

Cast included:

Jocasta	
Antigone	*Svetlana Beriosova*
The Sphinx	
Chorus	*Paul Bacchus*
	Jarlath Conroy
	Richard Vanstone
Messenger	*Hywel Jones*
Creon	*Edwin Manda*
Tiresias	*David March*
Oedipus	*Geoffrey Whitehead*

Directed by James Roose-Evans

Wanda Rotha, so often cast as glamorous queens on the stage, appeared as the septuagenarian translator of verses in *The Old Ones*

THE OLD MAN'S COMFORTS

Perry Pontac, a dramatist new to London, created a favourable impression with *The Old Man's Comforts*, presented at the Open Space Theatre. Ken Tynan is quoted as saying the play is more consistently witty than any first play he has ever seen. It is much influenced by Oscar Wilde; consequently the dialogue was a joy to listen to, with a succession of polished epigrams.

The plot concerned a wealthy old invalid only willing to leave his money to a person such as himself – one who has renounced the pleasures of the flesh and become morally and physically pure. Fenella Fielding and Neil Cunningham played superbly in the eccentric and extravagant style demanded by the writing.

A play by Perry Pontac. Presented at the Open Space Theatre on December 21, 1973. Designed by Robin Don.

Cast included:

Nurse Harge	*Petronella Ford*
Crotolon	*Malcolm Storry*
Fredonia	*Candida Fawsitt*
Turlock	*Anthony Milner*
Porges	*Neil Cunningham*
Lauerta	*Fenella Fielding*

Directed by Charles Marowitz

THE OLD ONES

Arnold Wesker's play at the Royal Court Theatre, *The Old Ones*, had no plot, but consisted of a succession of scenes of Jewish life in a big city. It offered superb opportunities for some splendid performances from some of our established leading players.

Wanda Rotha, so often seen as a glamorous queen, appeared as a faded seventy-year-old lonely creature, spending her lifetime on the useless translation of verses she knew she would never complete. Rose Hill made a poignant impact as a poor absent-minded soul who spent most of her time talking to herself.

Max Wall and George Pravda were argumentative brothers and Patience Collier, looking more than ever like Marie Rambert, was the focal point around which all the various personal relationships revolved. Douglas Heap designed a warren of hideously depressing bed-sitters in which most of the members of the community eked out their ghastly existence.

A play by Arnold Wesker. Presented by the English Stage Company at the Royal Court Theatre on August 8, 1972. Designed by Douglas Heap, with costumes by Harriet Geddes.

Cast included:

Emmanuel	*Max Wall*
Gerda	*Amelia Bayntun*
Boomy	*George Pravda*
Teressa	*Wanda Rotha*
Millie	*Rose Hill*
Sarah	*Patience Collier*
Rosa	*Susan Engel*
Martin	*James Hazeldine*
Rudi	*Leonard Fenton*
Jack	*George Tovey*

Directed by John Dexter

ON THE BOIL

A new musical by John Albery and John Gould, *On the Boil*, met with a favourable reception at Farnham Castle Theatre. The plot, highly suitable for comedy situations, concerns a university professor who discovered a love potion. Those who take it fall head over heels in love with the first person they meet – quite regardless of sex.

Martin Connor and Graham Berown, as two male laboratory assistants who take the potion, were responsible for much of the comedy. Angus Lennie gave a delightfully amusing performance as a businessman interested in the commercial possibilities of the love potion. The tunes were decidedly infectious and lingered in the memory.

A musical, with book and lyrics by John Albery and music by John Gould. Presented by the Farnham Repertory Company at the Castle Theatre, Farnham, on December 19, 1972. Designed by Paul Mayo. Choreography by Christopher Dunham and musical direction by John Gould.

Cast included:

Prof. Reginald Brown	*Peter Robert Scott*
John Makeshift	*Martin Connor*
Jim Green	*Graham Berown*
Helen Bradshaw	*Christine Edmonds*
Pamela Brown	*Joan Morrow*
Miss Murgatroyd	*Pamela Vezey*
Sir William Fosdyke	*Roger Ostime*
George Grubb	*Angus Lennie*
Princess Royal	*Annie Page*

Directed by Christopher Dunham

ONCE UPON A TIME . . .

David Frost's first venture into management proved memorable. At the Duke of York's for matinées only, he presented *Once Upon A Time . . .*', an entertainment conceived in excellent taste, with book and lyrics by Norman Newell, music by Roger Webb and designs by Tony Walton. The versatile cast included such seasoned players as Joyce Grant, Patsy Rowlands, Tim Curry and Kerry Gardner, as a gentle clown who is adored by the entire audience.

Gillian Lynne's sensitive direction and inventive choreography animated the action in the most magical fashion and the result was a production of rare enchantment which should not be allowed to fade into oblivion after one short season.

To Roger Webb's lively music, such immortal nursery rhyme characters as Goldilocks, Little Bo-Peep, Jack Frost, Little Red Riding Hood and the Queen of Hearts are all played with complete conviction by an admirable team of dedicated players.

An entertainment with book and lyrics by Norman Newell and music by Roger Webb. Designed by Tony Walton; choreographed by Gillian Lynne. Presented by David Frost, for Paradine Plays Ltd, at the Duke of York's Theatre on December 21, 1972. Musical Director – Martin Goldstein.

Cast included: *Tim Curry, David Delve, Rosemary Faith, Micky Feast, Lucy Fenwick, Keith Galloway, Kerry Gardner, Joyce Grant, Judy Gridley, Michael Howe, David Jennings, Geraldine Long, Brian Osborne, Tony Robinson, Patsy Rowlands, Marc Urquart* and *Liz Whiting*

Directed by Gillian Lynne

Brewster Mason as the Moor and Lisa Harrow as Desdemona in the Royal Shakespeare Company's production of *Othello* at the Aldwych. *Photograph by Philip Sayer*

OTHELLO

John Barton directed *Othello* for the Royal Shakespeare Company in a mid-Victorian setting at Stratford-upon-Avon in 1971 and the same production was brought to the Aldwych Theatre the following summer, proving how effectively his choice of period suits the play.

Emrys James scored a personal success by playing Iago as a Midlander who detested his home background, from which he can never quite escape. He resents the superiority of his public school superior officer and the atmosphere is soon tense with jealousy. His performance rather eclipsed Brewster Mason's Othello, though he spoke the Moor's lines with a fine appreciation of their beauty. The rest of the cast contributed memorable performances which fitted into Mr Barton's conception of the tragedy. They were all in the right key and colour.

A revival of the play by Shakespeare. The Royal Shakespeare Company's 1971 Stratford-upon-Avon production presented at the Aldwych Theatre on July 18, 1972. Designed by Julia Trevelyan Oman.

Cast included:

Othello	*Brewster Mason*
Iago	*Emrys James*
Cassio	*David Calder*
Desdemona	*Lisa Harrow*
Emilia	*Heather Canning*
Roderigo	*Roger Rees*
Bianca	*Lynn Dearth*

Directed by John Barton

161

OWNERS

Jill Bennett set out to appear in *Owners* by Caryl Churchill at the Royal Court Theatre Upstairs, but plans were changed as the result of her being involved in a car accident and Stephanie Bidmead took over the part after the original date for the first night had been postponed.

Fifteen rather baffling scenes dealt with a lady property speculator whose husband wishes to murder her, but he deputes the task to his assistant, who is more interested in suicide than murder. An excellent cast, including David Swift, Richard O'Callaghan, Anne Raitt, Lucinda Curtis, Eileen Devlin and Kenneth Cranham, gave able support to Stephanie Bidmead, but Nicholas Wright, who directed, was defeated in his attempt to create a smooth-running production from the author's obscure intentions.

A play by Caryl Churchill. Presented at the Royal Court Theatre Upstairs on December 6, 1973. Designed by Di Seymour.

Cast included:

Clegg	*David Swift*
Worsley	*Richard O'Callaghan*
Marion	*Stephanie Bidmead*
Alec	*Kenneth Cranham*
Lisa	*Anne Raitt*
Alec's mother	*Eileen Devlin*
Mrs Arlington	*Lucinda Curtis*

Directed by Nicholas Wright

A PAGAN PLACE

Dave Allen made an impressive appearance as a village doctor in *A Pagan Place* by Edna O'Brien, a sort of Irish *Under Milk Wood*, at the Royal Court Theatre. A young actress by the name of Veronica Quilligan, played a sensitive little girl who wandered through the episodic sketches of family and village life in the most enthralling fashion. But the quiet calm of Dave Allen's performance is what haunted the memory afterwards.

A play by Edna O'Brien. Presented at the Royal Court Theatre on November 2, 1972. Designed by Sean Kenney.

Cast included:

Creena	*Veronica Quilligan*
Nigger	*Declan Mulholland*
Con	*David Burke*
Josie	*Colette O'Neil*
Ambie	*Struan Rodger*
Miss Davitt	*Avril Elgar*
Father Declan	*David Daker*
Della	*Sheelagh Cullen*
Mr Holland	*Dermot Tuohy*
Caimin	*Patrick Dawson*
Aunt Bride	*Kitty Fitzgerald*
Petronella	*Sally Travers*
Dr Daly	*Dave Allen*
Lizzie	*Angela Crow*
Emma	*Brenda Fricker*
Guard Shaughnessey	*Donal Cox*
Eamonn	*Alex Farrell*
Nuns	*Avril Elgar*
	Sheelagh Cullen
	Diane Holland

Directed by Ronald Eyre

Veronica Quilligan and Sheelagh
Cullen in *A Pagan Place*.
Photograph by John Haynes

Hilary Tindall, Gwen Watford,
Ronald Leigh-Hunt, Robin Bailey,
Elspeth March and Megs Jenkins
in *Parents' Day*. *Photograph by
Reg Wilson*

THE PAPERTOWN PAPERCHASE

David Wood wrote his sixth ingenious and inventive children's play for the Worcester Swan Theatre Company at Christmas 1972, when *The Papertown Paperchase* met with considerable success. The original plot concerned the malevolent intentions of the Fireflies who inhabited the Land of Fire towards Papertown which they set out to destroy.

Mr Wood sets his story of adventure in such unusual places as Paperclip Forest, Scissors Gorge and Steaming Stepping Stones, all likely to stimulate the juvenile imagination. When the history of the Children's Theatre of the sixties and seventies comes to be written, Mr Wood's achievement will call for a very special chapter because he refuses to write down to young people in any shape or form and ignores the old nursery-rhyme stories which so many consider long out of date.

A Christmas musical by David Wood. Presented by the Worcester Repertory Company at the Swan Theatre, Worcester, on December 29, 1972. Designed by Louanne Harvey and choreographed by Judy Stephens. Musical director – Peter Washtell.

Cast included:
John Cunningham, John Bleasdale, Robert Baldwin, John A Cooper, Henry B Wall, Joy Ring, David Soames, Ian Ricketts, Chris Tranchell, Roger Mutton, Annette Woolett and Anton Phillips
Directed by Giles Block

PARENTS' DAY

Ronald Millar, one of our most distinguished popular playwrights, wrote *Parents' Day* in association with Robert Chetwyn, from a novel by Edward Candy. Perhaps there were too many cooks, but the resulting broth was not up to the usual Millar standard. It was a decided disappointment.

The play, it seemed, set out to comment on the generation gap, being set in a small progressive boarding-school on Parents' Day. The characters were no more than mouthpieces for the ideas of their particular generation on various subjects.

Elspeth March came off best because she had the most amusing lines and looked as majestic as an empress who refused to tolerate any obstacles or opposition. Such sterling players as Megs Jenkins, Gwen Watford, Ronald Leigh-Hunt and Robin Bailey worked like Trojans, but were defeated by the material.

A play by Ronald Millar, in association with Robert Chetwyn, from a novel by Edward Candy. Presented by John Gale, for Volcano Productions Ltd, at the Globe Theatre on July 12, 1972. Settings by Hutchinson Scott; music by Bruce Cole and lyrics by Howard Schumman.

Cast included:

Meg Lindsay	*Geraldine Newman*
Celia Spurgeon	*Cherith Mellor*
Janet Storrace	*Megs Jenkins*
Emma Branksome	*Gwen Watford*
Harry Branksome	*Robin Bailey*
Vincent Harker	*Ronald Leigh-Hunt*
Dinah Harker	*Hilary Tindall*
Mrs Muriel Daintry	*Elspeth March*
Helen Pinnegar	*Georgine Anderson*
Owen Pinnegar	*Peter Howell*
Tim Murdoch	*Guy Slater*

Directed by Robert Chetwyn

PEACE IN OUR TIME

John Spurling was commissioned by the Sheffield Crucible Theatre to write *Peace In Our Time*, a documentary-style play on the origins of the Second World War. The ghosts and monsters of the past made effective theatre, under the lively direction of Colin George. Michael Tudor Barnes was memorable as Hitler, played absolutely straight; Douglas Campbell as the flamboyant Mussolini, George Hagan as the sympathetic Chamberlain; James Smith as the icy Ribbentrop and Paul Angelis doubling Baldwin and Himmler all played their parts with considerable theatrical skill.

A play by John Spurling. Presented by the Crucible Theatre Trust Ltd and Yorkshire Television at the Crucible Theatre, Sheffield, on November 16, 1972. Designed by Rodney Ford.

Cast included: Michael Carter, Paul Lally, Michael Tudor Barnes, James Smith, Michael J Jackson, David Boyce, Neil Phillips, Preston Struthers, Paul Angelis, Ronald Cunliffe, James Taylor, John Price, Douglas Campbell, Rosemary Kingston, Terry Wale, George Hagan

Directed by Colin George

THE PERSIANS

The thrust stage of the Crucible Theatre at Sheffield was a great asset to the production of *The Persians* by Aeschylus, directed by Colin George in the European première of an adaptation by the American poet, John Lewin.

The designer, Tanya Moiseiwitsch, provided masks and costumes which made some of the players over seven feet in height in this version which had originally been commissioned by Tyrone Guthrie. Colin George showed his complete mastery of this stage, which is ideally suited to the larger-than-life approach to Greek tragedy.

Adaptation by John Lewis of the play by Aeschylus. Presented for the first time in Europe at the Sheffield Crucible Theatre on October 4, 1972. Designed by Tanya Moiseiwitsch. Music by Jeremy Barlow.

Cast included:

Queen Atossa	*Ann Casson*
King Darius	*Douglas Campbell*
King Xerxes	*Paul Angelis*
The Messenger	
	Michael Tudor Barnes
Chorus Leader	*George Hagan*

Directed by Colin George

PETER PAN

Robert Helpmann's new-approach production of *Peter Pan* returned to the Coliseum for a second Christmas season in 1972, staged by Alan Pinniger. Once again Dorothy Tutin proved to be the most outstanding Peter since the days of Jean Forbes-Robertson. She casts a spell over the house because she believes in the part so intensely and her slightly husky voice and breathy delivery never for one moment gave the impression that she was an actress simulating Barrie's immortal boy. Ron Moody played Captain Hook – a part he played at the Scala Theatre in 1966 – with immense gusto and made Barrie's villain as memorable as Dickens's Fagin.

A revival of the play by J M Barrie. Presented by Tom Arnold Presentations Ltd, in association with Howard & Wyndham Ltd and by arrangement with Sadler's Wells Trust (Coliseum) Ltd at the London Coliseum on December 26, 1972.
    The 1971 Robert Helpmann production, staged by Alan Pinniger with choreography by Royston Maldoom, music by Grant Foster, décor and costumes by Anthony Holland. Musical director – Derek Taverner.

Cast included:

Peter Pan	*Dorothy Tutin*
Mr Darling	} *Ron Moody*
Captain Hook	}
Mrs Darling	*Pauline Jameson*
Michael	*Marc Granger*
John	*Benedict Taylor*
Wendy	*Wendy Padbury*

Smee	*Ian Trigger*
Starkey	*Mischa de la Motte*

Cast also included: Peter O'Farrell, Iris Glow, Patsy Blower, David Arnold, Jonathan Kiley, Keith Lelliott, Jeremy Watts, Adam Richens, David Norfolk, Ray Edwards, Barry Rohde, Terry Etteridge, Jimmy Bell, Douglas Anderson, Robert Niko, Pater Salmon, Garry Ginivan, David Wells, Bill Owens, Barry Wilkinson, Namdi, Jane Lee, Bernard Jamieson, Richarde Mascall and Paul Barber

Directed by Alan Pinniger

Left: Lulu played the name-part in the Douglas Squires production of *Peter Pan* at the Manchester Opera House. *Photograph by Guttenberg Ltd*

Right: Timothy Davies as Slug, Thelma Whiteley as Greenfly and Melody Kane as Maggot, imprisoned in a flower pot in *The Plotters of Cabbage Patch Corner*

PETER PAN

When *Peter Pan* was only three Christmases old – in 1906 – Pauline Chase was playing Peter for the first time at the Duke of York's in London, while up in Manchester Zena Dare was playing the same part in a simultaneous production. History repeated itself in 1972 when Dorothy Tutin played Peter at the London Coliseum, while Lulu was appearing in the same part at Manchester Opera House.

The Robert Helpmann production was revived at the Coliseum, but Douglas Squires was responsible for the Manchester production and he created some lively choreography to suit Grant Foster's catchy score. Lulu never offended the traditionalists, as she played Peter with a boyish restlessness and faced Captain Hook with a touch of swagger which suited her personality. Anthony Sharp played Hook with restrained villainy.

A revival of the play by J M Barrie. Presented by Tom Arnold Presentations Ltd, in association with Howard & Wyndham Ltd at Manchester Opera House on December 19, 1972.

Music by Grant Foster and John Crook and choreography by Douglas Squires. Musical director – John Forsyth.

Cast included:

Peter Pan	*Lulu*
Mr Darling	
Captain Hook	*Anthony Sharp*
Mrs Darling	*Susan Hannay*
Wendy	*Prue Clarke*
Smee	*Brian Freeman*
Starkey	*Al Paige*

Cast also included: *Sean Flanagan, Alan Bone, Philip Tyler, Katya Aron, Malcolm Dixon, Simon Thompson, Peter Vaughan Clarke, Jane Wren, Lynn Fitzpatrick, Heather Seymour, Peter Duncan, Simon Barry, Philip Baldwin, Bryan Sweeney, David Buxton, Christopher Allen, Howard Trevor, Jack Youens, Michael Tarn, Bob Keazor, Jenny Turner* and *Peter Casillas*

Directed by Douglas Squires

THE PLOTTERS OF CABBAGE PATCH CORNER

David Wood has created one of the most imaginative children's plays with *The Plotters of Cabbage Patch Corner*, which returned to the London Christmas scene at the Shaw Theatre and is likely to be a very welcome annual visitor for many a year to come.

The cast consists of such endearing creatures as Glow Worm, Ladybird, Bumble Bee and in the background are the Voices of the Big Ones. The action, which has a message the younger generation will understand, takes place in the corner of a garden, in Slug's cabbage, Red Admiral's cocoon, Spider's house and on the compost heap. It is a milestone in children's entertainment and something which is very much of this day and age.

A musical play for children with book, music and lyrics by David Wood. Sets and costumes by Susie Caulcutt. Choreography by Maurice Lane. Musical direction by Peter Pontzen. Presented by Eddie Kulukundis for Knightsbridge Theatrical Productions Ltd at the Shaw Theatre, Euston Road, NW1 on December 6, 1972.

Cast included:

Glow Worm	*Robert McBain*
Ladybird	*Myvanwy Jenn*
Ant	*Stuart Lock*
Slug	*Timothy Davies*
Red Admiral	*Ben Aris*
Greenfly	*Thelma Whiteley*
Maggot	*Melody Kane*
Bumble Bee	*Larry Dann*
The Great Mushroom	*Donald Macdonald*
Spider	*Irene French*
Voices of the Big Ones	*Donald Macdonald*
	Irene French
Pianist	*Peter Pontzen*

Directed by Jonathan Lee

Daniel Massey, Dudley Jones and
John Standing in *Popkiss*

POPKISS

The idea of making a musical out of the Ben Travers farce *Rookery Nook*, turned out to be a good one. Called *Popkiss*, it opened at the Globe Theatre and provided an evening of nostalgic nonsense, away back in the world of plus-fours and cloche hats.

John Standing's expert tap-dancing and manipulation of his cane brought back memories of Jack Buchanan and Daniel Massey was highly amusing in the Ralph Lynn part. Mary Millar at her most decorative seized her big moment, selling lifeboat flags, while she sang 'Doing My Bit'. The Travers farce made an admirable transition to the musical stage because it had been treated by people who respected it as a superb example of the comedy of the 1920s. There was no question of vandalism.

A musical based on *Rookery Nook*, the farce by Ben Travers, with book lyrics by Michael Ashton and music by John Addinson and David Heneker. Designed by Robin Archer and choreographed by Malcolm Clare and David Drew. Musical direction by Raymond Bishop.

Presented by Donald Albery and Ian Hunter for Calabash Productions Ltd at the Globe Theatre on August 22, 1972.

Cast included:

Gertrude Twine	*Joan Sanderson*	Gerald Popkiss	*Daniel Massey*
Mrs Leverett	*Hazell Hughes*	Putz	*Peter Whitbread*
Harold Twine	*Dudley Jones*	Poppy Dickey	*Mary Millar*
Clive Popkiss	*John Standing*	Clara Popkiss	*Patricia Hodge*
Rhoda Marley	*Isla Blair*	Mrs Possett	*Susan Hardie*

Directed by Richard Cottrell

168

Ron Smerczak in the British
première of Friedrich
Dürrenmatt's *Portrait of a Planet*.
Photograph by John Vere Brown

PORTRAIT OF A PLANET

Friedrich Dürrenmatt's grimly
humorous play, *Portrait of a Planet*,
was given a Workshop Presentation at the Gardner Centre Theatre
of Sussex University in Brighton,
to open a tour.

The author opens and closes his
work with four gods who have no
real interest in the Earth or its
people. During the course of the
action, he discusses such subjects as
the Vietnam peace negotiations,
racial intolerance, power politics
and lunar exploitation. Each member of the cast played several
parts.

A play by Friedrich Dürrenmatt,
translated by James Kirkup. Presented by Prospect Theatre Company at the Gardner Centre Theatre
of the University of Sussex,
Brighton, on January 24, 1973.
Costume designs by Sue Yelland.

Cast included:

Adam	*Ron Smerczak*
Cain	*Michael Pennington*
Abel	*Glyn Grain*
Enoch	*Jonathan Hyde*
Eve	*Linda Marlowe*
Adah	*Vanessa Miles*
Zillah	*Jean Gilpin*
Naamah	*Judith Blake*

Directed by Kenny McBain

PRIVATE LIVES

John Gielgud's glitteringly sophisticated production of *Private Lives* at the Queen's Theatre brought Noël Coward back into the full glare of the limelight as an unequalled writer of light comedy. The passing of some forty years has not dimmed the lustre of this modern classic.

Maggie Smith played Gertrude Lawrence's old part of Amanda in masterly fashion, making every line sound like an amusing witticism. Robert Stephens, in Sir Noël's old role of Elyot Chase, matched every nuance of her playing and the first night was an unforgettable occasion with Sir Noël in a box to share and enjoy the ecstatic reception.

A revival of the play by Noël Coward. Presented by H M Tennent Ltd, by arrangement with Arthur Cantor, at the Queen's Theatre on September 21, 1972. Production designed by Anthony Powell, with costumes by Beatrice Dawson.

Cast included:

Sibyl Chase	*Polly Adams*
Elyot Chase	*Robert Stephens*
Victor Prynne	*James Villiers*
Amanda Prynne	*Maggie Smith*
Louise	*Cari Hedderwick*

Directed by John Gielgud

PULL BOTH ENDS

Television's popular dancing and singing group, The Young Generation, appeared in their first stage musical at the Piccadilly Theatre, *Pull Both Ends* – a show with the unusual setting of a Christmas Cracker factory.

It was a poor book and several critics suggested the corniest Christmas Cracker mottos were superior in quality to the dialogue of the show. The fifteen young girls and fifteen young boys of The Young Generation danced with tremendous brio and were scarcely ever off the stage.

The appealing leading lady, Christine Holmes, had a Sheila Hancock quality and immense attack, with red-headed Judy Bowen as a close runner-up for the laurels of the evening. Gerry Marsden's cheeky personality was well suited to this youthful escapade.

A musical with music and lyrics by John Schroeder and Anthony King and book by Brian Comport. Presented by Marilyn Davis for Present Productions Ltd, in association with David Missen, by arrangement with Donald Albery, at the Piccadilly Theatre on July 18, 1972. Designed by Malcolm Pride; choreography by Nigel Lythgoe; musical direction by

Christine Holmes and Judy Bowen
in *Pull Both Ends*. *Photograph by*
Tom Hustler

Alyn Ainsworth; conductor –
Don Savage.

Cast included:

Cindy Smith	*Christine Holmes*
Joe Miller	*Gerry Marsden*
Bill Kirby	*Miles Greenwood*
Fred Kirby	*Michael Cotterill*
Rita Brewster	*Judy Bowen*
Stanley Wibble	*Keith Smith*
J Hamilton-Smith	*John Hughes*

and *The Young Generation*

Directed by Leslie Lawton

THE RAGGED-TROUSERED PHILANTHROPISTS

The Lincoln Theatre Royal Company scored a popular success with an adaptation of Robert Tressell's famous novel, *The Ragged-trousered Philanthropists*, which pointed out that English workers cannot go on being treated like dirt and should stand up to fight their all-powerful employers.

The material was cleverly put together and set in an area where the rich ruled over the poor. Howard Lloyd-Lewis, assisted by Sue Dunderdale, helped to shoot the script with humour, which made it so much more palatable. As the Mayor of Mugsborough, Tim Stern headed a highly versatile company who played far more parts than there were players.

A play created by the Lincoln Company from the novel by Robert Tressell. Presented at Lincoln Theatre Royal on November 1, 1972. Designed by Terry Brown. Music compiled and arranged by Geoffrey Drew and lyrics by Tim Stern and Geoffrey Drew.

Cast included: Christopher Leaver, Tim Stern, Geoffrey Drew, Richard Albrecht, Reg Stewart, Robert Whelan, David Gilmore, Lindsey Franklin, Virginia Clarke and *Richard Anker*

Directed by Howard Lloyd-Lewis assisted by Sue Dunderdale

RAISING HELL

Leila Berg made a stage adaptation under the title of *Raising Hell* of her book, *Death of a Comprehensive*, and it was first staged at Salisbury Playhouse by Theatrescope, the travelling company based on the Playhouse, who presented it at various schools in the district.

A projector helped Paul Tomlinson in his imaginative direction of this production which gave a vivid impression of the background in which the parents and children lived in the part of London where Rising Hill School came into being. Frank Ellis played the headmaster whose policy was to take the fear of the teacher out of education and give priority to the child.

A documentary by Leila Berg. Presented by Theatrescope, the touring company of Salisbury Playhouse at Salisbury Playhouse and at schools in the district during December 1972. Settings by Neville Lewis and costumes by Barbara Wilson.

Cast included: David Beames, Frank Ellis, Laura Graham, Penny Jones, Robert Richards and *David Sadgrove*

Directed by Paul Tomlinson

THE REAL McCOY

Described as a rock opera based on Shakespeare's *Macbeth*, *The Real McCoy* was directed by John Hole at the Swan Theatre at Worcester. Set in Soho and Sidcup, it did not bear a close resemblance to the Shakespeare tragedy, being concerned with a London crime syndicate and a bank raid, complete with rope-ladder.

A dozen actors and a six-piece band, under the direction of Chris Littlewood, produced a shattering volume of sound. Anna Nicholas and John Gulliver played the McCoys with splendid attack and Merdelle Jordine and Christine Roberts were novel witch club hostesses.

A rock opera by John A Cooper, with two dialogues by Gael Turnbull. Presented by the Worcester Repertory Company at the Swan Theatre, Worcester, on October 4, 1972. Designed by Susanna Poigndestre. Musical director – Chris Littlewood.

Cast included:

A Busker	*John A Cooper*
Lila	*Merdelle Jordine*
Karen	*Christine Roberts*
Suzanna	*Susanna Gwynn*
Joe	*Tony Mann*
Reggie McCoy	*John Gulliver*
Ronnie Carfield	*Don Dryden*
Charles Duffield	*Kenneth Garner*
Lenny Lennox	*John Bleasdale*
Duncan	*Peter Powell*
Malcolm	*Derek Crewe*
Connie McCoy	*Anna Nicholas*
Maria Duffield	*Celia Imrie*

Directed by John Hole

Left: A scene from *Red is for Winter*. Photograph by Viking Studios Ltd

Left: A scene from *Red is for Winter*. Photograph by Viking Studios Ltd

Right: Susan Macready as Stella Faringford and John Fraser as Eustace Jackson in a revival of *The Return of the Prodigal*. Photograph by Frank Page Studios

RED IS FOR WINTER

Christopher Denys gave an heroic portrait of James Graham, Marquis of Montrose, commander of Charles I's army in Scotland during the Civil War in *Red is for Winter*, premièred at the Pitlochry Festival Theatre.

To tell the story Mr Denys used the technique he has neatly exploited in the past to dramatize the stories of the Repeal of the Corn Laws and the Tolpuddle Martyrs for schoolchildren.

Nineteen members of the Pitlochry Company played many and various parts and as and when necessary used costumes which hung on rail-racks on stage throughout the performance. This method meant the story, covering the period between 1612 and 1650 in England, Scotland and the Continent, could be unfolded at tremendous speed and the audience was swept up in the thrilling events. Alec Heggie dominated the proceedings as Montrose, who failed to appreciate the cynicism of politicians and kings.

A play by Christopher Denys. Presented at the Pitlochry Festival Theatre on July 17, 1972. Designed by Alan Stewart.

Cast included: Robert Aldous, Peter Ducrow, Alec Heggie, John Kesl, Ian Lindsay, Victor Lucas, Donald MacIver, Tony Roper, Christopher Saul, David Shackleton, Sheila Brownrigg, Alice Fraser, Jenny Galloway, Lois Hantz, Colette Kelly, Anne Mackenzie Davidson, Pamela Pitchford, Janet Spearman and *Sarah Stephenson*

Directed by Christopher Denys

THE RETURN OF THE PRODIGAL

Robert Chetwyn's distinguished production of *The Return of the Prodigal* by St John Hankin at the Thorndike Theatre at Leatherhead provided a rare chance to see this 1905 play concerning the Black Sheep of a well-to-do family. The rogue, charmingly played by John Fraser, offers his family the choice between keeping him for life or jeopardizing their social position by the disgrace of seeing him in the workhouse.

This stylish revival recalled yet another one – Peter Glenville's 1948 production with John Gielgud as Eustace in a company which included Sybil Thorndike, Irene Brown, Nora Nicholson, Rachel Kempson and Richard Goolden.

A revival of the play by St John Hankin. Presented at the Thorndike Theatre, Leatherhead, on January 23, 1973. Designed by Colin Winslow.

Cast included:

Samuel Jackson	*Tony Steedman*
Mrs Jackson	*Rosamond Burne*
Henry Jackson	*Neville Hughes*
Eustace Jackson	*John Fraser*
Violet Jackson	*Bonnie Hurren*
Sir John Faringford	*John Crocker*
Lady Faringford	*Sheila Keith*
Stella Faringford	*Susan Macready*
Dr Glaisher	*Lennard Pearce*
Rev Cyrill Pratt	*Geoffrey Edwards*
Mrs Pratt	*Hazel Douglas*
Baines	*Nicholas McArdle*
Footmen	*Robert Meadwell*
	John Wilkinson

Directed by Robert Chetwyn

172

Left: Joan O'Hara, Eileen Colgan, Olu Jacobs and Barney MacKenna in the Dublin Abbey Theatre production of *Richard's Cork Leg*

Right: Frances Cuka as Queen Elizabeth and Richard Briers in the name-part in the Prospect Theatre Company's production of *Richard III*. *Photograph by Mark Gudgeon*

RICHARD'S CORK LEG

From the Abbey Theatre in Dublin to the Royal Court Theatre in Sloane Square came *Richard's Cork Leg*, which featured The Dubliners, Ireland's most popular folk-group. Alan Simpson, who directed the production, seen earlier at the Dublin Theatre Festival of 1972, was responsible for creating this entertainment out of Brendan Behan's papers, discovered after his death. He found sketches, typically ribald Behan lyrics and other suggestions for plays which might have been written. The material amounted to jottings in a dramatist's notebook, rather than memorable work such as we admired in this writer's best plays. Eileen Colgan and Joan O'Hara were the leading ladies.

An entertainment by Brendan Behan, with material edited and compiled by Alan Simpson. Presented at the Royal Court Theatre, by arrangement with Noel Pearson, on September 19, 1972. Designed by Wendy Shea.

Cast included:

Maria Concepta	*Eileen Colgan*
Rose of Lima	*Joan O'Hara*
Cronin	*Luke Kelly*
Hero Hogan	*Ronnie Drew*
Motician	*Olu Jacobs*
Mrs Cronin	*Fionnuala Kenny*
Mrs Mallarkey	*Angela Newman*
Deidre Mallarkey	*Dearbhla Molloy*
and The Dubliners	

Directed by Alan Simpson

RICHARD III

Richard Briers, after establishing himself as one of the most popular light comedians of our time, turned to Shakespeare and appeared in the name-part of Richard III in the Prospect Theatre production of *Richard III* which opened at the MacRobert Centre of the University of Stirling.

His interpretation was both fluent and persuasive; there was no suggestion of the black, evil, melodramatic king about his performance. There was a decided streak of genuine humanity in the foundation upon which he built the character.

Derek Jacobi's superbly spoken Buckingham was an outstanding feature of this production, so ably directed by Toby Robertson. The lamenting ladies were well played by Marilyn Taylerson as Lady Anne, Antonia Pemberton as Queen Margaret and Frances Cuka as Queen Elizabeth.

A revival of the play by Shakespeare. Presented by the Prospect Theatre Company at the MacRobert Centre of the University of Stirling on October 11, 1972. Designed by Kenneth Rowell. Music by Carl Davis.

Cast included:

King Edward IV	*Michael Atkinson*
George, Duke of Clarence	*Simon Gough*
Richard, Duke of Gloucester	*Richard Briers*
Sir Robert Brackenbury	*Timothy Peters*
Lord Hastings	*Christopher Burgess*
Lady Anne	*Marilyn Taylerson*
Queen Elizabeth	*Frances Cuka*
Duke of Buckingham	*Derek Jacobi*
Lord Stanley	*Michael Goodliffe*
Queen Margaret	*Antonia Pemberton*
Jane Shore	*Jennifer Tudor*
Lord Mayor of London	*Willoughby Goddard*

Directed by Toby Robertson and Kenny McBain

THE RIVALS

The London Theatre Company's spring drama season intended to attract a new straight theatre public to Sadler's Wells Theatre in Islington, concluded with a disappointing revival of *The Rivals*, directed by Malcolm Taylor.

In spite of having Maxine Audley as Mrs Malaprop, Anthony Sharp as Sir Anthony Absolute, Philip Bond as Captain Absolute, Richard Kay as Faulkland and David Jason as Acres, all giving worthy performances, the production lacked that sense of style which is so essential to Sheridan's comedy.

A revival of the play by R B Sheridan. Presented by the London Theatre Company at Sadler's Wells Theatre on May 1, 1972. Designed by Suzanne Billings, with lighting by Neville Currier.

Cast included:

Errand Boy	*Helen Bernat*
Maid	*Harriet Philpin*
Fag	*John F Landry*
Thomas	*Roger Elliott*
Lucy	*Jo Warne*
Captain Absolute	*Philip Bond*
Lydia Languish	*Anne Rutter*
Julia	*Linda Gardner*
Mrs Malaprop	*Maxine Audley*
Sir Anthony Absolute	
	Anthony Sharp
Faulkland	*Richard Kay*
Acres	*David Jason*
Sir Lucius O'Trigger	
	Jonathan Adams
David	*Michael Bilton*
Harpsichordist	*Trevor Smith*

Directed by Malcolm Taylor

ROBIN HOOD

One of the special delights of the pantomime season is the ever-enchanting Victorian production of *Robin Hood* to be seen at the Players' Theatre, under the Arches between Charing Cross Station and Hungerford Bridge.

An adaptation by Denis Martin from Burnand's 1862 extravaganza. The score was a mosaic of melodies by Bizet, Massenet, Sullivan, Saint-Saëns, Donizetti, Handel, Offenbach, and other immortals. Reginald Woolley created astonishingly beautiful stage pictures, which gave the impression that the tiny Players' stage was about the size of Drury Lane. Dashing Sheila Mathews played Robin in the style of those much-adored Principal Boys who were pantomime heroes before the male teenage pop-stars chased them into oblivion.

A pantomime by F C Burnand (1862), adapted by Denis Martin, with lyrics by Maurice Browning. Presented at the Players' Theatre on December 12, 1972. Scenery by Reginald Woolley, costumes by Reginald Hanson. Dances and musical items staged by Doreen Hermitage.

Cast included: Clifton Todd, Eleanor McCready, Pauline Antony, Jenny Wren, Jonathan Adams, Michael Darbyshire, Loraine Hart, Alan Rebbeck, Mike Fields, Sheila Mathews, Erich Vietheer, Annie Leake, Arthur Sweet, Bernice Adams, Dinah Harris, Margaret Lake, Joan Ryan, David Barclay, David Rayner and *Colin Richmond*

Directed by Don Gemmell

174

Jenny Wren as Maid Marian,
Michael Darbyshire as the Sheriff
of Nottingham, Sheila Mathews
as Robin Hood and Jonathan
Adams as Sir Gilbert in the
Victorian pantomime, *Robin Hood.*
Photograph by Jeremy Grayson

ROBINSON CRUSOE

From France, Le Grand Magic Circus came to the Round House to present *Robinson Crusoe* that proved to be a mildly amusing anarchic happening based on the story of Robinson Crusoe. Scenes from Crusoe's early life were played in booths round the area, in people's seats, and occasionally up aloft.

The dreams of the shipwrecked Crusoe were burlesque fantasies of civilized society which emphasized the solitude of Crusoe and Man in general. The dialogue was badly reproduced, but the music came over with gusto.

A musical spectacle presented by David Aukin, by arrangement with the Round House Trust Ltd at the Round House, Chalk Farm, and performed by Le Grand Magic Circus et ses Animaux Tristes from Paris on December 20, 1972. Scenario by Jerome Savary, lyrics by Roland Topor, music by Magic Circus and sets by Michel Lebois, Philippe Caron and Patrick Chauveau.

Directed by Jerome Savary

ROCK CARMEN

Bizet's opera, after being transformed into the *Carmen Jones* film and a highly dramatic Roland Petit ballet, appeared at the Round House as *Rock Carmen*.

This new Carmen seems to do all her shopping in Carnaby Street and bears no relation to the immortal creature conceived by Mérimée and sung on the opera stage with such brio by Calvé. Escamillo, the toreador, is transformed into Ed the rock superstar and the lovestricken soldier Don José is now a campus policeman. They were played by Terri Stevens, Robert Coleby and Davy Clinton, with a pop festival as the background for the final tragedy instead of the bull-ring of the Bizet version. It was a gimmick version which offered no compensations. The music was by Michael Hughes and the book and lyrics by Herb Hendler.

A musical freely adapted from Bizet's and Mérimée's *Carmen*. Presented by Buck Spurr and Herb Hendler, in association with the London Rock Carmen Company and Videocassette Enterprises at the Round House, Chalk Farm, on July 13, 1972. Lighting and sets by Joe Lights. Choreography by Irving Davies. Costumes by Michéle Deliss. Music by Michael Hughes; book and lyrics by Herb Hendler; musical direction by John Hawkins and Jonathan Cohen.

Cast included:

Carmen	*Terri Stevens*
Joe	*Davy Clinton*
Ed	*Robert Coleby*
Michelle	*Elaine Paige*

Directed by Irving Davies.

RULING THE ROOST

The Actors' Company, a group of experienced actors who combined to play both leading and supporting roles in their own company, presented Feydeau's *Ruling the Roost* at Billingham Forum before proceeding to the 1972 Edinburgh International Festival.

Two pieces of casting of minor parts give an idea of the policy of this new group. Ian McKellen appeared as a pimply page-boy and John Tordoff as an over-familiar family retainer. Richard Cottrell, who translated the farce from the French, directed the production with tremendous gusto, getting a remarkably sensitive response from these actors who have chosen to work together in complete defiance of the star system.

An English translation by Richard Cottrell for *Le Dindon* by Georges Feydeau. Presented by the Cambridge Theatre Company with the Actors' Company at Billingham Forum on August 22 before proceeding to the 1972 Edinburgh International Festival. Designed by Robin Archer.

Cast included:

Vatelin	*Tenniel Evans*
Lucienne	*Moira Redmond*
Pontagnac	*Ronnie Stevens*
Clotilde	*Marian Diamond*
Redillon	*Robin Ellis*
Armandine	*Caroline Blakiston*
Pinchard	*Robert Eddison*
Madame Pinchard	*Margery Mason*
Soldignac	*Frank Middlemass*
Maggy	*Sheila Reid*
Hotel Manager	*Edward Petherbridge*
The Maid	*Felicity Kendal*

176

The Page-boy	*Ian McKellen*
First Police Inspector	
	Jack Shepherd
Second Inspector	*Juan Moreno*
Jean	*Matthew Long*
Gerome	*John Tordoff*

Directed by Richard Cottrell

THE RUPERT CHRISTMAS SHOW

Rupert appeared for the first time on the Christmas scene at the Royalty Theatre in *The Rupert Christmas Show,* based on one of A E Bestall's cartoon stories, *Rupert and the Paperfall,* by Ken Martyne.

Diane Robillard brought Rupert to life on the stage with her ingenious movement and uncanny understanding of the motivation of the cartoon character.

The story concerned lost lists of birthday presents for Rupert's friends, but all ended happily in this show which had colourful scenery and jolly songs to appeal to the younger generation.

An entertainment by Ken Martyne, based on *Rupert and the Paperfall* by A E Bestall. Songs and music by Mike McNaught and Ken Martyne; sets by Derek Cousins; special heads and costumes by Dimitris Stephanides; costumes by Karmian Huddy. Musical Director – Grant Hossack. Presented by Dimension Productions Ltd, by arrangement with Beaverbrook Newspapers Ltd, at the Royalty Theatre on December 18, 1972.

Cast included: Clive Bennett, Diane Robillard, David Wheldon-Williams, Christopher Ryan, Anne Salingar, Richard Olley, Martin Reynalds, Chrissy Roberts, Reginald Jessup, Laurie Webb, Dougie Mann and *Kelly Worrow.*

Directed by Ken Martyne

THE RUPERT SHOW

Believing there is a good public for children's plays outside the Christmas season, *The Rupert Show* was presented at the Victoria Palace in July for morning and afternoon performances.

Ken Martyne dramatized stories concerning the little bear who has delighted *Daily Express* readers for more than forty years and in the Victoria Palace show Rupert took Simple Simon to the court of Old King Cole. Diane Robillard played Rupert behind a convincing mask and David Cullen's catchy tunes made the show a sure success with the young generation.

An entertainment for children, based on the Rupert Books, adapted by Ken Martyne. Orchestrations, Vocal Direction and Musical Direction by David Cullen; songs and music by Cullen and Martyne and designs by Derek Cousins.

Presented by Dimension Productions Ltd, by arrangement with Beaverbrook Newspapers Ltd, at the Victoria Palace Theatre on July 24, 1972.

Cast included:

Rupert	*Diane Robillard*

Other parts played by: *David Delve, Rosemary Faith, Anne Salinger, Howard Benbrook, Rita McKerrow, Godfrey Charles, Clive Bennett, Kalman Glass, Neville Ware, Reginala Jessup* and *Rob Stuart*

Directed by Ken Martyne

Jeremy James-Taylor as Leandro, Jim Dale as Scapino and Ian Charleson as Ottavio in the Young Vic's production of *Scapino*. *Photograph by Reg Wilson*

SCAPINO

It is doubtful if the Young Vic has ever staged a more successful show than *Scapino*, that loose stage adaptation of Molière's breezy farce, *Les Fourberies de Scapin*, which opened this enterprising playhouse for the young in 1970.

Frank Dunlop's captivating production, with Jim Dale repeating his irresistibly comic performance in the name-part, made an admirable contribution to the British Theatre's Fanfare for Europe at the beginning of 1973, when Britain entered the Common Market. The entire company were inspired by Mr Dale's clowning and were responsible for a brio rarely attained by British players.

A revival of the free adaptation of Molière's *Les Fourberies de Scapin*. Presented at the Young Vic on December 29, 1972, being the same production which opened the Young Vic in September 1970. Setting by Carl Toms and music by Jim Dale.

Cast included:

Scapino	*Jim Dale*
Waiters	*Ray Davis*
	José Moreno
Waitress	*Barbara Courtney*
Carlo	*Andrew Robertson*
Ottavio	*Ian Charleson*
Sylvestro	*Gavin Reed*
Giacinta	*Mel Martin*
Argante	*Richard Kane*
Geronte	*Peter Bayliss*
Leandro	*Jeremy James-Taylor*
Zerbinetta	*Ursula Mohan*
Nurse	*Lotti Taylor*

Directed by Frank Dunlop

THE SCHOOL FOR SCANDAL

Jonathan Miller directed *The School for Scandal* for the National Theatre at the Old Vic without the stylish elegance play-goers normally associate with Sheridan's masterpiece. There was a rundown look about the designs and a coarseness about Mr Miller's approach to Sheridan's world of fashion.

Denis Quilley and Malcolm Reid scored memorable personal successes as the scandalmongers, Crabtree and Backbite. Paul Curran as Sir Peter and Louise Purnell as Lady Teazle played the screen scene superbly and in the Olivier tradition Mr Curran was deeply moved and aghast.

A revival of the play by Richard Brinsley Sheridan. Presented by the National Theatre at the Old Vic on May 11, 1972. Settings by Patrick Robertson and costumes by Rosemary Vercoe.

Cast included:

Lady Sneerwell	*Sheila Burrell*
Snake	*Benjamin Whitrow*
Joseph Surface	*Ronald Pickup*
Mrs Candour	*Mary Griffiths*
Crabtree	*Denis Quilley*
Sir Benjamin Backbite	
	Malcolm Reid
Sir Peter Teazle	*Paul Curran*
Lady Teazle	*Louise Purnell*
Charles Surface	*John Shrapnel*
Moses	*Stephen Greif*

Directed by Jonathan Miller

Malcolm Reid as Sir Benjamin
Backbite, Mary Griffiths as Mrs
Candour and Sheila Burrell as Lady
Sneerwell in National Theatre's
production of *The School for Scandal*

A SENSE OF DETACHMENT

John Osborne's *A Sense of Detachment* at the Royal Court Theatre was not really a play, but an assembly of six characters occupying the stage and reacting to each other. The world would appear to be in ruins, but in spite of all the devastation and the bleak outlook, Osborne points out that man still has the desire to go on.

A football supporter in a box and another man in the stalls effectively interrupted the dialogue from time to time, but the most memorable performance of the evening came from Rachel Kempson as an elderly English gentlewoman reading extracts from a sex-shop sales catalogue concerning sexual perversions.

A play by John Osborne. Presented with Michael White at the Royal Court Theatre on December 4, 1972. Designed by Nadine Baylis.

Cast included:

Chairman	*Nigel Hawthorne*
Chap	*John Standing*
Girl	*Denise Coffey*
Older Lady	*Rachel Kempson*
Father	*Hugh Hastings*
Grandfather	*Ralph Michael*
First Man	*Terence Frisby*
First Man's Wife	*Jeni Barnett*
Second Man	*David Hill*
Stage Manager	*Peter Jolly*

Directed by Frank Dunlop

THE SHADOW OF A GUNMAN

The rarely-played O'Casey play, *The Shadow of a Gunman*, seemed more significant than ever when revived at the Young Vic while the Ulster troubles were at their height in Belfast and Londonderry. Though O'Casey calls it a tragedy, Peter James directed it as a comedy. Eric Shorter proclaimed the production as one of the funniest evenings in London.

The farcical element was superbly played by Peter McEnery and Niall Buggy; and Susan Sheers and June Watson were equally at home in their parts. Possibly Miss Sheers was a little too serious as the martyred Minnie Powell.

On the open stage at the Young Vic it was difficult to convey the atmosphere of a raided tenement, which is essential to the staging of O'Casey's play.

A revival of the play by Sean O'Casey. Presented at the Young Vic on July 3, 1972. Designed by Brenda Hartill Moores.

Cast included:

Donal	*Peter McEnery*
Minnie Powell	*Susan Sheers*

Directed by Peter James

Lauverne Gray with the chorus of
Smilin' Through.   *Photograph by
Stuart Robinson*

SMILIN' THROUGH

John Hanson, with the looks of an old-time matinée idol, and a voice capable of belting numbers across the footlights into the largest theatres, wrote the music and lyrics of *Smilin' Through* at the Prince of Wales Theatre.

Based on the former stage and screen classic, Mr Hanson's musical has a flavour of the musical comedies of the 1920s, with its derivative music and banal lyrics proclaiming 'Life's a Song, When You're Young', and costumes and scenery reminiscent of tasteless Number Two touring shows of long, long ago.

The corny First World War story, with flashbacks to 1884, slowly creaked its way through rousing male choruses of *The Student Prince* and *Desert Song*, vintage and tear-jerking scenes played in a crude melodramatic style which suited the unimaginative book.

A musical based on the stage and film success by Jane Murfin and Jane Cowl, by arrangement with Emile Littler. Book by John Hanson and Constance Cox; music and lyrics by John Hanson and title-song by Arthur A Penn.

Presented by Leslie Grade, in association with the Yvonne Arnaud Theatre, Guildford, and by arrangement with Bernard Delfont, at the Prince of Wales Theatre on July 5, 1972. Designs by Pamela Ingram; costumes by Margaret Graham; choreography by David Gardiner; orchestrations by Ronald Hamner and musical direction by Derek Taverner.

Cast included:

John Carteret	*John Hanson*
Kathleen Dungannon ⎱	*Lauverne*
Maureen Clare ⎰	*Gray*
Dr Owen Harding	*Tony Adams*
Kenneth Wayne ⎱	*Glyn Worsnip*
Jimmy Wayne ⎰	
Ellen	*Carole Doree*
Willie Ainley	*Freddie Eldrett*

Directed by David Gardiner

181

STAND AND DELIVER

The highwayman, Jack Sheppard, is the hero of *Stand and Deliver!*, the bawdy musical by Monty Norman and Wolf Mankowitz, given a spectacular and bustling production by Wendy Toye at the Edinburgh Lyceum.

Nicky Henson was ideally cast as Jack, making a sensational escape from Newgate Jail, in one of the most successful scenes in the production. Anna Dawson, as Jack's coquettish high society lover was contrasted with Sammie Winmill as his admirer from the whorehouse. The strong cast did this new work full justice and made the most of the appealing musical numbers.

A musical on the life of Jack Sheppard, with story, music and lyrics by Monty Norman, book by Wolf Mankowitz, designs by Peter Whiteman and orchestrations by Alan Tew. Presented at the Edinburgh Lyceum Theatre, by arrangement with Bernard Delfont and John Gale, on September 20, 1972. Choreographer – Wendy Toye. Musical director – Robert Stewart.

Cast included:

Jack Sheppard	*Nicky Henson*
Jonathan Wild	*Derek Godfrey*
Edgeworth Bess	*Sammie Winmill*
Lady Arabella Harvey	
	Anna Dawson
Lord Harvey	*Paul Hardwick*
Blueskin ⎫	
Turnkey ⎬	*James Caincross*
Mrs Frome	*Pamela Cundell*

Directed by Wendy Toye

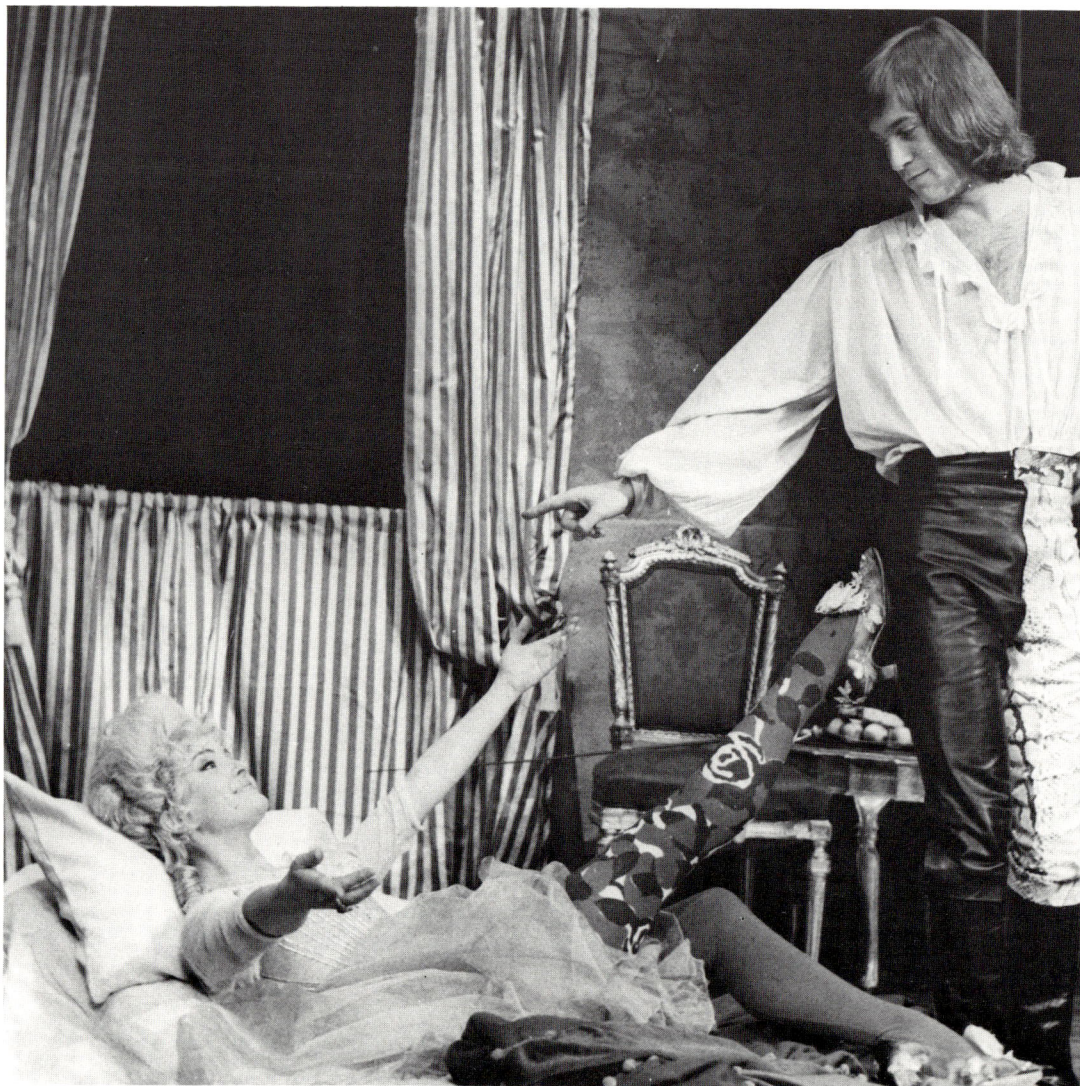

182

Gerald Harper had four leading ladies in the Francis Durbridge thriller, *Suddenly at Home*, which opened at the Fortune Theatre in September 1971. In June 1972,

Kate O'Mara, Patricia Dermott, Rachel Herbert and Patricia Shakesby took over from the actresses who had created the parts. *Photograph by Zöe Dominic*

SUZANNA ANDLER

Eileen Atkins in the name-part of Suzanna Andler, in *Suzanna Andler* seen at the Cambridge Arts Theatre, is on stage throughout the close on two-hour duration of the play. Marguerite Duras has written a conversation-piece rather than a play, set in a villa to be let above the Mediterranean at St Tropez, décor which offers Berkeley Sutcliffe a golden opportunity to recapture the beauty of that part of the world.

Suzanna Andler is the no-longer-loved wife of a very rich man, who is not seen in the play. She has a long duologue with her husband's mistress, played by Lynn Farleigh, and more than one duologue with a man with whom she is having a casual affair – played by John Stride.

Howard Sackler directed the piece at a snail's pace, with over-long pauses which did not help to grip the attention of the audience.

A play by Marguerite Duras, translated by Barbara Bray. Presented by H M Tennent Ltd and David Conville Productions Ltd, in association with Leonard S Field and the Yvonne Arnaud Theatre at the Arts Theatre, Cambridge, on September 18, 1972, and at the Aldwych Theatre on March 7, 1973, with Dinsdale Landen as Michael Cayre. Designed by Berkeley Sutcliffe.

Cast included;

Suzanna Andler	*Eileen Atkins*
Riviere	*Stanley Lebor*
Michael Cayre	*John Stride*
Monique Combes	*Lynn Farleigh*

Directed by Howard Sackler

The final moments of *A Tailor for Ladies*. Alec Heggie and Lois Hantz are in the centre of the picture.
Photograph by Viking Studios Ltd

A TAILOR FOR LADIES

Christopher Denys, Director of Productions at the Pitlochry Festival Theatre for the third year in succession, opened the 1972 season with his own production and translation of *A Tailor for Ladies* by Georges Feydeau, who was only twenty-four when he wrote this, his first work for the theatre which showed real signs of significance.

The Pitlochry Company accepted the challenge of playing French farce with a real sense of fun. Alec Heggie as Gaylord Puff, the couturier; Robert Aldous as the Irish expatriate and Ian Lindsay as Detective Serjeant Beaulocq all added to the joy of the occasion.

The British stage première of the farce by Georges Feydeau adapted by Christopher Denys. Presented at the Pitlochry Festival Theatre, as the opening production of the 1972 season on April 29. Designed by Helen Wilkinson.

Cast included:

Daniel Moulineaux	*Alec Heggie*
Yvonne Moulineaux	*Lois Hantz*
Bassinet	*Peter Ducrow*
Anatole Aubin	*Victor Lucas*
Suzanne Aubin	*Sarah Stephenson*
Madame Aigreville	
	Pamela Pitchford
O'Higgins	*Robert Aldous*
Beaulocq	*Ian Lindsa*
Argent	*John Kes*
Rosa Pichinette	*Alice Frase*

Directed by Christopher Denys

Rupert Frazer in the name-part in
Tamburlaine The Great presented by
the Glasgow Citizens' Theatre.
Photograph by Diane Tammes

TAMBURLAINE THE GREAT

The Glasgow Citizens' Theatre staged Christopher Marlowe's *Tamburlaine the Great* at Edinburgh's Assembly Hall during the 1972 International Festival. Under the direction of Keith Hack, they presented a highly melodramatic Twopence Coloured version, with babies tossed on spears, fake blood spurting from actors' bodies and dying kings hauled up in cages.

The designer, Philip Prowse, chained skeletons to pillars arranged for fountains of blood to astound the onlooker and favoured a jutting stage which resembled the prow of a pirate ship decorated with chains and instruments of torture.

Three actors shared the part of Tamburlaine – Rupert Frazer, Jeffery Kissoon and Mike Gwilym – playing an act apiece, which made it difficult to suggest any character progression.

A revival of the play by Christopher Marlowe. Presented by the Citizens' Theatre of Glasgow at the Edinburgh Assembly Hall on August 23 as part of the 1972 Edinburgh International Festival. Designed by Philip Prowse.

Cast included:

Mycetes	*Murray Salem*
Cosroe	*Lewis Collins*
Theridamas	*James Aubrey*
Bajazeth	*Ian McDiarmid*
Tamburlaine	*Rupert Frazer*
	Jeffery Kissoon
	Mike Gwilym
Techelles	*David Yelland*
Usumcasane	*Chris Brown*
Agydas	*Douglas Heard*
Soldan of Egypt	*Jonathan Levy*
Amyras	*Colin Haigh*
Calyphas	*Jeremy Blake*
Celebinus	*Laurance Rudic*
Callapine	*Jonathan Kent*
Zenocrate	*Paola Dionisotti*
Zabina	*Jill Spurrier*
Olympia	*Angela Chadfield*
Anippe	*Celia Foxe*

Directed by Keith Hack

Left: Joan Plowright as Katharina and Anthony Hopkins as Petruchio in Jonathan Miller's production of *The Taming of the Shrew*. *Photograph by John Timbers*

Top right: Ian Lindsay, Alice Fraser and Victor Lucas in Molière's *Tartuffe* presented at the Pitlochry Festival Theatre. *Photograph by Viking Studios Ltd*

Bottom right: Sarah Stephenson, Pamela Pitchford and Victor Lucas in *Tartuffe*. *Photograph by Viking Studios Ltd*

THE TAMING OF THE SHREW

Joan Plowright was eager to play Katharina in *The Taming of the Shrew* and when she agreed to do so at the Chichester Festival Theatre we are told she asked the director, Jonathan Miller, of *Beyond the Fringe* fame, to discover a new way of presenting Shakespeare's classic.

Mr Miller cut the Christopher Sly induction and concentrated upon the woman-taming sequences of the play. One had the impression that he believed *The Taming of the Shrew* was not really a comedy and had lectured the cast to that effect during rehearsal. They appeared bewildered by the Miller theories on the play and there were far fewer laughs than one would have expected, though Miss Plowright and her Petruchio, Anthony Hopkins, came off best in the long run, as most of Mr Miller's atten-tion was focused on their scenes.

The grim setting by Patrick Robertson was variously described by the London critics as a waiting-room, an empty rehearsal room and an uncompleted block of matt-black offices.

A revival of the play by Shake-speare. Presented at the Chichester Festival Theatre on July 5, 1972. Settings by Patrick Robertson, costumes by Rosemary Vercoe and music by Carl Davis.

Cast included:

Katharina	*Joan Plowright*
Petruchio	*Anthony Hopkins*
Baptista	*William Mervyn*
Bianca	*Susan Tracy*
Gremio	*Brian Hayes*
Tranio	*Richard Cornish*
Grumio	*Harold Innocent*
Lucentio	*Paul Hastings*

Directed by Jonathan Miller

TARTUFFE or THE IMPOSTOR

The team-work of the players and the tempo of Christopher Denys's direction made a delightful enter-tainment of Molière's *Tartuffe* at the Pitlochry Festival Theatre. Ian Lindsay carried Tartuffe's sleek hypocrisy to absurd heights, con-trasting with the trusting foolish-ness of Victor Lucas's Orgon. This polished and stylish production was presented with tremendous verve, and it enjoyed a short Scottish tour before the Pitlochry season opened.

A revival of the play by Molière in an English version by Richard Wilbur. Presented at the Pitlochry Festival Theatre on May 8, 1972. Designed by Helen Wilkinson.

Cast included:

Mme Pernelle	*Sheila Brownrigg*
Orgon	*Victor Lucas*
Elmire	*Alice Fraser*
Damis	*Donald MacIver*
Mariane	*Sarah Stephenson*
Valère	*Christopher Saul*
Cléante	*Robert Aldous*
Tartuffe	*Ian Lindsay*
Dorine	*Pamela Pitchford*

Directed by Christopher Denys

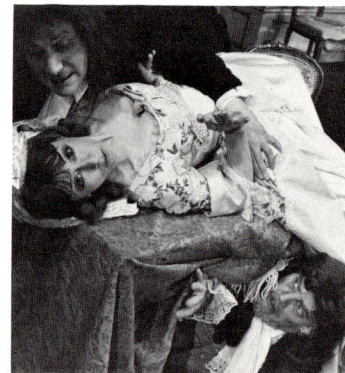

186

Michael Denison as Prospero and
Celia Bannerman as Miranda in
The Tempest. Photograph by
Zoë Dominic

THE TEMPEST

When Richard Digby Day directed *The Tempest* at the Open Air Theatre in Regent's Park, he borrowed the Royal Ballet's pocket-sized dancer, Wayne Sleep, to play the part of Ariel. It was a splendid choice, as Mr Sleep has a strong voice capable of doing justice to Shakespeare's verse. Not since the days of Leslie French has the Open Air Theatre seen so spiritual an Ariel.

The designer, Kit Surrey, built an impressive cavernous rock to provide a dwelling for the inhabitants of the Island. Michael Denison played Prospero with a quiet dignity and the comedy was provided by the unselfish teamwork of Ian Talbot as Trinculo and James Bree as Stephano.

A revival of the play by Shakespeare. Presented by David Conville for the New Shakespeare Company at the Open Air Theatre, Regent's Park, on May 30, 1972. Scenery by Kit Surrey, with costumes by Hugh Durant and choreography by David Drew.

Cast included:

Prospero	*Michael Denison*
Caliban	*Gregory Floy*
Trinculo	*Ian Talbot*
Stephano	*James Bree*
Ariel	*Wayne Sleep*
Miranda	*Celia Bannerman*

Directed by Richard Digby Day

THAT'S NO LADY – THAT'S MY HUSBAND

Francis Matthews, after a long television commitment as Paul Temple, returned to the stage at the Guildford Yvonne Arnaud Theatre in *That's No Lady – That's My Husband*, an amusing comedy by Tony Lesser in which a company executive decides to switch roles and become the lady of the house when his highly successful wife accepts a job as a £7,000-a-year television editor.

Mr Matthews gave a delightful performance as the disintegrating housekeeper, with Clive Morton as his doctor-father and Prunella Scales as the bright wife.

A play by Tony Lesser. Presented at the Yvonne Arnaud Theatre, Guildford, on August 22, 1972. Designed by Geoffrey Tozer.

Cast included:

Charles Plummer	*Clive Morton*
Hilary Plummer	*Prunella Scales*
Pat Plummer	*Francis Matthews*
Bobbie	*Leon Green*
Brutus Griffin	*Roger Mutton*

Directed by William Franklyn

THE THREE ARROWS

The Actors' Company, consisting of a group of experienced players who believe in equal pay and responsibility for all in the company, presented the première of *The Three Arrows* by Iris Murdoch, directed by Noel Willman. Set in medieval Japan, it deals with the eternal problems of political intrigue and frustrated love. Ian McKellen played a political prisoner, with John Tordoff as the Emperor, Frank Middlemass as the General who made all the important decisions, encouraged by his ambitious mother, played by Margery Mason. Robert Eddison was a most imposing old Zen teacher and Marian Diamond a shy Crown Princess.

A play by Iris Murdoch. Presented by the Cambridge Theatre Company and performed by the Actors' Company at the Arts Theatre, Cambridge, on October 17, 1972. Designed by Hutchinson Scott.

Cast included:

Prince Hirakawa	*Matthew Long*
Prince Tenjiku	*Tenniel Evans*
Prince Yoremitsu	*Ian McKellen*
Taihito	*John Tordoff*
General Musashi	*Frank Middlemass*
Rokuni	*Margery Mason*
Keiko	*Marian Diamond*
Kuritsubo	*Caroline Blakiston*
Ayame	*Sheila Reid*
Father Akita	*Robert Eddison*
Okano	*Jack Shepherd*
Norikura	*Juan Moreno*
Tokusan	*Ronnie Stevens*

Directed by Noel Willman

THREE SISTERS

Under the artistic direction of Robin Phillips, the newly-formed Company Theatre, started operations at Greenwich Theatre at the beginning of 1973, for what promised to be exciting productions of works by Chekhov, Lorca, Ibsen, Vanbrugh, Garson Kanin and James Saunders. The season opened with Elisaveta Fen's translation of *Three Sisters* by Chekhov.

R B Marriott admitted he had never seen the heartbreak and personal loneliness in the play so well realized, with such imagination and trueness of feeling and expression. Joy Parker as Olga, Gwen Watford as Masha and Mia Farrow as Irena gave performances likely to haunt the memory for many a day.

A play by Anton Chekhov, translated by Elisaveta Fen. Presented at Greenwich Theatre on January 25, 1973. Designs by Roger Butlin and costumes by Daphne Dare.

Cast included:

Andrey	*Norman Rodway*
Natasha	*Ann Firbank*
Olga	*Joy Parker*
Masha	*Gwen Watford*
Irena	*Mia Farrow*
Koolyghin	*Vernon Dobtcheff*
Vershinin	*Keith Baxter*
Toozenbach	*Roger Hammond*
Soliony	*Charles Dance*
Chebutykin	*Frank Gatliff*
Fedotik	*Jonathan Elsom*
Rodé	*Peter Gordon*
Ferapont	*John Rogan*
Anfisa	*Sylvia Coleridge*

Directed by Robin Phillips

THROUGH THE LOOKING GLASS

Felicity Douglas was responsible for a masterly adaptation to the stage of Lewis Carroll's *Through the Looking Glass*, warmly welcomed at the Ashcroft Theatre in Croydon. Alison Frazer was the very personification of the John Tenniel drawings of the immortal little girl. Dulcie Gray made a memorably scatty White Queen, with Michael Denison equally impressive as the White Knight and as Tweedledee. Michael Graham Cox was larger than life as Humpty Dumpty and he also played Tweedledum and the Red Knight with a sensitivity which made an instant appeal to the young audience. These artists obviously enjoy playing to children in such finely-written works which provide them with such rewarding engagements.

An adaptation by Felicity Douglas of the story by Lewis Carroll. Presented at the Ashcroft Theatre, Croydon, in association with the Cambridge Theatre Company, on December 26, 1972. Designed by Paul Ford, choreographed by Maggy Maxwell and orchestrated by Malcolm Rudland. Musical director – Malcolm Rudland.

Cast included:

Alice	*Alison Frazer*
Tiger Lily	*John Halstead*
Daisy	*Kleshna Handel*
Daisy	*Jill Streatfeild*
Rose	*Jill Stanford*
Beetle	*Susan Bown*
Red Queen	*Daphne Anderson*
Goat	*John Vine*
Train Guard	*Hamish Patrick*
Gentleman in Newspaper	*Stanley Bates*
Engine Driver	*John Halstead*
White Queen	*Dulcie Gray*
Tweedledum	*Michael Graham Cox*
Tweedledee	*Michael Denison*
Walrus	*Stanley Bates*
Carpenter	*Kleshna Handel*
Red King	*John Vine*
Humpty Dumpty	*Michael Graham Cox*
White King	*Henry Moxon*
Haigha	*John Halstead*
Hatta	*Stanley Bates*
White Bishop	*Hamish Patrick*
Red Castle	*John Vine*
Lion	*Kleshna Handel*
Unicorn	*Jill Streatfeild*
Red Knight	*Michael Graham Cox*
White Knight	*Michael Denison*
Frog Footman	*Henry Moxon*

Directed by Felicity Douglas

TIME AND TIME AGAIN

Set in a suburban conservatory and garden, Alan Ayckbourn's five-hander conversation-piece at the Comedy Theatre, *Time and Time Again*, defied definition. It may not have been a play by textbook standards, but it added up to two and a quarter hours of delightful fooling. It would not mean much on paper, but expertly played by such comedy-craftsmen as Tom Courtenay, Cheryl Kennedy, Bridget Turner, Barry Andrews and Michael Robbins, under the imaginative direction of Eric Thompson, it kept the audience constantly amused.

A play by Alan Ayckbourn. Presented by Michael Codron at the Comedy Theatre on August 16, 1972. Designed by Alan Tagg.

Cast included:

Leonard	*Tom Courtenay*
Graham	*Michael Robbins*
Joan	*Cheryl Kennedy*
Anna	*Bridget Turner*
Peter	*Barry Andrews*

Directed by Eric Thompson

190

Ian McKellen as Giovanni and Robert Eddison as Bonaventura in *'Tis Pity She's a Whore* presented by the Cambridge Theatre Company. *Photograph by Zoë Dominic*

'TIS PITY SHE'S A WHORE

At the 1972 Edinburgh International Festival the newly-formed Actors' Company presented the John Ford tragedy, *'Tis Pity She's A Whore*, directed by David Giles.

There were several magnificent performances, notably Ian McKellen and Felicity Kendal as the brother and sister in love, and Robert Eddison as the Friar who attempts to divert the brother from his incestuous relationship.

At Edinburgh the production was played so broadly that the audience tended to laugh in the wrong places and some of the minor characters gave the impression of playing for laughs. There seemed to be some uncertainty over the presentation of the more extravagant dramatic situations.

A revival of the play by John Ford. Presented by the Cambridge Theatre Company and performed by the Actors' Company at the 1972 Edinburgh International Festival, followed by a season at the Arts Theatre, Cambridge, opening on October 5. Designed by Kenneth Mellor.

Cast included:

Bonaventura	*Robert Eddison*
A Cardinal	*Juan Moreno*
Soranzo	*Edward Petherbridge*
Florio	*Frank Middlemass*
Donedo	*Tenniel Evans*
Grimaldi	*Robin Ellis*
Giovanni	*Ian McKellen*
Bergetto	*John Tordoff*
Richardetto	*Ronnie Stevens*
Vasques	*Jack Shepherd*
Poggio	*Mathew Long*
Annabella	*Felicity Kendal*
Hippolita	*Moira Redmond*
Philotis	*Sheila Reid*
Putana	*Margery Mason*

Directed by David Giles

TOAD OF TOAD HALL

For more than ten Christmases Richard Goolden has played to perfection the part of Mole in A A Milne's sensitive and faithful adaptation of *The Wind in the Willows*, known to play-goers as *Toad of Toad Hall*. At the Jeannetta Cochrane Theatre revival in 1972 it was obvious from the deep sincerity of Richard Goolden's performance that he agrees with A A Milne about the original work; 'it is what I call a Household Book – a book which everybody in the household loves and quotes continually ever afterwards.'

This ingenious adaptation has been a regular Christmas attraction on the London stage for the past forty years and in this latest revival there were memorable performances by Ian Talbot as Toad, Nikolas Simmonds as Ratty and Richard Wilson as Badger.

A revival of a play adapted by A A Milne from Kenneth Grahame's book, with music by H Fraser-Simson. Presented by David Conville and Charles Ross at the Jeannetta Cochrane Theatre on December 16, 1972. Décor by Peter Rice, choreography by Sally Gilpin and musical direction by Tony Stenson.

Cast included:

Mole	*Richard Goolden*
Water Rat	*Nikolas Simmonds*
Badger	*Richard Wilson*
Toad	*Ian Talbot*
Judge	*Paddy Ward*
Washerwoman	*Muriel Barker*
Bargewoman	*Pamela Manson*

Directed by Peter Watson

Left: Adam Walton as Tom, with the boys of Rugby School in *Tom Brown's Schooldays.*

Right: Roy Dotrice as Dr Arnold and Judith Bruce as Mary Penrose the School Matron in *Tom Brown's Schooldays.* *Photographs by Zoë Dominic*

TOM BROWN'S SCHOOLDAYS

Peter Coe, director of *Tom Brown's Schooldays*, has a flair for getting exciting theatrical performances out of groups of young people. The success of *Oliver!* owed a great deal to this unique aspect of Mr Coe's power as a director.

He recalls those famous Gang Show ensembles in the Rugby School sequences in the musical version of *Tom Brown's Schooldays*, which turned out to be a rather patchy affair at the Cambridge Theatre.

Roy Dotrice, with little or no singing voice, was rather ineffective as Dr Arnold, the Headmaster, and Judith Bruce made the most of the songs allocated to the Matron, a rather strange choice of character for the leading lady. Ray Davis stole the show in the small part of Obadiah the porter, a bright personality who brought scenes to life whenever he was on stage. Christopher Guard was effectively sinister as Flashman the Bully.

A musical freely based on the story by Thomas Hughes. Presented by Gordon Mills and Harold Davison for MAM, in association with Joe Vegoda at the Cambridge Theatre on May 9, 1972.

Book and lyrics by Joan Maitland and Jack Maitland; music by Chris Andrews; settings by Michael Knight; costumes by Ingeborg; choreography by Leo Kharibian and musical direction by Alan Bradan.

Cast included:

Dr Arnold	*Roy Dotrice*
Mary Penrose	*Judith Bruce*
Tom Brown	*Adam Walton*
East	*Richard Willis*
Flashman	*Christopher Guard*
Obadiah	*Ray Davis*
Margery	*Trudi Van Doorn*

Directed by Peter Coe

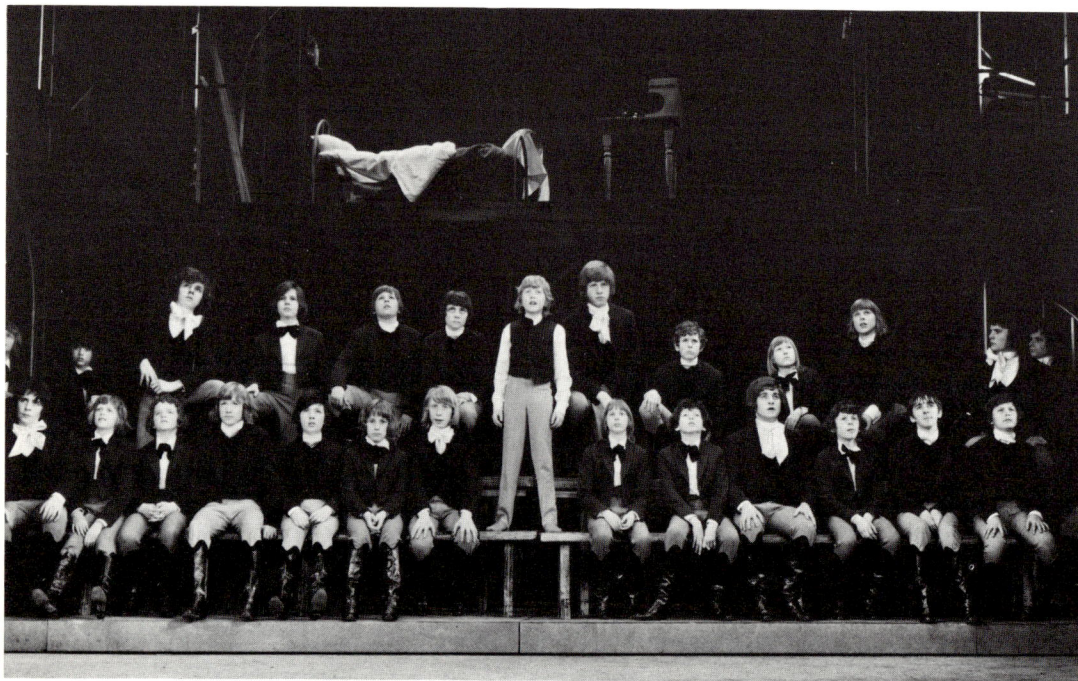

Billy Franks as Jim Hawkins and Christopher Benjamin as Long John Silver in *Treasure Island* at the Mermaid Theatre. *Photograph by Douglas H. Jeffrey*

A TOUCH OF PURPLE

The cast, headed by Maxine Audley, Gerard Heinz, Ray Barrett and Gillian Rhind struggled to bring life to *A Touch of Purple*, a thriller seen at the Globe Theatre, but it was a losing battle against unconvincing characterization on the part of the author, Elleston Trevor. The story concerns people suspected of murdering a woman who owned a Richmond antique shop, but it lacked any real interest.

A play by Elleston Trevor. Presented by Bill Kenwright for David Gordon Productions and Leon Gluckman at the Globe Theatre on October 18, 1972. Designed by Tim Goodchild.

Cast included:

Max Weiner	*Gerard Heinz*
Kate Weiner	*Maxine Audley*
Jo Weiner	*Gillian Rhind*
Police Constable	*Philip Hatton*
Police Sergeant	*Denis Nolan*
Fairey	*Ray Barrett*
Dr Wells	*Bernard Horsfall*
Geoffrey	*Ian Masters*

Directed by Philip Grout

TREASURE ISLAND

The traditional Mermaid Theatre production of *Treasure Island* with its instant transformation scenes was staged at the Mermaid Theatre for the 1972 Christmas season with more emphasis on fights, realistically staged by Juan Moreno, in bloody and full-blooded style.

Christopher Benjamin, as Long John Silver, was obviously inspired by his distinguished predecessor, Bernard Miles, who created the part in the original production of this version at the Mermaid in 1959. Impressive performances were given by Laurie Payne, as the upstanding Captain Smollett, Richard Hampton as the treacherous Israel Hands and George Benson as a dogmatic Squire Trelawney.

A play by Bernard Miles, Peter Coe and Josephine Wilson, adapted from the book by Robert Louis Stevenson. Revived by the Mermaid Theatre Trust at the Mermaid Theatre on December 18, 1972. Designed by Adrian Vaux.

Cast included:

Jim Hawkins	*Billy Franks*
Black Dog	*Juan Moreno*
Ben Gunn / Blind Pew	*Anthony Edwards*
Tom / Dr Livesey	*James Warwick*
Squire Trelawney	*George Benson*
Redruth	*Antony Viccars*
Long John Silver	*Christopher Benjamin*
Captain Smollett	*Laurie Payne*
Israel Hands	*Richard Hampton*

Directed by Sally Miles

TRELAWNY

Julian Slade's musical version of
Pinero's backstage play, *Trelawny
of the Wells*, proved a hit when it
went to Sadler's Wells Theatre in
Islington, the actual setting of the
Pinero story, for a limited summer
season. The musical was called
simply *Trelawny*. It transferred to
the Prince of Wales Theatre.

The Bristol Old Vic production,
designed by Alexander McPherson,
caught all the romantic atmosphere
of the gas-lit theatre of the 1860s,
but the musical numbers charmed
the ear only at spasmodic intervals
and the young and attractive
Gemma Craven was not quite
ready to seize the tremendous
chance the name-part offered her.

Elizabeth Power as Avonia Bunn
had far more panache. Looking
rather like Maggie Smith, she
caught the spirit of the artificial
Victorian style of acting and put
over her numbers with tremendous
brio. Ian Richardson won sympathy in the Tom Robertson part
of the modern playwright yearning
for an opportunity to sweep away
the ridiculous plays so popular at
the time. Max Adrian was suitably
melodramatic as the snobbish Sir
William Gower.

A musical adapted from Pinero's
play, *Trelawny of the Wells*, by
Aubrey Woods, George Rowell
and Julian Slade. Presented by
Veronica Flint-Shipman and Cameron Mackintosh in the Bristol Old
Vic production at Sadler's Wells
Theatre on June 27, 1972, and later
at the Prince of Wales Theatre.

Book by Aubrey Woods; music

and lyrics by Julian Slade; designs
by Alexander McPherson and
choreography by Bob Stevenson.

Cast included:

Tom Wrench	*Ian Richardson*
Rose Trelawny	*Gemma Craven*
Avonia Bunn	*Elizabeth Power*
Ferdinand Gadd	*David Morton*
Augusta Colpoys	*Teddy Green*
James Telfer	*John Gower*
Mrs Telfer	*Betty Benfield*
Sir William Gower	*Max Adrian*
Miss Trafalgar Gower	*Joyce Carey*
Arthur Gower	*John Watts*

Directed by Val May

TWELFTH NIGHT

Vanessa Redgrave made one of her all-too-rare stage appearances when she appeared as Viola in Michael Bakewell's traditional, ungimmicky production of *Twelfth Night* at the Shaw Theatre in Euston Road. She simulated an appealing boyish quality which she blended with girlish gaucherie.

Nyree Dawn Porter, with a reputation much enhanced by television successes, made a somewhat chilly Olivia, Ann Beach was a spirited Maria, John Turner made a sensitive Orsino, Peter Jeffrey's Malvolio was as pompous as one would expect, Jonathan Cecil's Sir Andrew was the silly-ass-Englishman always popular on

the stage, contrasting neatly with the boisterous Sir Toby of Windsor Davies. Oscar Quitak's Feste touched the heart as so few of Shakespeare's Fools are able to do.

The costumes and settings were dull and uninspired, not worthy of the highly talented team engaged for this production.

A revival of the play by Shakespeare. A Dolphin Theatre production presented at the Shaw Theatre on May 16, 1972. Designed by Christopher Lawrence.

Cast included:

Orsino	*John Turner*
Sebastian	*Norman Eshley*
Sir Toby Belch	*Windsor Davies*
Sir Andrew Aguecheek	
	Jonathan Cecil
Malvolio	*Peter Jeffrey*
Feste	*Oscar Quitak*
Olivia	*Nyree Dawn Porter*
Viola	*Vanessa Redgrave*
Maria	*Ann Beach*

Directed by Michael Bakewell

TWELFTH NIGHT

Giles Havergal directed the Glasgow Citizens' Theatre Company in an off-beat production of *Twelfth Night*, presented at Edinburgh's Assembly Hall during the 1972 Edinburgh International Festival.

Viola and Sebastian were played with pleasing effect by the same actor, Jeremy Blake. In the outrageously comic scenes, Sir Andrew, Sir Toby and Malvolio vied with each other, showing off their untraditional garb and Olivia chose dark sun-glasses of outsize proportions instead of her usual veil. The audience roared their appreciative enjoyment of the comedy, but there were times when the romantic allure of the play was sacrificed to the gimmicks devised by Giles Havergal, inventive though they were.

A revival of the play by Shakespeare. Presented by the Glasgow Citizens' Theatre at the Edinburgh Assembly Hall on September 1, as part of the 1972 Edinburgh International Festival. Designed by Philip Prowse.

Cast included:

Orsino	*Jonathan Kent*
Olivia	*Celia Fox*
Viola	*Jeremy Blake*
Feste	*Chris Brown*
Sir Toby Belch	*Ian McDiarmid*
Sir Andrew Aguecheek	
	James Aubrey
Maria	*Angela Chadfield*
Malvolio	*Mike Gwilym*
Sebastian	*Jeremy Blake*
Antonio	*Douglas Heard*

Directed by Giles Havergal

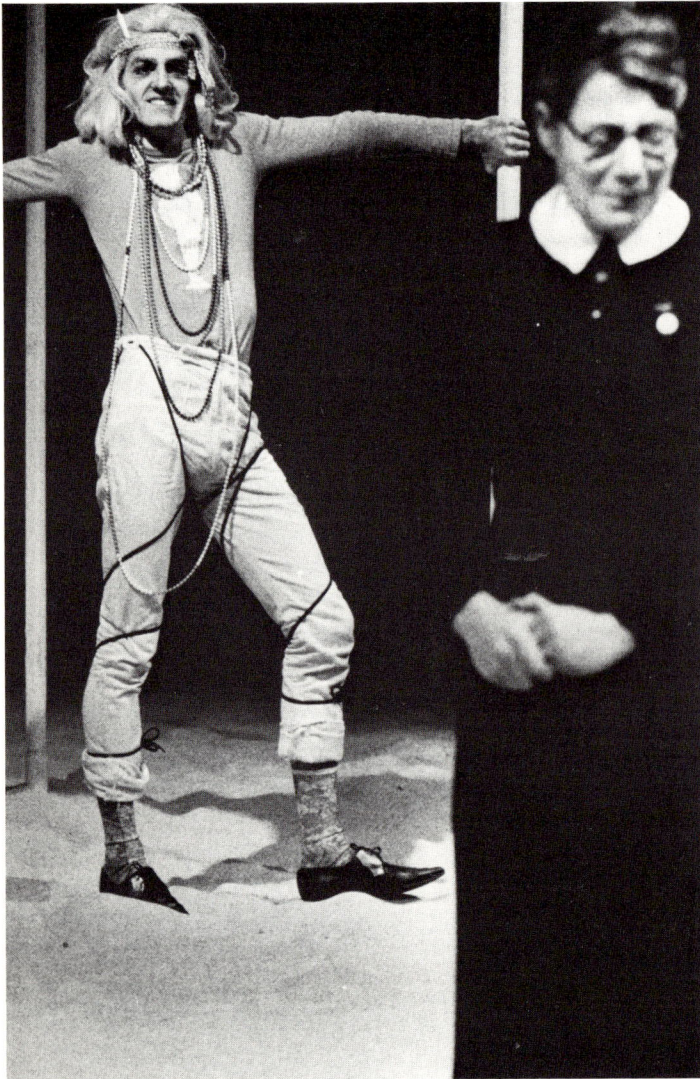

Left: Mike Gwilym as Malvolio and Angela Chadfield as Maria in The Glasgow Citizens' Theatre production of *Twelfth Night*. *Photograph by Diane Tammes*

Right: James Bree as Feste in *Twelfth Night* at the Open Air Theatre in Regent's Park. *Photograph by John Timbers*

TWELFTH NIGHT

David Conville's acceptable and straightforward production of *Twelfth Night* was the fortieth birthday production at the Open Air Theatre in Regent's Park.

All those years ago Jean Forbes-Robertson was Viola and on this 1972 occasion her daughter, Joanna van Gyseghem, played Olivia in the most touching fashion. Celia Bannerman projected the vocal beauty of Viola and Michael Denison brought an impressive imperious quality to his interpretation of Malvolio.

In the early seasons at Regent's Park the scenery was left to Nature, to a magnificent cluster of trees which were so cunningly and magically floodlit, but now Kit Surrey has created a picturesque façade and a stone-garden veranda against which the Watteau-style figures in Tim Goodchild creations, make a most pleasing picture.

A revival of the play by Shakespeare. Presented by David Conville for the New Shakespeare Company at the Open Air Theatre, Regent's Park, on July 12, 1972. Sets by Kit Surrey and costumes by Hugh Durrant. Music for the songs by James Bernard.

Cast included:

Orsino	*Darryl Kavann*
Viola	*Celia Bannerman*
Sir Toby Belch	*Hugh Manning*
Sir Andrew Aguecheek	
	Nigel Jeffcoat
Maria	*Janie Booth*
Malvolio	*Michael Denison*
Olivia	*Joanna van Gyseghem*
Feste	*James Bree*
Sebastian	*Nigel Bradshaw*

Directed by David Conville

Left: Joanna van Gyseghem as Olivia and Michael Denison as Malvolio in *Twelfth Night* at the Regent's Park Open Air Theatre. *Photograph by John Timbers*

Right: Patrick Cargill who appeared in *Two and Two Make Sex*. *Photograph by Crispian Woodgate*

TWO AND TWO MAKE SEX

Patrick Cargill, the supreme farçeur of the contemporary British theatre, worked wonders with the material supplied by Richard Harris and Leslie Darbon in their *Two and Two Make Sex* at Richmond Theatre. He gave a highly entertaining performance, but the play was rather slow and one had to wait a long time for the one outstandingly hilarious scene.

A play by Richard Harris and Leslie Darbon. Presented at Richmond Theatre on September 4, 1972. Designed by John C Piper.

Cast included:

Jane	*Barbara Flynn*
George	*Patrick Cargill*
Clare	*Jane Downs*
Ruth	*Diana King*
Nick	*Ian Lavender*
Jane's Father	*Jack Allen*

Directed by Jan Butlin

Peter Ustinov as the Archbishop and Brian Bedford as the General in *The Unknown Soldier and his Wife*. Photograph by Zoë Dominic

THE UNKNOWN SOLDIER AND HIS WIFE

The opening production for the New London Theatre in Drury Lane, occupying the site of the old Winter Garden, was the first London presentation of *The Unknown Soldier and His Wife* by Peter Ustinov, directed by the author who also played the leading part of the Archbishop.

Taking the futility of war as his theme, Peter Ustinov showed the reasons for devastating wars in the time of the Romans, the Crusades and at the French Revolution. The same types come down the ages – the tyrant, the inventor, the ever-pregnant girl and her soldier-husband.

The over-long play was repetitive in theme, coming right down to the air-raid sirens of our own day. Brian Bedford played a succession of tyrants most effectively. The wide-open stage suited the episodic style of Peter Ustinov's production.

A play by Peter Ustinov presented by Bernard Delfont in Alexander H Cohen's production to open the New London Theatre, built on the site of the Winter Garden Theatre, Drury Lane, London, on January 11, 1973. Scenery and costumes by Motley, lighting by Robert Ornbo, music by David Shire. Musical director – Raymond Bishop.

The play was originally presented by Alexander H Cohen for the New York Lincoln Center Festival in 1967. It was first seen in this country at the Chichester Festival Theatre on May 22, 1968.

Cast included

Television Engineer	Peter Abbott
Sergeant	Mark Kingston
Bugler	David Rhys Anderson
General	Brian Bedford
Rebel	Brett Usher
Wife	Tamara Ustinov
Archbishop	Peter Ustinov
14768	Stuart Mingall
71696	Christopher Muncke
Unknown Soldier	Miles Anderson
94343	David Quilter
Enemy Leader	Jeffry Wickham
Woman	Margaret Robertson
Reinforcements	Peter Abbott
	Alan Granville
	Barry McGinn
	Ronald O'Neill

Directed by Peter Ustinov

198

During the summer of 1972 Michael Redgrave took over from Alec Guinness the part of Father in *A Voyage Round My Father* by John Mortimer at the Haymarket Theatre. Sir Alec had to leave the cast to fulfil a film commitment

THE VICAR OF SOHO

The infamous Rev. Harold Davidson, Rector of Stiffkey, was the subject of a musical, *The Vicar of Soho*.

George Benson made a sympathetic figure of the Vicar and James Bolam was the hit of the evening with his song and dance routine.

The dialogue and lyrics were often flat, but the plot was colourful enough, considering the Vicar used to pick up penniless girls arriving at London railway stations, and later appeared in Blackpool side-shows, finally agreeing to appear in a lion's den at Skegness, where he died from injuries inflicted by the animals.

A musical with book and lyrics by Stuart Douglass and music by Tony Russell. Presented by the Gardner Centre at University of Sussex, Brighton, on August 2, 1972. Additional music by Iwan Williams; designed by Brenda Hartill Moores; choreography by Noel Tovey and musical direction by Peter Durrent.

Cast included:

Rev. Harold Davidson	*George Benson*
Showman	
Ronnie	
Newspaper seller	*James Bolam*
Luke Gannon	
Rose Ellis	*Anna Barry*

Other parts by: *Cristina Avery, Katherine Barker, Jeremy Child, Hilary Crane, Jon Croft, Jill Lidstone, James Warwick, Sammie Winmill*

Directed by Gordon McDougall

WAS HE ANYONE?

Six of the cast of N F Simpson's
fantasy, *Was He Anyone?* at the
Royal Court Theatre Upstairs
played thirty-four parts between
them, with Carol Gillies playing
only one – the wife of a man
drowning in the middle of the
Mediterranean. The author deals
with the preoccupations of the
National Help You Out Com-
mittee concerning the victim; the
action covers $27\frac{1}{2}$ months and it
gave N F Simpson an opportunity
to express his opinions on such
subjects as bureaucracy, red tape
and do-gooders.

A play by N F Simpson. Presented
at the Royal Court Theatre Upstairs on July 5, 1972. Designed by
Harriet Geddes.

Cast included:
  Geoffrey Chater, Stanley Lebor,
  Yvonne Antrobus, Carol Gillies,
  Rowena Cooper, Richard Kay and
  June Brown
Directed by Nicholas Wright

Lana Morris and Philip Bond in
When the Wind Blows

WHEN THE WIND BLOWS

Richard Digby-Day was responsible for an ingenious production of a thriller by Brian Clemens, *When the Wind Blows*, premièred at York Theatre Royal. Half a dozen young people are gathered together for a birthday party in a converted windmill, with the sails creaking past the window.

The shocks included the introduction of Grand Guignol horror and a male full-frontal nude which was quite acceptable in the context, and a finale which the first-night audience found to be a mighty surprise.

A play by Brian Clemens. Presented at the Yvonne Arnaud Theatre, Guildford, on January 16, 1973, after a première at York Theatre Royal with a different cast. Designed by Brian Currah.

Cast included:

Ann Marsh	*Helen Weir*
Jenny Rayner	*Lana Morris*
Maggie Miller	*Vanessa Kempster*
Peter Rayner	*Alex Davion*
Terry Dexter	*Philip Bond*
Andy Flewin	*Keith Varnier*
Steve Turner	*Peter Mantle*

Directed by Richard Digby-Day

WHILE THE SUN SHINES

Terence Rattigan wrote *While the Sun Shines* in 1942, the darkest year of the war. He was on a three-week leave in borrowed rooms in Albany, which gave him the set for the comedy he was determined to write in order to enjoy his leave and raise his morale. The result was an instant hit, which ran for more than a thousand performances.

When the Hampstead Theatre Club revived the comedy thirty years later, with a highly efficient cast, directed by Alec McCowen, it proved as amusing as ever and showed every sign of another long run in the West End, had a suitable theatre been available.

A revival of the play by Terence Rattigan. Presented at the Hampstead Theatre Club on December 18, 1972. Designed by Saul Radomsky.

Cast included:

Horton	*Jeffrey Segal*
Earl of Harpenden	*Michael Culver*
Lieutenant Mulvaney	
	Stephen Bradley
Lady Elizabeth Randall	
	Doran Godwin
Duke of Ayr and Stirling	
	John Stratton
Lieutenant Colbert	
	Richard Warwick
Mabel Crum	*Anna Calder Marshall*

Directed by Alec McCowen

WHO KILLED JACK ROBIN?

Tudor Gates wrote a thriller concerning the personal combat on a psychological level between an intelligent criminal and a remorselessly pursuing detective in *Who Killed Jack Robin?* at Richmond Theatre.

Lee Montague played the likeable crook, with Colin Douglas as his casual but formidable opponent. After a shock opening, the adversaries plot their moves by thinking more than one move ahead, until the criminal makes his inevitable mistake.

A play by Tudor Gates. Presented by Richmond Theatre Productions Ltd, by arrangement with Charles Ross, at Richmond on August 7, 1972. Designed by John C Piper.

Cast included:

Dr Adcock	*John Breslin*
Supt. Pratt	*Colin Douglas*
Jack Robin	*Lee Montague*
Christine	*Elizabeth Wallace*

Directed by Philip Grout

WHO THOUGHT IT?

That highly individual Yorkshire-born actor, Edward Petherbridge, seemed to have been inspired by both Ruth Draper and Marcel Marceau when he appeared in a one-man show at the Arts Theatre Club called *Who Thought It?* by Colin Bennet and Alex Durant.

This mixture of mime, monologue and poetry revealed Mr Petherbridge as a personality with a lively, out of the ordinary sense of humour, who finds fun in subjects as far apart as vultures and toreadors and wears masks with an air of accomplishment.

Michael Aldridge, Eleanor Bron,
Amanda Barrie and John Bird in
Who's Who? *Photograph by Stuart
Robinson*

WHO'S WHO?

Michael Aldridge, John Bird,
Amanda Barrie and Eleanor Bron
exploited their attractive stage
personalities in *Who's Who?*, an
enigmatic farce by Keith Waterhouse and Willis Hall at the
Yvonne Arnaud Theatre in Guildford.

It is a comedy of errors, involv-
ing a whole lot of curious doubts.
Mr White and Mr Black both turn
up in Brighton for a weekend.
Are they joined by their girlfriends,
or aren't they? Do their wives
join them, or don't they? Lies
were twisted to truth and truth to
lies in the most fascinating manner
by these masters of light comedy,
in a soufflé which had the advantage
of Robert Chetwyn's expert direction.

A play by Keith Waterhouse and
Willis Hall. Presented at the
Yvonne Arnaud Theatre, Guild-
ford, on September 26, 1972.
Designed by Hutchinson Scott.

Cast included:

Timothy Black	*Michael Aldridge*
Bernard White	*John Bird*
Helen Brown	*Amanda Barrie*
Joanna	*Eleanor Bron*

Directed by Robert Chetwyn

Fulton Mackay, Callum Mill and
John Cairney in *Willie Rough*

WILLIE ROUGH

Willie Rough, the first play to be written by Bill Bryden, Associate Director of the Lyceum Theatre of Edinburgh, was revived at the Lyceum in October, after a promising first season earlier in the year.

James Grant in the name-part, played a Shop Steward and Trade Union Organizer in a Clyde shipyard, who opposed the First World War. He wrote what he felt to be the truth in a conflict between socialism and patriotism, but was accused of treason and sent to prison. After his release, he found himself on his own. Joseph Brady, John Cairney, Fulton Mackay, Callum Mill, Roddy McMillan and Clare Richards contributed to the deep impression made by Mr Bryden's play.

A revival of the play by Bill Bryden. Presented at the Lyceum Theatre, Edinburgh, on October 18, 1972. Designed by Geoffrey Scott, with costumes by Deirdre Clancy.

Cast included:

Willie Rough	*James Grant*
Hughie	*Fulton Mackay*
Eddie	*Callum Mill*
Jake Adams	*Roddy MacMillan*
Bernadette	*Clare Richards*
Pat Gatens	*Joseph Brady*
Charlie McGrath	*John Cairney*

Directed by Bill Bryden

Frank Thornton, Maria Charles and
Ronald Radd in *Winnie the Pooh*.
Photograph by Sophie Baker

WINNIE THE POOH

A A Milne's imaginative story, *Winnie the Pooh*, never seems to grow stale and it turned up at the Phoenix Theatre as fresh as ever, with the enchanting Sarah Sutton captivating the juvenile audience with her endearing performance as Roo. Frank Thornton played Eeyore as dolefully as the author would have wished and Ronald Radd played Pooh in splendid fashion.

A play adapted from the A A Milne story by Julian Slade. Presented by Veronica Flint-Shipman at the Phoenix Theatre on December 18, 1972. Settings by Derek Cousins, costumes by Tim Goodchild and choreography by Bridget Espinosa. Music by H Fraser-Simson, with additional music by Julian Slade.

Cast included: John O'Farrell, Ronald Radd, Trevor T Smith, Frank Thornton, Maria Charles, Eric Dodson, Ann Windsor, Sarah Sutton, Wayne Sleep, Audrey Leybourne, Chris Melville, Jini Steel, Peter Boyce, Bill Bradley, Kenneth Caswell and Joshua Le Touzel

Directed by Malcolm Farquhar

WORLD THEATRE SEASON
Ninth Season at the Aldwych, 1972

THE WIZARD OF OZ

Harold Arlen's haunting melodies, written for the Judy Garland film, *The Wizard of Oz*, proved as captivating as ever when a stage version of the enchanting story was revived at the Victoria Palace for a Christmas matinée season. The charm of this old-time production might have been more potent without so much audience participation and the introduction of a Dalek.

Diane Raynor made a winsome Dorothy, blown by a whirlwind from Kansas to the other end of the rainbow, where she met Tony Sympson as the Wizard, Geoffrey Hughes as the Lion, Frank Marlborough as the Scarecrow and Sam Kelly as the Tin Man – all admirably cast.

A play with book by L Frank Baum and music and lyrics by Harold Arlen and E Y Harburg. Presented by Paul Elliott and Duncan C Weldon for Triumph Theatre Productions at the Victoria Palace Theatre on December 26, 1972. Choreography by Garry Tabbutt. Musical director – Bert Hayes.

Cast included:
Dorothy   *Diane Raynor*
Sorceress of the North
           Angela Ryder
Wicked Witch of the West
           Brian Hewitt-Jones
Scarecrow   *Frank Marlborough*
Tin Man   *Sam Kelly*
Cowardly Lion   *Geoffrey Hughes*
Wizard of Oz   *Tony Sympson*
Directed by Bryan C Wolfe

THE KATHAKALI DRAMA COMPANY

From India Peter Daubeny brought the Kathakali Drama Company to the Aldwych, as part of the Ninth World Theatre Season in dramas from the two great Hindu epics – *The Ramayana* and *The Mahabharata*. Selections from these great works made up nine different programmes, which were played in repertoire.

The players wore elaborate make-up and vividly decorated costumes, but even with the aid of informative programmes and the simultaneous translation system, it was not easy to follow the plot of their legends, even though the works had been cut to a length suitable for presentation before Western audiences.

An actor of the Kathakali Theatre
of Southern India

Eduardo De Filippo as the
Neapolitan tramway worker in
*Napoli Milionaria.   Photograph by
Antonia Cesareo*

NAPOLI MILIONARIA

Eduardo de Filippo, one of Italy's
supreme comic actors, brought his
own company to the Aldwych to
appear in his own play set in war-
scarred Naples – *Napoli Milionaria* –
as part of the 1972 World Theatre
Season.

This slight, pathetic-looking
veteran of seventy-two years hardly
ever smiles. He has a Chaplinesque
pathos and a flair for understate-
ment, which makes his comedy
both amusing and serious at the
same time.

Napoli Milionaria tells of a
soldier who returns from two years
in a German prisoner-of-war camp
to discover his black-marketeering
wife has made a fortune, but
money has turned her head and the
family has fallen apart.

Pupella Maggio gave an ex-
plosive gesticulating performance
as the wife, in vivid contrast to
Eduardo de Filippo's skilled natur-
alistic behaviourism which won the
sympathy of the house.

A play by Eduardo de Filippo.
Presented by the Eduardo de
Filippo Company at the Aldwych
on May 8, 1972, as part of the 1972
World Theatre Season, under the
artistic direction of Peter Daubeny.
Designed by Bruno Garofalo.

Cast included:
Gennaro Jovine   *Eduardo de Filippo*
Amalia Jovine   *Pupella Maggio*
Errico   *Franco D'Amato*
Brigadiere Ciappa
                      Giuseppe Anatrelli
Riccardo   *Luca Della Porta*
Directed by Eduardo de Filippo

THE POSSESSED

The Ninth World Theatre Season ended in triumph at the Aldwych with a visit from the Stary Theatre Company from Cracow in *The Possessed*, Andrzej Wajda's dramatization of Dostoevsky's novel. It was a stunning, chilling and mind-piercing experience, as the Polish players, under Wajda's direction, demonstrated the shattering effect of magnificent Total Theatre.

Raving sounds punctuated the scenes, some of them ending with blood-freezing effects as the company wove some fine individual performances into a superbly bal-anced ensemble. To single out individual players would be unfair because the company achieved such a remarkable degree of team-work.

A new dramatization by Andrzej Wajda from the novel by Dosto-evsky, based on the adaptation by Albert Camus, in a Polish trans-lation by Joanna Guze.

Performed by the Cracow Stary Theatre Company from Poland, as part of the Ninth World Theatre Season, under the artistic direction of Peter Daubeny, at the Aldwych Theatre on May 29, 1972. Settings by Andrzej Wajda and costumes by Krystyna Zachwatowicz.

Cast included:

Nicholas Stavrogin	*Jan Nowicki*
Alexey Kirilov	*Andrzej Kozak*
Ivan Shatov	*Aleksander Fabisiak*
Lisa Drozdov	*Hanna Halcewicz*
Maria Timofeyevna Lebyatkin	*Izabela Olszewska*
Barbara Petrovna Stavrogin	*Zofia Niwinska*
Stepan Trofimovich Verhovensky	*Wiktor Sadecki*
Peter Stepanovich Verkhovensky	*Wojciech Pszoniak*

Directed by Andrzej Wajda

THE ORESTEIA

The National Theatre of Greece came to the Aldwych to give the world première of their modern Greek version of *The Oresteia* by Aeschylus, directed by Takis Mou-zenides. The trilogy consisted of *Agamemnon*, *The Choephori* (The Libation Bearers) and *The Eumen-ides* (The Benign Ones).

The settings by Kleovoulos Klonis were simple and evocative but the handling of the Chorus was quite inspired and inspiring; their chanting and their ingeniously choreographed sequences gave the plays the quality of compelling dance-dramas.

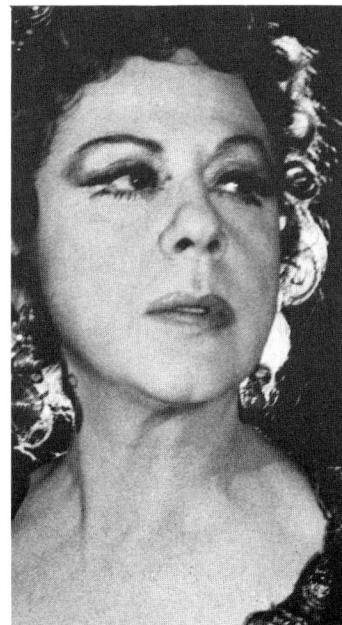

Helen Hadjiarghyri as Electra with the Chorus in *The Choephori*, in the National Theatre of Greece's production of *The Oresteia*

The outstanding players were Mary Aroni as Clytemnestra, Vassili Kanakis as Agamemnon, Nikos Kazis as Aegisthus, Chriss Politis as Orestes, Helen Hadjiarghyri as Electra and Kostas Kosmopoulos as the First Chorus Leader who all helped to make this production an unforgettable theatrical experience.

The world première of a new translation into modern Greek by Tassos Roussos of *The Oresteia* by Aeschylus – the trilogy consisting of *Agamemnon*, played alone, and *The Choephori* and *The Eumenides*, played as a double-bill. Presented by the National Theatre of Greece at the Aldwych, as part of the 1972 World Theatre Season, under the direction of Peter Daubeny – *Agamemnon* being presented on April 25 and the double-bill following on April 27, 1972. The set was designed by Kleovoulos Klonis; choreography by Zouzou Nicoloudi; costumes by Dionyssis Fotopoulos and music by Stefanos Vassiliadis.

Casts included:

Clytemnestra	*Mary Aroni*
Agamemnon	*Vassili Kanakis*
Cassandra	*Kakia Panayiotou*
Aegisthus	*Nikos Kazis*
First Chorus Leaders	
	Kostas Kosmopoulos
	Zetta Kondyli
Orestes	*Chriss Politis*
Electra	*Helen Hadjiarghryi*
Apollo	*Vassili Kanakis*

Directed by Takis Mouzenides

Welcome Msomi in the name-part
of his own play, *Umabatha*.
Photograph by Barry Comber

UMABATHA

Peter Daubeny's Ninth World
Theatre Season opened with a
smash-hit, *Umabatha*, an original
Zulu play by a Zulu writer, played
by the Natal Theatre Workshop
Company from South Africa, who
were the first Zulu company to be
seen outside South Africa.

Umabatha was based on the
theme of *Macbeth* and followed the
Shakespeare story very closely, but
was not a translation of the Shakespeare text. In some respects it was
crude and naïve, but the finely-
built Zulu warriors, with their
shields and assegais, made a
tremendous impact upon the audience with their war dances.

Bare-breasted women sang and
wailed in turn and Welcome
Msomi, the author, headed the cast
of this exciting dance-drama which
packed the theatre for every
performance.

A Zulu drama on the theme of
Macbeth by Welcome Msomi. Presented by the Natal Theatre Workshop Company at the Aldwych
Theatre on April 3, 1972, as the
opening production of the World
Theatre Season, under the artistic
direction of Peter Daubeny.

Cast included:

Mabatha	*Welcome Msomi*
Kamadonsela	*Daphne Hlomuka*
Dangane	*Khulekani Magubane*
Bhangane	*Lawrence Sithole*
Kamakhawulana	
	Ntombiyenkosi Mhlongo

Directed by Pieter Scholtz

Victor Garcia's trampoline setting
for the Nuria Espert Company's
production of Lorca's *Yerma*

YERMA

Nuria Espert, Spain's leading
tragedienne, returned to London,
this time to play the name-part in
Yerma, Federico García Lorca's
poignant story of the childless wife
who strangles her husband. The
production was part of the World
Theatre Season.

It was played on a gigantic
trampoline, designed by Victor
Garcia, who also directed the play.
The setting stole the reviews; in
turn it suggested the Granada
mountainside, the sail of a ship
seen in Yerma's nightmare, a
living womb, and a beating heart.
It served to make the simple
tragedy of a Spanish farmer and his
frustrated wife something timeless
and abstract.

It caught the imagination of
London play-goers who filled the
theatre at every performance.

A play by Federico García Lorca.
Presented by the Nuria Espert
Company from Spain at the
Aldwych Theatre Season, under the
artistic direction of Peter Daubeny,
on April 17, 1972. Set and costumes designed by Victor Garcia
and Fabian Puig. The production
returned to the Aldwych Theatre
on April 2, 1973.

Cast included:

Yerma	*Nuria Espert*
Juan	*José Luis Pellicena*
Old Pagan Woman	*Amparo Valle*
Dolores	*Paloma Lorena*
Victor	*Daniel Dicenta*

Directed by Victor Garcia

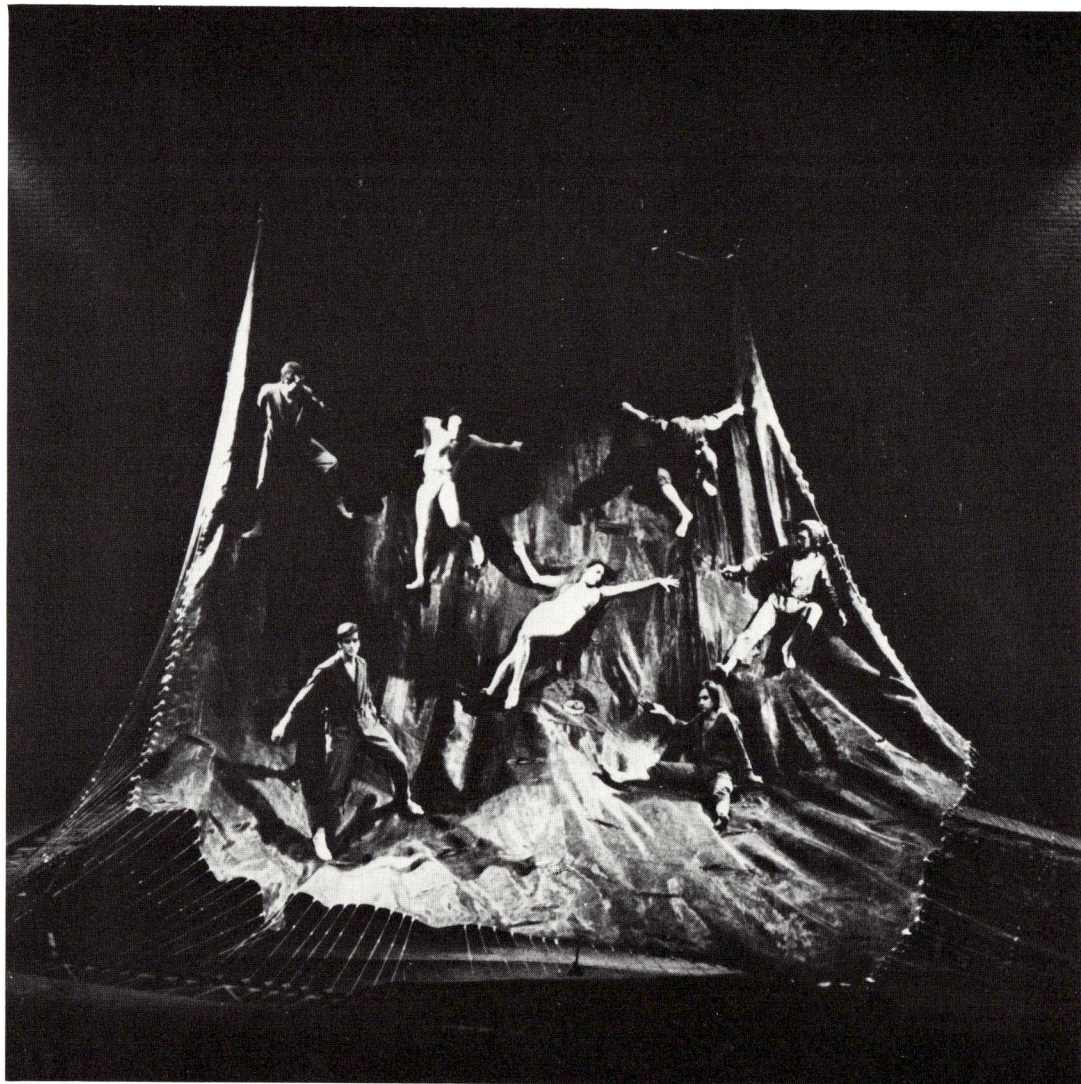

Roddy McMillan and John Grieve
in *The Bevellers*

THE BEVELLERS

Roddy McMillan wrote a play about work in a dying craft in *The Bevellers*, set in a basement shop below the streets of Glasgow where men are involved in various stages of bevelling glass from glass plate to framed mirror.

Andrew Byatt played a boy spending his first day at the craft of glass bevelling, surrounded by mirrors, machinery and broken glass and confronted by the violence and humour of the men he meets – the bevellers of the title. It was not a documentary, but a remarkable, accurately observed account of a day in a strange underground world. The author, once a beveller himself, played the kindly foreman.

A play by Roddy McMillan. Presented by the Royal Lyceum Theatre Company at the Lyceum Theatre, Edinburgh, on February 16, 1973. Designed by Geoffrey Scott, with costume designs by Deirdre Clancy.

Cast included:

Bob Darnley	*Roddy McMillan*
Norrie Beaton	*Andrew Byatt*
Dan Matchett	*William Armour*
Peter Laidlaw	*John Grieve*
Charlie Weir	*Jackie Farrell*
Joe Crosby	*Paul Young*
Leslie Skinner	*John Young*
Alex Freer	*Leonard Maguire*
Nancy Blair	*Mary McCusker*

Directed by Bill Bryden

THE LIARS

Henry Arthur Jones, once a close rival of Pinero, has been sadly neglected by the professional theatre. The Mercury Theatre at Colchester were congratulated for their enterprise in reviving *The Liars*, not seen on the professional stage since 1917. This stylish comedy, which put Victorian women in their place as creatures not worth taking seriously, made an entertaining evening and was well worth the imaginative direction David Buxton lavished upon the production.

A revival of a play by Henry Arthur Jones. Presented at the Mercury Theatre, Colchester, on February 13, 1973. Designed by Sheila Godbolt.

Cast included:

Freddie Tatton	*Peter Laird*
Archibald Coke	*John Harwood*
Mrs Crespin	*Monica Stewart*
Sir Christopher Deering	
	Victor Lucas
George Nepean	*Ronald Forfar*
Lady Rosamund	*Pamela Ruddock*
Dolly Coke	*Barrie Shore*
Lady Jessica	*Susan Tebbs*
Gilbert Nepean	*Roger Forbes*
Gadsby	*Philip Boyd*
Edward Falkner	*Philip Voss*
Ferris	*Katie Flower*
Waiter	*Nicholson Jensen*
Footman at the Tattons	
	Robert Flockhart
Taplin	*Nicholas Jensen*

Directed by David Buxton

CADENZA

Just before he died in 1972, Alec Coppel put the finishing touches to his last thriller *Cadenza* which Allan Davis directed at the Thorndike Theatre, Leatherhead. The author was rather proud of having written a modern thriller in which the telephone bell hardly ever rang.

The story concerns a missing hostess. Dinner guests arrive at a Mayfair flat; it is empty; the candles are newly lit; the dinner is cooking; a cigarette smoulders in the ashtray, but there is no hostess to welcome them.

Stuart Damon, Barbara Shelley, John Turner, Sebastian Breaks and Jennifer Watts struggled valiantly with what proved to be a plot which was not thick enough to last out an evening.

A play by Alec Coppel from a story by Alec Coppel and Myra Coppel. Presented at the Thorndike Theatre, Leatherhead, on February 13, 1973. Designed by Colin Winslow. Songs by Richard Kayne.

Cast included:

Helen Jacklin	*Barbara Shelley*
Charles Jacklin	*Sebastian Breaks*
Eddie Payne	*Stuart Damon*
Mordacai	*John Turner*
Miss Nash	*Jennifer Watts*

Directed by Allan Davis

ONLY A GAME

Peter Gilmore played the part of a star footballer in physical and moral decline in *Only a Game*, Barrie Keeffe's play presented by the Dolphin Theatre Company at the Shaw Theatre, Euston Road. The author had rich material: the footballer's knee operations, his mistress who became pregnant, and his marriage drifting on the rocks, but he did not use it as well as he might have done and we did not get to know the characters as deeply as we would have liked. Jan Waters gave a moving performance as the wife who wondered whether it was really worth trying to save the marriage.

A play by Barrie Keeffe. Presented by the Dolphin Theatre Company at the Shaw Theatre, Euston, on March 20, 1973. Designed by Christopher Lawrence.

Cast included:

Murray Fearn	*Peter Gilmore*
Elanor	*Jan Waters*
Gloria	*Elaine Donnelly*
Jimmy Jones	*Freddie Earlle*
Arnold Fearn	*Basil Lord*
Mrs Summerfield	
	Daphne Anderson
Harry Richards	*Ivan Beavis*
Alan Turner	*Karl Howman*
Specialist	*Colin Jeavons*
The voice of	*Jimmy Hill*

Directed by Michael Croft

SAY GOODNIGHT TO GRANDMA

Madge Ryan gave a towering performance as a terrifyingly possessive mother in *Say Goodnight to Grandma*. The author himself gave a moving and convincing performance as her young married son, with Stephanie Turner winning sympathy as the young wife fighting a seemingly losing battle against her ruthless monster of a mother-in-law.

Highly dramatic was the party which the mother cunningly arranged to further isolate her daughter-in-law when she invited old-time pals from the son's social club, grown men who had not really grown up. The wife tried to beat the mother at her own game but as the curtain fell one shuddered at the thought of what would happen the next morning and in the years to come.

A play by Colin Welland. Presented by Ray Cooney Productions at the St Martin's Theatre on March 29, 1973. Setting by Peter Rice.

Cast included:

Mrs Weston	*Madge Ryan*
Jean Weston	*Stephanie Turner*
Tony Weston	*Colin Welland*
Mrs Mahoney	*Doreen Keogh*
Ray	*Patrick Durkin*
Harry	*Shaun Curry*
Phil	*Paul Luty*
Eric	*Geoffrey Hughes*
Ken	*John Lesley*

Directed by Patrick Dromgoole

Diana Rigg as Célimène in Tony Harrison's version of *Le Misanthrope* by Molière. *Photograph by Zoë Dominic*

MAN OF DESTINY

The Open Space Theatre gave us a rare opportunity of seeing a revival of *Man of Destiny*, the curtain-raiser Bernard Shaw wrote for Irving and Ellen Terry. It was never seen at the Lyceum, getting no further than provoking a storm of acrimonious discussion between the famous actor and the dramatist who insisted Ellen Terry was wasting her time under his management.

David Schofield and Diana Quick played Napoleon and the Strange Lady in a rather throwaway style and at times discovered some unconscious humour in the lines.

A revival of a play by Bernard Shaw. Presented at the Open Space Theatre on January 17, 1973. Designed by Robin Don.

Cast included:

Giuseppe	*Dallas Cavell*
Napoleon	*David Schofield*
Lieutenant	*Malcolm Storry*
Strange Lady	*Diana Quick*

Directed by Jeremy Young

ROOTED

Suburban Sydney is the setting for *Rooted* by Alexander Buzo, which Hampstead Theatre Club imported from Australia. It was a rather tame affair concerning a wife eager to turn her husband out of their new flat, to make way for the big-noise glamour-boy who seemed to wield considerable power in the city. The cast, under Pam Brighton's valiant direction, did all they could to gain and hold the attention of the audience, but they fought a losing battle.

A play by Alexander Buzo. Presented at the Hampstead Theatre Club on March 5, 1973. Designed by William Dudley.

Cast included:

Gary	*Christopher Mitchell*
Bentley	*Philip Jackson*
Sandy	*Jenny Agutter*
Diane	*Kay Barlow*
Richard	*Nigel Terry*

Directed by Pam Brighton

THE MISANTHROPE

The National Theatre scored a major triumph with their production of *The Misanthrope*. The Molière masterpiece, freshly adapted by Tony Harrison, brilliantly designed by Tanya Moiseiwitsch and imaginatively directed by John Dexter, was daringly and successfully translated into the reign of de Gaulle. The experiment worked magnificently, with casting to match.

Alec McCowen scored the most spectacular success of his career, leading the critic Frank Marcus to say this young actor's achievement could perhaps be equalled but not surpassed by Olivier. Diana Rigg as Célimène was breathtakingly seductive. Other outstanding contributions on the acting side came from Gawn Grainger, Nicholas Clay, Alan MacNaughtan, Gillian Barge and Jeremy Clyde. Tony Harrison will obviously be invited to translate and transpose more Molière to the English stage, giving people with no knowledge of French a chance to appreciate the exact English equivalent of the French classics.

A play by Molière in an English version by Tony Harrison. Presented by the National Theatre at the Old Vic on February 23, 1973. Designed by Tanya Moiseiwitsch, with music arranged by Marc Wilkinson.

Cast included:

Alceste	*Alec McCowen*
Philinte	*Alan MacNaughtan*
Oronte	*Gawn Grainger*
Célimène	*Diana Rigg*
Eliante	*Jeanne Watts*
Arsinoé	*Gillian Barge*
Acaste	*Nicholas Clay*
Clitandre	*Jeremy Clyde*
Basque	*Paul Curran*
Official of Academie	*Clive Merrison*
Dubois	*James Hayes*

Directed by John Dexter

Vladek Sheybal as Gustav Mahler
and Edith Macarthur as Alma
Mahler in Maurice Rowdon's
Mahler

NIGHTFALL

Derek Martinus skilfully directed *Nightfall*, a play for two actors by Burton Graham. It says much for the technique and understanding of the two actors – Hugh Burden and Patrick Barr – that they were able to hold the attention of the audience at the Adeline Genée Theatre, East Grinstead, for two hours while they coped with the situation of both being ex-husbands of a successful novelist.

A play by Burton Graham. Presented by Bill Kenwright for David Gordon Productions, by arrangement with Myles Byrne Productions Ltd at the Adeline Genée Theatre, East Grinstead, on March 1, 1973.

Cast included:
Jonas   *Hugh Burden*
James   *Patrick Barr*
Directed by Derek Martinus

MAHLER

Gustav Mahler, the composer and conductor, married Alma Schindler, daughter of a fashionable Court painter and nineteen years his junior, when he was forty-two. By the time he was fifty he died after suffering a long period of failing health.

In his play *Mahler* seen at the Arts Theatre Club, Maurice Rowdon brought the two figures together after death to discuss their brief married life and to reflect on what it might have been in the Vienna of legendary waltzes. Vladek Sheybal, the Polish actor better known on the screen than on the stage, gave some indication of the dark depths of the composer's mind, but the author had not probed deep enough to give him material worthy of his understanding.

A play by Maurice Rowdon. Presented by Portslade Productions Ltd at the Arts Theatre Club on February 14, 1973. Setting by Kit Surrey and musical concept by Peter Paul Koprowski. Dance arranged by Sally Gilpin.
Cast included:
Gustav Mahler   *Vladek Sheybal*
Alma Mahler   *Edith Macarthur*
Directed by Peter Watson

TWIGS

Twigs, seen at the Coventry Belgrade Theatre, was imported from America, and consisted of four sketches by George Furth. Moira Lister, the pivot character of all four plays, had ample scope to display her versatility, and had excellent support from Karl Held, Alan Tilvern, Lionel Murton, Harry Towb, Barry Martin, Elliott Sullivan and Hilary Minster. The settings, four contrasting kitchens, were designed by Terry Parsons.

A play by George Furth. Presented by Paul Elliott and Duncan C Weldon for Triumph Theatre Productions at the Belgrade Theatre, Coventry, on February 20, 1973. Designed by Terry Parsons.

Cast included:

Emily	
Celia	
Dorothy	*Moira Lister*
Ma	
Frank	*Karl Held*
Phil	*Alan Tilvern*
Swede	*Lionel Murton*
Lou	*Harry Towb*
Ned	*Barry Martin*
Pa	*Elliott Sullivan*
Priest	*Hilary Minster*

Directed by Brian Murray

WHAT EVERY WOMAN KNOWS

Straight from playing Barrie's Peter Pan, Dorothy Tutin appeared as Maggie Wylie, one of Barrie's most attractive leading ladies in *What Every Woman Knows* at Brighton's Theatre Royal. She gave the most captivating performance as the Little Cherub who sits aloft to look after the career of John Shand.

Straight from his splendid performance as Stanhope in *Journey's End*, Peter Egan made an equally impressive impact as John Shand, the humourless young Scot who imagined he was entirely self-made in his career as an M.P. Cathleen Nesbitt brought tremendous style to the Comtesse de la Brière and Gordon Jackson's David Wylie was as good and wholesome as Scots oats. Amanda Murray's Lady Sybil had an artificial charm which could never hope to captivate a man for very long. This is just what Barrie intended.

A revival of a play by J M Barrie. Presented by Roger Clifford and Craig Macdonald, in association with Anthony M Chardet, by arrangement with Julie C Daugherty, at Brighton Theatre Royal on February 27, 1973. Setting and costume designs by Peter Farmer.

Cast included:

Alick Wylie	*Archie Duncan*
James Wylie	*Boyd Mackenzie*
David Wylie	*Gordon Jackson*
Maggie Wylie	*Dorothy Tutin*
John Shand	*Peter Egan*
Comtesse de la Brière	*Cathleen Nesbitt*
Lady Sybil Tenterden	*Amanda Murray*
Mr Feikie	*Stanley Lloyd*
Mr Venables	*Lockwood West*
Grace	*Carol Marsh*
Thomas	*Stanley Lloyd*

Directed by Clifford Williams

A PRIVATE MATTER

Originally presented at Nottingham Playhouse in 1972 *A Life of The General*, Ronald Mavor's absorbing play eventually reached the West End as *A Private Matter*. Alastair Sim played the Cambridge don wishing to write the life of a famous general whose career came to a mysterious end as the result of a sensational incident which was hushed up as a nervous breakdown.

There are only four characters in this lively discussion play which had all the suspense of a thriller, thanks to the masterly direction of Ian McKellen. Apart from the biographer, played by Alastair Sim, there was the General's widow, a woman torn by conflict and loyalty, vividly played by Dorothy Reynolds, and her two contrasting sons – the stuffy one brought to life by Peter Cellier and the extrovert by Derek Fowlds.

A play by Ronald Mavor. Presented by H. M. Tennent and Knightsbridge Theatrical Productions Ltd at Brighton Theatre Royal on January 15, 1973, and at the Vaudeville Theatre on February 21, 1973. Designed by Hutchinson Scott.

Cast included:

Anne	*Dorothy Reynolds*
Anthony	*Derek Fowlds*
Christopher	*Peter Cellier*
Mervun Dakyns	*Alastair Sim*

Directed by Ian McKellen

Dorothy Reynolds and Alastair Sim
in *A Private Matter*.   *Photograph
by Angus McBean*

George Benson as William and Simon Ward as Valentine in the Cambridge Theatre Company's production of *You Never Can Tell*. Photograph by Chris J Arthur, Trans World Eye

WHO WERE YOU WITH LAST NIGHT?

Perth Theatre presented the première of *Who Were You With Last Night?* by Kerry Lee, a comedy-thriller which made an amusing evening. Ann Kennedy played a rich and seductive young woman seeking revenge on her husband who parted from her five years ago.

The fun really set in when she bribed a man to shoot him dead on the fifth anniversary of their separation. The author provided a number of rewarding parts for the cast who revelled in their opportunities – Roger Hume as a comic policeman, Bruce Bennett as the young man from the escort agency and Ron Bain as his admirer.

A play by Kerry Lee Crabbe. Presented at Perth Theatre on February 21, 1973. Designed by Helen Wilkinson.

Cast included:

Lorna	*Ann Kennedy*
Rudi	*Richard Denning*
Detective Sergeant Trotter	
	Roger Hume
Tony	*Ron Bain*
Eddie	*Bruce Bennett*
Angie } Trixie }	*Jeni Angus*
Private Dick	*Roger Kemp*

Directed by Nicolas Kemp

YOU NEVER CAN TELL

Shaw's *You Never Can Tell* was given a sparkling revival by the Cambridge Theatre Company at the Cambridge Arts Theatre under the direction of Derek Goldby who inspired some masterly, unselfish team-work from the cast.

Simon Ward as the self-assured and witty wooer of Celia Bannerman's Gloria was a joy; Margaret Courtenay's Mrs Clandon had superb stage presence and she projected the performance with tremendous vigour. George Benson never missed a trick in the plum part of William. It was a joyous evening by a troupe of most accomplished players.

A revival of a play by Bernard Shaw. Presented by the Cambridge Theatre Company at the Arts Theatre, Cambridge, on February 12, 1973. Designed by Pauline Whitehouse, with dances arranged by Gary Downie.

Cast included:

Dolly	*Gillian Bailey*
Valentine	*Simon Ward*
Parlourmaid	*Pamela Farbrother*
Philip	*Richard Everett*
Mrs Clandon	*Margaret Courtenay*
Gloria	*Celia Bannerman*
Crampton	*John Phillips*
M'Comas	*Brian Hayes*
William	*George Benson*
Bohun	*Harold Innocent*
Waiters	*John Gillett*
	David Janes

Directed by Derek Goldby

SARAH B. DIVINE

An American satirical show, *Sarah B. Divine* by Tom Eyen, was based on incidents in the life of Sarah Bernhardt. In London it was chosen as a vehicle for the popular drag artists, Rogers and Starr. Little was discovered about the Divine Sarah and the purpose seemed to be to show her success as the personification of the star-making system, Hollywood fashion.

A play by Tom Eyen. Presented at the Jeannetta Cochrane Theatre, Bloomsbury, on March 19, 1973. Additional material by Pam Gems, choreography by Sue Lefton and music and musical direction by Jeremy Nicholas. Songs by David Ashton.

Cast included:

Maurice Bernhardt	*David Ashton*
Sarah Bernhardt	*Ann Mitchell*
Sarah Bernhardt	*Pat Quinn*
Jason	
M. Dumas	
M. Pitou	*Denis Lawson*
Armand	
Prince Henri de Ligne	
Eleonora Duse	
Judith Van Hard	*Roy Starr*
Mme Nathalie	
Oscar Wilde	
Fifi d'Amour	
Ellen Terry	*Michael Rogers*
Bosie	
Stage Manager	*Robert Philips*
Louis Richepin	

Directed by Robert Walker

Frances Tomelty as Glafira and
Colin Douglas as Yegor Bulichov
in *The White Raven.* *Photograph by
Allan Hurst*

THE WHITE RAVEN

Maxim Gorky's *Yegor Bulichev*, the second play in an unfinished trilogy about the crumbling of the Russian bourgeoisie, was splendidly translated by Moura Budberg, that great authority on Tsarist Russia, and presented as *The White Raven* at Nottingham Playhouse, under the lively direction of Stuart Burge.

The entire production was dominated by Colin Douglas as the snarling bear of gigantic proportions, dying of cancer of the liver. This mightly figure dwarfed all the other characters in the play, as a sort of Russian Falstaff, living in a society fading into oblivion. The play provided a vivid impression of the end of the Romanov era and all it stood for.

A play by Maxim Gorky, translated by Moura Budberg. Presented by the Nottingham Playhouse Company at Nottingham Playhouse on February 14, 1973. Settings by

Patrick Robertson and costumes by Rosemary Vercoe.

Cast included:

Xenia	*Peggy Marshall*
Glafira	*Frances Tomelty*
Shura	*Angela Pleasence*
Varvara	*Eve Belton*
Zvonzov	*Sean McCarthy*
Yegor Bulichov	*Colin Douglas*
Pavlin	*David Blake Kelly*
Donat	*Tony Rohr*
Bashkin	*Desmond Perry*
Doctor	*Jon Whatson*
Tiatin	*Philip Donaghy*
Vassili Dostigaev	*Arthur Cox*
Elisaveta	*Phillada Sewell*
Jakov Laptiev	*Jarlath Conroy*
Alexei	*Graham Schofield*
Tonia	*Fidelma Murphy*
Melania	*Hazel Hughes*
Trumpeter	*Ron Cook*
Taissia	*Fidelma Murphy*
Mokroussov	*Tony Rohr*
Zobunova	*Valerie Lilley*
Propatei	*Donal McCann*

Directed by Stuart Burge

WOYZECK

Charles Marowitz's adaptation and direction of Georg Büchner's *Woyzeck* was a rather tricksy affair at the Open Space Theatre, where it was seen prior to representing Great Britain at the Festival of Experimental Theatres, sponsored by the Associazione Teatri of Italy.

The play lasted about seventy-five minutes with no interval. It was incomplete at the author's death at the age of twenty-three and is generally regarded as the first example of a working-class tragedy. It influenced the early work of Bertolt Brecht, but the Open Space production was unimaginative and depressing.

A play by Georg Büchner, freely adapted by Charles Marowitz. Costumes by Lindy Hemming and choreography by Gillian Gregory. Presented at the Open Space Theatre on February 19, 1973.

Cast included:

Woyzeck	*David Schofield*
Captain	*Dallas Cavall*
Marie	*Carol Drinkwater*
Andrez	*Tim Morand*
Barker	*Anthony Milner*
Drum Major	*Malcolm Storry*
Doctor	*Milo Sperber*
Sergeant	*Preston Struthers*
Margaret	*Lesley Ward*
Soldier/Doctor	*John Burgess*
Soldier/Dancer	*Adam Shand-Kidd*
Malcontent	*Anthony Milner*
Dancers	*Maxine Sperber*
	Karen Rabinowitz

Directed by Charles Marowitz

UP SPAGHETTI JUNCTION!

Malcolm Totten, with the able assistance of many collaborators in *Up Spaghetti Junction!* devised a show to reflect the history and character of Birmingham. Every member of the company brought his own view of Birmingham to the show. The music was by Jon Raven, the songwriter who has been used to drawing upon the industrial Midlands in his career as a folklorist. The slides and back projections were by Paul Hill, former Midlands Press Photographer of the Year.

An entertainment devised by Malcolm Totten, written by John Clarke, David Edgar, Malcolm Totten and David Turner, with music by Jon Raven, arranged by Don Shearman. Designed by Hugh Durrant, choreographed by Lucy Fenwick and musical direction by Don Shearman.

Presented at the Birmingham Repertory Theatre on February 23, 1973.

Contributors: Gareth Armstrong, John Baddeley, Eileen Barry, Jenny Cryst, Susan Derrick, Michael Hadley, Linal Haft, Paul Henry, Olu Jacobs, Mandy Jenner, David King, Geoffrey Leesley, Raymond Llewellyn, Kevin McNally, Frank Moorey, Robert O'Mahoney, Jon Raven, Colin Starkey, Marcia Warren, Holly Wilson and Pinkerton's Bicycles.

Directed by Michael Simpson and Christopher Honer

SMALL CRAFT WARNINGS

Tennessee Williams parades a collection of life's failures gathered in a Southern Californian bar in *Small Craft Warnings*. The play gave Elaine Stritch the opportunity to make her first appearance in a straight play on the London stage at Hampstead Theatre Club. The production later transferred to the Comedy Theatre.

Nothing happens during the action, but the dramatist's master hand held the interest of the audience. Miss Stritch played an ageing beautician, living in a trailer with a flashy young man she is keeping, admirably played by Edward Judd. In a well chosen cast, which was well directed by Vivian Matalon, George Pravda played a failed doctor, Tony Beckley a cynical homosexual, Eric Deacon his attractive American boy friend, Frances de la Tour a sex-hungry slut and Peter Jones the bar-keeper with a compassionate eye on his regular clientèle.

A play by Tennessee Williams. Presented at Hampstead Theatre Club on January 29, 1973, and at the Comedy Theatre on March 13, 1973. Designed by Saul Radomsky.
Cast included:

Leona Dawson	*Elaine Stritch*
Monk	*Peter Jones*
Doc	*George Pravda*
Bill	*Edward Judd*
Violet	*Frances de la Tour*
Steve	*James Berwick*
Quentin	*Tony Beckley*
Bobby	*Eric Deacon*
Tony	*John Bay*

Directed by Vivian Matalon

A DOLL'S HOUSE

The return of Claire Bloom to the London stage after an absence of eight years was quite an event. Having been hailed in America as Ibsen's Nora and Hedda, she chose Nora in *A Doll's House* to make her reappearance at the Criterion Theatre.

Perhaps we have seen too many great Noras on the London stage, and in consequence Miss Bloom's conception lacked depth. She looked like an exquisite Victorian porcelain figurine, but a Nora incapable of any really deep thinking. The critic Frank Marcus amusingly suggested that after closing the door decorously behind her, she would return the next morning.

Colin Blakely brought new life to the husband and Nora Nicholson's old nurse was an exquisite cameo capable of leaving lasting memories.

A new adaptation by Christopher Hampton of the play by Henrik Ibsen. Bernard Delfont and Michael White, by arrangement with Donald Albery, presented the Hillard Elkins production at the Criterion Theatre on February 20, 1973. Setting by John Bury, with costumes by Beatrice Dawson.
Cast included:

Torvald Helmer	*Colin Blakely*
Nora	*Claire Bloom*
Dr Rank	*Anton Rodgers*
Mrs Kristine Linde	*Stephanie Bidmead*
Nils Krogstad	*Peter Woodthorpe*
Anne-Marie	*Nora Nicholson*
Helene	*Dorothy Baird*

Directed by Patrick Garland

222

Left: Ron Cook as Pug, Michael Johnson as Meercraft and Arthur Cox as Fitzdotterel in *The Devil is an Ass.* *Photograph by Allan Hurst*

Right: Raymond Campbell, Stephen Rea and Carmel McSharry in *The Freedom of the City*

THE DEVIL IS AN ASS

Ben Jonson's parody morality play, *The Devil is an Ass*, does not appear to have been given a full scale professional production since 1663, until it was staged at Nottingham Playhouse in the spring of 1973, adapted by Peter Barnes.

Mr Barnes treated the text as an art expert would restore an old painting, replacing obsolete words with others of equal precision, beauty and force, retaining meaning that is clear to contemporary audiences.

The play, cut down from the original running time of four hours, struck a chillingly authentic modern note, with Meercraft's money-making schemes. This satire was a romp at the expense of confidence tricksters.

A play by Ben Jonson, adapted by Peter Barnes. Presented at Nottingham Playhouse on March 14, 1973. Costumes designed by John Napier and setting by Patrick Robertson.

Cast included:

Satan	*David Blake Kelly*
Pug	*Ron Cook*
Iniquity	*Jarlath Conroy*
Fitzdotterel	*Arthur Cox*
Meercraft	*Donal McCann*
Everill	*Sean McCarthy*
Wittipol	*Michael Johnson*
Manly	*Graham Schofield*
Engine	*Desmond Perry*
Trains	*Jon Whatson*
Gilthead	*David Blake Kelly*
Plutarchus	*Jarlath Conroy*
Sir Paul Eitherside	*Colin Douglas*
Ambler	*Tony Rohr*
Sledge	*Paul Weingott*
Shackles	*Desmond Perry*
Mrs Fitzdotterel	*Fidelma Murphy*
Lady Eitherside	*Hazel Hughes*
Lady Tailbush	*Valerie Lilley*
Pitfall	*Meg Davies*

Directed by Stuart Burge

THE FREEDOM OF THE CITY

Brian Friel, the Irish writer, sets his play *The Freedom of the City* in the Londonderry of 1970 and he takes a human rather than a political point of view in this work which was seen at the Royal Court Theatre and at the Abbey Theatre in Dublin at the same time, while the Ulster troubles were at their height.

After the dispersal of an unauthorised Civil Rights March, three demonstrators – a mother of eleven children, a decent, intelligent boy and a young social rebel – take refuge in the Guildhall. Eventually they are senselessly and needlessly killed by British soldiers. They are not revolutionary martyrs, which is what makes Mr Friel's play such a moving experience. They were played by Carmel McSharry, Raymond Campbell and Stephen Rea, under the sensitive direction of Albert Finney.

A play by Brian Friel. Presented by the Royal Court Theatre and Memorial Enterprises Ltd at the Royal Court Theatre on February 27, 1973. Setting designed by Douglas Heap and costumes by Harriet Geddes.

Cast included:

Elizabeth Doherty	*Carmel McSharry*
Michael Hegarty	*Raymond Campbell*
Adrian Fitzgerald	*Stephen Rea*
The Judge	*Basil Dignam*
Judge's Clerk	*Anthony Nash*
Court Usher	*Catherine Harding*
Professor Cupley	*Matthew Guinness*
Doctor Winbourne	*Alex McCrindle*
The Brigadier	*Louis Haslar*
Corporal	*Nick Llewellyn*
Soldier	*David Atkinson*
The Priest	*Peter Adair*
Liam O'Kelly	*George Shane*
Balladeer	*Michael O'Hagan*
The Lecturer	*Bob Sherman*

Directed by Albert Finney

GAUNT

Within a stone's throw from John of Gaunt's own Lancaster Castle, the Duke's Playhouse at Lancaster staged *Gaunt*, an allegory by David Pownall which traced the rise and fall of the House of Lancaster.

This highly dramatic play, written with considerable humour, skilfully directed by Peter Oyston, with impressive scenes and costumes by Laurie Dennett and Paul Miller, centred round Gaunt in Purgatory. The leading part was magnificently played by Michael David, with William Zappa as his Fool. Many of the players in the company were called upon to play several parts, which they did with considerable versatility.

A play by David Pownall. Presented at the Duke's Playhouse, Lancaster, on February 28, 1973. Designed by Laurie Dennett, with costumes by Paul Miller, music by Stephen Boxer and dances devised and directed by Michael Melia.

Cast included:

Gaunt	*Michael David*
Heron	*William Zappa*
Henry IV	*Ben Cross*
Henry V	*Michael Melia*
Henry VI	*Stephen Boxer*
Henry VII	*Stephen Boxer*
Gloucester	*Alan Collins*
Beaufort	*Ben Cross*
Suffolk	*Michael Melia*
Edward IV	*Michael Melia*
Richard III	*Ben Cross*
Richard of York	*Michael Melia*
Peny	*Stephen MacKenna*
Daunse	*John Golder*
Flie-Away	*Charles Haggith*
Sunshine	*Christine Noonan*
Heads	*John Cording*
Queen	*Celia Gregory*
Scroop	*Alan Collins*
Lollard	*Charles Haggith*
Priest	*Alan Collins*

Directed by Peter Oyston

HANS KOHLHAAS

Frederick Proud directed *Hans Kohlhaas*, a play by James Saunders based on a story by Heinrich Von Kleist, along Brechtian lines at Greenwich Theatre.

When not speaking, the players sat on either side of the bare acting area, wearing rehearsal costume. The story concerned a 16th-century horse-dealer, whose fury concerning the fate of two of his animals by a feudal lord leads to a peasants' revolt. Richard Moore and Jonathan Elsom, June Jago and Peter Howell lent admirable support.

Cast included:

Hans Kohlhaas	*Richard Moore*
Sternbald	*Peter Gordon*
The Tollkeeper Martin Luther Elector of Brandenburg	*Frank Gatliff*
The Steward Henkel Hinz	*John Rogan*
The Junker	*Jonathan Elsom*
Elizabeth	*June Jago*
The Lawyer Elector of Saxony John Frederick	*Trevor Baxter*
Governor of Brandenburg Kunz	*Alan Helm*
Sheriff of Wittenburg Prince Meissen	*Charles Dance*
Count Wrede Lord Chancellor of Saxony	*Peter Howell*

Directed by Frederick Proud

IS YOUR DOCTOR REALLY NECESSARY?

Theatre Workshop presented a bouncing musical at Stratford Theatre Royal called *Is Your Doctor Really Necessary?*, a Ken Hill satire on the medical profession. He poked fun at the rivalry between professional doctors and the manufacturers of patent medicines, both of whom were out to make money. Their first aim is not to cure a patient, because more money can be made by keeping them in need of treatment and pills.

Tony Macaulay wrote some lively tunes.

A play by Ken Hill with songs by Tony Macaulay. Presented by Theatre Workshop at the Theatre Royal, Stratford East, on February 14, 1973. Setting by Guy Hodgkinson and Mark Pritchard, costumes by Willie Burt and choreography by Judith Paris.

Cast included:

Dr Haversham O'Mara	*Maxwell Shaw*
Sir Harvey Springett	*Brian Murphy*
Nurse	*Diane Langton*
Hemsley	*Griffith Davies*
Minister of Health	*Avis Bunnage*
Stilson	*Larry Dann*
Wilson	*Trevor Smith*
Miss Birch	*Toni Palmer*
J.G.	*Ron Hackett*
Dr Gilbert Gamble	*Kenneth Scott*
Alice	*Valerie Walsh*

Directed by Ken Hill

Robert Eddison as Father Anthony
Perfect and Barrie Shore as
Christine Smith in *The Prodigal
Daughter*. *Photograph by
Photovogue*

HAPPY AS A SANDBAG

Ken Lee's musical collage of life on
the home front during World War
Two, *Happy as a Sandbag,* was
directed by Philip Hedley at
Leicester's Phoenix Theatre. There
was no satire in this revue, which
set out, to chronicle the times,
touching on the Armed Forces,
the Land Army, Neville Chamberlain's declaration of war, Churchill's
blood, sweat and tears speech and
Lord Haw Haw's advice to sur-
render. It was pleasingly nostalgic
and highly entertaining.

A revue by Ken Lee. Presented by
the Leicester Theatre Trust Ltd at
the Phoenix Theatre, Leicester, on
February 7, 1973. Setting by Paul
Wright, choreography by Catherine
Crutchley, musical arrangements by
Ian Kellam and musical direction
by Peter Durrent.

Cast included: *Catherine Crutchley,
Penelope Nice, Gwen Taylor, Chris-
tine Welch, David Firth, Martin
Friend, Arthur Griffiths, Christo-
pher Godwin, Darryl Kavann and
Roy Macready.*
Directed by Philip Hedley

THE PRODIGAL DAUGHTER

The presence of Robert Eddison
added lustre to the cast of *The
Prodigal Daughter*.

The agonising dilemmas facing
the priesthood today are brought
into focus by Mr Turner whose
play concerns three Roman Catholic
priests in a rambling old-fashioned
presbytery, where they are joined
by a new housekeeper, a non-
Catholic who is very much in tune
with the times. Much of the comedy
stems from how the housekeeper
solves some of their problems.

A play by David Turner. Presented
at the Mercury Theatre, Colchester, on March 6, 1973. Designed by Alasdair Burman.

Cast included:
Father Anthony Perfect
                    Robert Eddison
Father Geoffrey Vernon
                    Charles Kay
Father Michael   *Barry Warren*
Christine Smith   *Barrie Shore*
Patrick O'Donnell *Anthony Barnett*
Mary Fallon   *Katie Flower*
Directed by David Buxton

Sally Ann Howes, Jim Smilie
and Kenneth Nelson in *Lover*.
Photograph by Godfrey Argent

LOVER

Brian Clemens calls his play *Lover*, a thriller which opened at the St Martin's Theatre. It had many ingredients of a thriller. Yet Mr Clemens's play lacked any suggestion of suspense and any development of story-line. His characters included a lovely artist's model, the only woman in the cast, admirably played by Sally Ann Howes, an infatuated Italian admirer, an elderly fashion photographer and his younger rival, two police constables with rather strange intentions and a sinister hall-porter, played in dark tones by Max Wall. There was no sort of story jig-saw into which these strange characters fit. They just came and went without leaving any exciting impression upon the audience.

A play by Brian Clemens. Presented by Peter Saunders at the St Martin's Theatre on March 8, 1973. Décor by Anthony Holland, with dresses by Clive.
Cast included:

Murchison	*Max Wall*
Terry Cleaves	*Kenneth Nelson*
Bruno Varella	*Jim Smilie*
Suzy Martin	*Sally Ann Howes*
Greg Miles	*Jeremy Hawk*
Constable Richard Lovell	
	Roger Lloyd Pack
Constable Henry Venner	
	Derren Nesbitt
Peter	*Christopher Strauli*
Directed by Philip Grout	

226

Freddie Jones as Peer Gynt and
Shelagh Fraser as Mrs Gynt (Aase)
in James Kirkup's new version of
Peer Gynt, by Ibsen.   *Photograph by
Ian Dickson*

PEER GYNT

James Kirkup, who has travelled
widely in Sweden, Lapland, Denmark and Norway, was responsible
for the new version of Ibsen's
Peer Gynt, presented by the Tyneside Theatre Company at Newcastle
University Theatre. His aim was to
reduce the play to about one third
of its length, to condense the action
and the endless discussions and
monologues and to reduce the
number of characters and settings.
He succeeded admirably and also
brought out the extraordinary
modernity of Ibsen's masterpiece –
its modernity of style, feeling and
ideas which make it so relevant to
the present time. He preserved the
essence of *Peer Gynt* and reduced it
to a manageable length.

Freddie Jones made an impressive, modern-looking Peer in rag-
ged overalls and a tattered shirt,
heading a cast of sixteen who played
some seventy characters between
them in John Fraser's superb set
which captured the chilling winds
moaning over the rugged mountainside. Greig's music was replaced by Keith Statham's score
which heightened the mysterious
gloom of the far North.

A play by Henrik Ibsen in a new
version by James Kirkup. Presented by the Tyneside Theatre
Company at the University Theatre,
Newcastle-upon-Tyne on January
30, 1973. Designed by John Fraser,
with music by Keith Statham.

Cast included:

Peer Gynt	*Freddie Jones*
Ragman	*Michael Burrell*
Solveig	*Soracha Cusack*
Mrs Gynt	*Shelagh Fraser*
Various parts	

*Tim Barlow, Antoinette Biggerstaff,
Philip Bowen, James Carter, Char-
mian Doré, Karl Johnson, Arthur
Kelly, Jeannette Lewis, Mary Ruther-
ford, Dennis Scott, Robin Soans,
Bill Wallis*

Directed by Gareth Morgan with
Ian Giles and Nick Heppel

227

LEAVE HIM TO HEAVEN

A lively musical by Ken Lee, *Leave Him to Heaven*, presented by the Theatre Royal Company of Lincoln, concerned the ageing Hollywood star, Conway Tearle. Geoffrey Drew gave a magnetic performance suggesting the dying teddy-boy and with some thirty rock n' roll numbers to put across, the company excelled themselves, reliving the '50s and the '60s in a dynamic three-hour show.

A musical play by Ken Lee. Presented by the Lincoln Theatre Company at the Lincoln Theatre Royal on February 28, 1973. Designed by Terry Brown and choreographed by Pat Adams. Musical director – Ian Smith.

Cast included:

Conway Tearle   *Geoffrey Drew*
Other parts: *Richard Albrecht, Virginia Clarke, Clare Duushka, Lindsay Franklin, David Gilmore, Christopher Leaver, Sue O'Brien, Paddy Stern, Tim Stern, Reg Stewart, Clare Venables*

Directed by Howard Lloyd-Lewis assisted by Sue Dunderdale

CHICHESTER FESTIVAL SEASON 1973

The eighth and last Chichester Festival Season under the direction of John Clements opened on May 9, 1973 and ran to September 15, 1973.

The opening production was the first performance in this country of the new Anouilh comedy, *The Director of the Opera*, with John Clements in the name-part and June Jago, Richard Pearson, Maureen O'Brien, Ciaran Madden and Penelope Wilton in a cast of seventeen. Peter Dews was responsible for the direction, Alan Tagg for the setting designs and Margaret Furse for the costumes.

The Seagull by Chekhov followed on May 23, with Irene Worth as Madame Arkadina, Robert Stephens as Trigorin, Richard Pearson as Sorin, Ralph Michael as Dorn, Maureen O'Brien as Nina and Peter Eyre as Konstantin. Jonathan Miller directed, with sets by Patrick Robertson and costumes by Beatrice Dawson.

R Loves J, a musical based on *Romanoff and Juliet* by Peter Ustinov, had its première on July 11, under the direction of Wendy Toye, with Topol of *Fiddler on the Roof* fame in the leading part. Peter Ustinov was responsible for the book, Alexander Faris for the music, Julian More for the lyrics and Tim Goodchild for sets and costumes.

Dandy Dick, the Pinero farce, opened on July 25, directed by

John Clements, with Alastair Sim and Patricia Routledge renewing the highly successful comedy partnership which started in the Chichester production of Pinero's *The Magistrate* in 1969. Alan Tagg designed the sets for *Dandy Dick* and Margaret Furse the costumes.

Since taking over the direction of the Chichester Festival Theatre from Laurence Olivier in 1966, John Clements has presented thirty-two plays, eight of which transferred successfully to the West End. He extended the season from its original nine weeks to the present nineteen and enhanced the reputation of the Chichester Festival as one of the great international theatrical attractions. Keith Michell is to take care of the direction of the Chichester Festival in 1974.

PITLOCHRY FESTIVAL 1973

23rd Season from April 21 to September 29

April 21 *The Venetian Twins* by Carlo Goldoni, adapted by Jac Alder
April 23 *The Secretary Bird* by William Douglas Home
April 26 *Easter* by August Strindberg in a new version by Michael Meyer
April 30 *Ten Little Niggers* by Agatha Christie
May 18 *Who's Afraid of Virginia Woolf?* by Edward Albee
June 11 *The Busybody* by Mrs Susannah Centlivre
July 2 *Schellenbrack* by Tom Gallacher
July 23 *Old Times* by Harold Pinter

Donald MacKechnie was appointed director of productions and he was assisted by Brian Shelton, who was responsible for *The Busybody*, and Colin Macintyre who staged *The Secretary Bird*. Alan Stewart was Head of Design.

The company consisted of players all new to Pitlochry and included Brendan Barry, Deborah Benzimra, Milton Cadman, Liza Evans, Roger Forbes, Lionel Guyett, Denise Hirst, Andrew Jolly, Colin Kaye, Jeanette Lewis, Bruce Montague, Madeleine Newbury and Norma Streader.

The Festival Director was Kenneth Ireland.

Timothy Dalton and Estelle Kohler as the star-crossed lovers in *Romeo and Juliet* which opened the Royal Shakespeare Company's 1973 season at Stratford-upon-Avon, directed by Terry Hands.

ROMEO AND JULIET

Zeffirelli's sun-baked Veronese production of *Romeo and Juliet* at the Old Vic in 1960 with John Stride and Judi Dench, and Gielgud's earlier poetic production at the New Theatre when he alternated Romeo and Mercutio with Olivier, to the Juliet of Peggy Ashcroft, have become legends still discussed with affection by all who love the theatre.

What about Terry Hands's current production which opened the 1973 Royal Shakespeare Season at Stratford-upon-Avon, played in grim Farrah-designed sets which looked like the inside of a prison – all darkness, iron bars and stark ugliness? It gave the impression that the director set out to be perversely different, no matter what the ensuing results would be.

The Italian colour, the romance, the magic of the Balcony Scene were all brushed aside as 'old hat'. Precious little was created to compensate the play-goer for such heavy losses. Estelle Kohler and Timothy Dalton as the lovers, Beatrix Lehmann as the Nurse, Tony Church as the Friar and Brenda Bruce as Lady Capulet survived to make the best possible impression under the circumstances.

A play by Shakespeare. Presented by the Royal Shakespeare Company at the Royal Shakespeare Theatre, Stratford-upon-Avon, as the opening production of the 1973 Stratford Season, on March 28. Designed by Farrah. Music by Ian Kellam. Dances by John Broome.

Cast included:

Escalus	*Clement McCallin*
Mercutio	*Bernard Lloyd*
Paris	*Anthony Pedley*
Montague	*Richard Mayes*
Lady Montague	*Janet Whiteside*
Romeo	*Timothy Dalton*
Benvolio	*Peter Machin*
Capulet	*Jeffery Dench*
Lady Capulet	*Brenda Bruce*
Juliet	*Estelle Kohler*
Tybalt	*David Suchet*
Nurse	*Beatrix Lehmann*
Friar Laurence	*Tony Church*
Friar John	*John Abbott*
Rosaline	*Janet Chappell*
Apothecary	*Robert Ashby*
Chorus	*Clement McCallin*

Directed by Terry Hands

SAVAGES

Richard Hampton's *Savages* at the Royal Court Theatre, rather than a play, was an exposure of the plight of Brazil, showing how the so-called Indians or original inhabitants of the country have been exploited by a tyrannous military régime – one which executes criminals, often following ghastly torture, to save the nation the cost of keeping them in prison.

Paul Scofield headed the cast as a British diplomat, with Tom Conti as his captor. The play was a result of Mr Hampton's visit to Brazil, where he discovered sixty per cent of industries are in foreign hands and the hourly wage rate in industry amounts to thirteen pence, almost the lowest in Latin America. A play by Christopher Hampton. Presented by the Royal Court Theatre and Michael Codron at the Royal Court Theatre on April 12, 1973. Designed by Jocelyn Herbert and Andrew Sanders.

Cast included:

Alan West	*Paul Scofield*
Mrs West	*Rona Anderson*
Carlos	*Tom Conti*
Crawshaw	*Michael Pennington*
General	*Leonard Kavanagh*
Attorney-General	*Gordon Sterne*
Investigator	
Ataide Pereira	*Glyn Grain*
Major Brigg	*A. J. Brown*
Chief	*Frank Singuineau*
Bert	
Elmer Penn	*Geoffrey Palmer*
Kumai	*Terence Burns*
Pilot	*Leonard Kavanagh*
Co-pilot	*Glyn Grain*

Directed by Robert Kidd

G.B.

A satirical revue, with Moral Re-armament colouring, was directed by Henry Cass at the Westminster Theatre, written by Alan Thornhill, Michael Henderson and H S Williams, with pleasing music by Kathleen Johnson.

There was amusing comment on working to rule on the railways, a bank hold-up and television interviewing. The outstanding number in the show was Michael Orchelin's mimed impression of an angler, and the vivid personality of Delia Sainsbury would be an asset to any show.

A revue with words by Alan Thornhill. Michael Henderson and Hugh Steadman Williams and music by Kathleen Johnson. Settings by Cameron Johnson, costumes by Dorothy Phillips, musical staging by Bridget Espinosa, musical arrangement by David Palmer and musical direction by Louis Mordish.

Presented by Westminster Productions Ltd, in association with Moral Re-Armament at the Westminster Theatre on March 6, 1973.

Cast included: Gladstone Adderley, Chris Channer, Imogen Claire, Penny Croft, Mike Fields, Helena Leahy, Michel Orphelin, Gordon Reid, Delia Sainsbury, Kenneth Shanley and Donald Scott.

Directed by Henry Cass

COLLABORATORS

John Mortimer disappointed his admirers with *Collaborators*, the story of a failed marriage, at the Duchess Theatre. There were moments when the author seemed to concentrate too much upon autobiographical details and the play suffered in consequence. Glenda Jackson and John Wood, as the wife and husband, executed an amusing dance, ingeniously choreographed by Malcolm Goddard, but it had no relation whatsoever to the play. Joss Ackland was at home as Mr Mortimer's caricature of an American film director.

A play by John Mortimer. Presented by Michael Codron at the Duchess Theatre on April 17, 1973. Designed by Michael O'Flaherty, with costumes supervised by Elizabeth Waller. Dances arranged by Malcolm Goddard.

Cast included:

Henry Winter	*John Wood*
Katherine Winter	*Glenda Jackson*
Sam Brown	*Joss Ackland*
Griselda Griffin	*Gloria Connell*

Directed by Eric Thompson

LE MALADE IMAGINAIRE

Molière's last play, *Le Malade Imaginaire*, was presented by the Comédie Française at the Aldwych Theatre for their first contribution to the Tenth World Theatre Season, under the artistic direction of Peter Daubeny. Jacques Charon, doyen of the Comédie Française, appeared as Argan, the last part Molière ever played. M. Charon's performance is one of the great comic creations of the contemporary international stage. John Barber gave a masterly description of him as 'a large brooding man, with the face of an old market-woman who has just been short-changed'.

A play by Molière. Presented by the Comédie Française at the Aldwych Theatre on April 16, 1973, as part of the Tenth World Theatre Season, under the artistic direction of Peter Daubeny. Sets and costumes by Jacques Marillier and music by Michel Magne.

Cast included:

Argan	*Jacques Charon*
Béralde	*Jacques Toja*
Diafoirus	*René Arrieu*
M. Purgon	*François Beaulieu*
Fleurant	*Marcel Tristani*
Cléante	*Jean-Noël Sissia*
M. Bonnefoy	*Dominique Rozan*
Thomas Diafoirus	*Francis Perrin*
Toinette	*Françoise Seigner*
Béline	*Bérengère Dautun*
Angélique	*Catherine Hiegel*
Louison	*Emmanuelle Milloux*

Directed by Jean-Laurent Cochet

THE HOUSE OF BERNARDA ALBA

Robin Phillips stressed the grim oppression of the story Lorca unfolds in *The House of Bernarda Alba*, in which the mother mourns her husband's death by enforcing an eight-year chastity period upon her daughters. In this Greenwich Theatre production they were all dressed in black, 'like crows beating their wings against the cage of tradition', to quote the evocative words of Frank Marcus.

Tom Stoppard's English version brought new life to the lines and the performance was notable for the impressive contributions of Mia Farrow as Adela and Sylvia Coleridge as the old, crazed woman of the strange household.

A play by Federico Garcia Lorca in an English version by Tom Stoppard. Presented at Greenwich Theatre on March 22, 1973. Designed by Daphne Dare. Music by Charles Dance.

Cast included:

Bernarda	*June Jago*
Maria Josefa	*Sylvia Coleridge*
Augustias	*Ann Firbank*
Magdalena	*Penelope Keith*
Amelia	*Helen Weir*
Martirio	*Morag Hood*
Adela	*Mia Farrow*
La Poncia	*Patience Collier*
Prudencia	
Beggar Woman	*Rosamund Burne*
Maid	*Josephine Gordon*

Directed by Robin Phillips

Helen Weir, Morag Hood and Mia
Farrow in *The House of Bernarda
Alba* by Lorca.   *Photograph by
S C Moreton-Prichard*

IN THE JUNGLE OF CITIES

Keith Hack, until recently Associate Director of the Glasgow Citizens' Theatre, brought together a company of fourteen young actors, most of whom had been working together for two years or more, and opened a short season at The Place in Euston with Bertolt Brecht's *In the Jungle of Cities*.

The Brecht play of 1923 seemed to date rather badly. It is a strip-cartoon concerning the story of a battle between Joe, an honest bookshop assistant and Shlink, a sinister Malayan timber tycoon. The production was staged as a boxing-match and turned out to be an attack on the business world of Chicago in 1912, though a number of Kurt Weill songs, written for other productions, were introduced as a welcome nostalgic touch.

A play by Bertolt Brecht, translated and adapted by Keith Hack, with music by Kurt Weill. Presented by Showman Productions Ltd at The Place, Euston, on March 15, 1973. Designed by Maria Bjornson.

Cast included:

George Garga	*James Aubrey*
John Garga	*Gregory Floy*
Mae Garga	*Geoff Lerway*
Marie Garga	*Julie Covington*
Jane Larry	*Cheryl Campbell*
C Shlink	*Christopher Ryan*
Skinny	*Rupert Frazer*
'King' the Gorilla	*Jonathan Kent*
J Finnay, the Worm	
	Ian McDiarmid
C Maynes	*Constantin de Goguel*
Whore	*Patti Love*
Joe, the pianist	*Michael Garrett*

Directed by Keith Hack

LITTLE MAN – WHAT NOW?

To open his Tenth – and last for the time being – World Theatre Season at the Aldwych Theatre on March 26, 1973, Peter Daubeny invited a company new to London – from the Bochum Schauspielhaus, under the imaginative direction of Peter Zadek.

They presented his lively production of *Little Man – What Now?*, the moving story of Lämmchen and Pinneberg and the ceaseless misfortunes they had to face during the early 1930s in Germany. Incredibly, they survived, with the satisfaction of knowing they still had each other.

Hannelore Hoger and Heinrich Giskes gave convincing and unflagging performances as the young lovers, scarcely off stage during Peter Zadek's breathless, episodic production. Dramatic sequences were separated by gaudy interludes provided by a dozen Swedish glamour girls of Dietrich's *Blue Angel* vintage, singing and dancing agreeably raucous tunes of Berlin's decadent pre-Nazi years.

A revue by Peter Zadek and Tankred Dorst, adapted to the stage from Hans Fallada's novel. Music by Erwin Bootz and Peter Raben; décor by Georg Wakhevitch; costumes by Georg Wakhevitch and Jeanne Renucci and choreography by Tutte Lemkow, assisted by Fay Werner.

Presented as the opening production of the Tenth World Theatre Season, under the artistic direction of Peter Daubeny, at the Aldwych Theatre on March 26, 1973 and performed by the company from Bochum Schauspielhaus in West Germany.

Cast included: Hannelore Hoger, Heinrich Giskes, Brigitte Mira, Klaus Höhne, Hans Mahnke, Rosel Zech, Karl-Heinz Vosgerau, Ulrich Woldgruber, Werner Dahms, Werner Eichhorn, Hermann Lause, Liesel Alex, Karl Friedrich, Tana Schanzara, Everhard Steib, Franz Gesein, Tamara Kafka, Hans Hirschmüller and Wolfgang Feige.

Directed by Peter Zadek

Paul Moriarty as the Mouth and Diana Quick as the Mother in a scene from *The Screens* by Jean Genet, presented at the Bristol Old Vic's New Vic Studio.
Photograph by Derek Balmer

THE SCREENS

Jean Genet wrote *The Screens* with ninety-seven speaking parts to be shared among thirty to forty actors, but gave permission for a shortened English version to be prepared specially for a Bristol New Vic Studio production using only nine actors.

On this vast canvas Genet expressed his highly personal opinions of the Algerian War which lasted from 1954 to 1962. His anti-hero is an arsonist, a jailbird, a traitor and a saint who betrays his people. The script presented the director with a Herculean challenge and Walter Donohue and his company were to be congratulated upon accepting it and doing as good a job as they did.

A play by Jean Genet, translated by Bernard Frechtman and adapted by Howard Brenton. Presented by the Bristol Old Vic Company in the New Vic Studio on March 20, 1973. Designed by Christopher Dyer.

Cast included: Tom Chadbon, Charlotte Cornwell, Paul Moriarty, Diana Quick, William Hoyland, Kate Nelligan, Lewis Michael, John Nettles and Tim Pigott-Smith.

Directed by Walter Donohue

LIEBELEI

To mark their first visit to London, the Vienna Burgtheater brought their famous Gerhard Klingenberg production of Schnitzler's *Liebelei* to the Aldwych Theatre as part of Peter Daubeny's 1973 World Theatre Season.

The fragile, ballerina-like Maresa Hörbiger, daughter of Paula Wessely, film idol of a generation or so ago, played with immense sensitivity the tragic Christine, daughter of a theatre violinist who was betrayed by a rich philanderer of Vienna's Naughty Nineties. She worshipped the young man, but to him she was no more than a passing infatuation. When she discovered he was eventually killed in a duel as the result of an affair with a married woman, the bitter revelation made suicide inevitable.

Attila Hörbiger, Maresa Hörbiger's real-life father, also appeared as her father in the play, an impressive figure vainly endeavouring to persuade her that she could never find happiness with a member of the aristocracy.

A play by Arthur Schnitzler. Presented by the Vienna Burgtheater at the Aldwych Theatre on April 9, 1973, as part of the Tenth World Theatre Season.

Cast included:

Hans Weiring	*Atilla Hörbiger*
Christine	*Maresa Hörbiger*
Mizi Schlager	*Sylvia Lukan*
Katharina Binder	*Ida Krottendorf*
Fritz Lobheimer	*Wolfgang Hübsch*
Theodor Kaiser	*Michael Heltau*
A Gentleman	*Paul Hoffman*

Directed by Gerhard Klingenberg

BORN YESTERDAY

In 1947, London play-goers were bewitched by Yolande Donlan's legendary performance as Billie Dawn, the eternal dumb blonde of Garson Kanin's *Born Yesterday*, and at Greenwich on April 19, 1973, Lynn Redgrave had no easy task in creating the character anew. Eschewing the tender side of Billie's nature, Miss Redgrave showed her as rather a toughy; undoubtedly an ex-chorus girl, also unlikely to put up with the rough handling she gets from her protector Harry Brock.

Her timing, however, was immaculate, pointing the lines effectively, and at its best in her poker-faced sorting of cards in the game of gin-rummy with Brock. A little learning is a dangerous thing, and she communicated this fact with devastating effect.

The Director was the playwright Tom Stoppard, but although he was sensitive to details, in general his direction lacked the pace essential for the quickfire dialogue.

Cast included:

Billie Dawn	*Lynn Redgrave*
Harry Brock	*Dave King*
Paul Verrall	*Bob Sherman*
Ed Devery	*John Rogan*
Senator Norval Hedges	*Ronald Adam*
Mrs Hedges	*Ann Firbank*
Eddie Brock	*Peter Gordon*
Assistant Manager	*Charles Dance*
Helen	*Josephine Gordon*
A Bellhop	*Ray Aucott*
Another Bellhop	*Elroy Josephs*

Directed by Tom Stoppard assisted by Robin Phillips

233

THE STARVING RICH

Stanley Price had a good idea for a farcical comedy in *The Starving Rich*, which originated at the Windsor Theatre Royal and visited Brighton Royal during a provincial tour.

Paul Rogers played a millionaire big businessman staying at a health clinic, starving on lemon juice to the tune of £150 a week. An intruder appears in his luxurious private room in the person of Roy Kinnear, a crook who has stolen a vast fortune in gold bars. He is on the run and seeking refuge.

Somehow the story got too involved and far too improbable, without measuring up to the glittering nonsense of the Rix farces. There were times when the comedy was very forced, despite the splendid technical accomplishment of the two leading players. It was a squib which rather backfired.

A play by Stanley Price. Presented by Tom Arnold Presentations Ltd, in association with Bill Kenright, Clement Scott Gilbert and Richard Schulman, during the course of a tour, at the Brighton Theatre Royal on March 26, 1973. Set designed by Richard Berry. Décor and costumes by Susie Caulcutt.

Cast included:

Clare Simpson	*Vivienne Martin*
Maurice Fisher	*Paul Rogers*
Esther Fisher	*Vanda Godsell*
Frederick Murdoch	*Roy Hepworth*
Mr Sterling	*Anthony Dawes*
Joe O'Brien	*Roy Kinnear*
Inspector Ferguson	*Robert McBain*

Directed by Jonathan Lynn

THE UNSEEN HAND

An excellent cast performed *The Unseen Hand*, presented at the Royal Court Theatre Upstairs, but the work itself was a confusing mixture of science-fiction, fantasy and parable. It was set in Azusa, a town in the USA that has everything from A to Z and concerns rogues from the bad old days of the Wild West and a creature from another planet whose head was branded with the mark of a red hand, through which he was partially controlled by his masters, the sorcerers of Nogoland. The cast was enlivened by the presence of a baseball cheer-leader, fresh from being whipped and assaulted by members of his own team. It was all quite fantastical.

A play by Sam Shepard. Presented at the Royal Court Theatre Upstairs on March 12, 1973. Designed by Brian Thomson.

Cast included:

Blue Mosphan	*Warren Clarke*
Willie	*Richard O'Brien*
Cisco Morphan	*Tony Sibbald*
The Kid	*Clive Endersby*
Sycamore Morphan	*Christopher Malcolm*

Directed by Jim Sharman

HELLO AND GOODBYE

Janet Suzman and Ben Kingsley gave blazingly realistic performances as brother and sister in Athol Fugard's *Hello and Goodbye* at the Islington King's Head Theatre Club. They are two unhappy creatures, united for a few hours after years of separation. The boy has become unhinged as a result of the isolation he endured while looking after his crippled father while she escaped to Johannesburg where she became a whore. Their brief union is brought about by the father's death, but soon they return to their former way of life.

A play by Athol Fugard. Presented at the King's Head Theatre Club, Islington, on March 22, 1973. Designed by John Scully.

Hester Smit	*Janet Suzman*
Johnnie Smit	*Ben Kingsley*

Directed by Peter Stevenson

RICHARD III

Young Terry Hands, Associate Director of the Royal Shakespeare Company, holds the distinction of being the first Englishman to direct a play at the Comédie Française. He was invited to direct Shakespeare's *Richard III*, with Robert Hirsch in the name-part, and this highly inventive production was presented at the Aldwych Theatre as part of the 1973 World Theatre Season. Using different materials, Farrah designed the production in fifteen shades of black, against an atmospheric back-cloth of black chains and prison bars.

Robert Hirsch's virtuoso performance as Richard, almost operatic in its flamboyance, became decidedly intimate when he came to the edge of the apron stage and whispered his soliloquies to the audience. There was a rare quality of humour in his conception of Richard; dressed in black leather breeches, with a steel legging to support his twisted leg and a black glove to hide his withered hand. His face belonged to a man who had known much mental and physical suffering, yet his smile had infinite charm. The memory of his performance will be cherished by all fortunate enough to have seen it.

A play by Shakespeare. Presented by the Comédie Française at the Aldwych Theatre on April 23, 1973, as part of the Tenth World Theatre Season, under the artistic direction of Peter Daubeny. Sets and costumes by Farrah. Music by Guy Woolfenden.

Cast included:

Buckingham	*Jacques Charon*
Richard	*Robert Hirsch*
Bishop of Ely	*Jacques Eyser*
Catesby	*Simon Eine*
Edward IV	*François*
Ghost of Henry IV	*Chaumette*
Lord Stanley	*Michel Etcheverry*
Brackenbury	*René Camoin*
Clarence	*Michel Duchaussoy*
Richmond	*François Beaulieu*
Vaughan	*Marco-Behar*
Grey	*Marcel Tristani*
Lovel	*Jean-Noël Sissia*
Ratcliffe	*Nicolas Silberg*

Lord Hastings	*Hervé Sand*
Queen Margaret	*Denise Gence*
Queen Elizabeth	*Catherine Samie*
Lady Anne	*Ludmila Mikael*
Jane Shore	*Virginie Pradal*
Elizabeth Plantagenet	*Martine Carlier*
Duchess of York	*Aline Bertrand*
Clarence's son	*Didier Attar*
Clarence's daughter	*Marie-Carole Favand*
Prince of Wales	*Gérard Malabat*
Duke of York	*Pascal Sellier*

Directed by Terry Hands

TWO GENTLEMEN OF VERONA

The New York Shakespeare Festival production of the rock musical, *Two Gentlemen of Verona*, based on the Shakespeare play, opened at the Phoenix Theatre under the direction of Mel Shapiro. Excellent songs, strongly and deftly reflecting varying moods. Brenda Arnau became a star overnight as Sylvia and Derek Griffith, Veronica Clifford, Samuel E Wright and Ray C Davis were outstanding.

Presented by Michael White, in association with Robert Stigwood, at the Phoenix Theatre, on April 26, 1973. Setting by Ming Cho Lee, costumes by Theoni V Aldredge and choreography by Dennis Nahat.

Cast included:

Thurio	*Derek Griffiths*
Lucette	*Veronica Clifford*
Speed	*Michael Staniforth*
Valentine	*Samuel E Wright*
Proteus	*Ray C Davis*
Julia	*Jean Gilbert*
Launce	*Benny Lee*
Antonio	*Terence Conoley*
Crab	*Muldoon*
Duke of Milan	*Keefe West*
Sylvia	*Brenda Arnau*
Tavern Host	*Terence Conoley*
Eglamour	*Minoo Golvala*

Directed by Mel Shapiro

Richard Pasco in the name-part in
Richard II, presented by the Royal
Shakespeare Company at the Royal
Shakespeare Theatre, Stratford-
upon-Avon during the 1973 season.
Photograph by Donald Cooper

RICHARD II

The novelty of the Royal Shake-speare Company's 1973 season at Stratford-upon-Avon was John Barton's production of *Richard II*, with Richard Pasco and Ian Richardson brilliantly alternating the parts of Richard and Boling-broke, two roles which have never previously been shared.

A play by Shakespeare. Presented at the Royal Shakespeare Theatre, Stratford-upon-Avon, on April 10, 1973. Designed by Timothy O'Brien and Tazeena Firth. Music adapted from traditional sources by David Hersey.

Cast included:

Richard II	*Richard Pasco*
Henry Bolingbroke	*Ian Richardson*
Queen Isabel	*Janet Chappell*
John of Gaunt	*Tony Church*
Duke of York	*Sebastian Shaw*
Duchess of York	*Beatrix Lehmann*
Duchess of Gloucester	*Janet Whiteside*
Thomas Mowbray	*Denis Holmes*
The Lord Marshall	*Richard Mayes*
Messenger to York	*David Suchet*
Duke of Aumerle	*Nickolas Grace*
Sir John Bushy	*Robert Ashby*
Sir Henry Greene	*Ray Armstrong*
Bishop of Carlisle	*Brian Glover*
Abbott of Westminster	*Robert Ashby*
Earl of Northumberland	*Clement McCallin*
Hotspur	*John Abbott*
Lord Ross	*Charles Keating*
Lord Willoughby	*Gavin Campbell*
Sir Piers of Exton	*Anthony Pedley*
First Gardener	*Denis Holmes*
Second Gardener	*Peter Machin*
Third Gardener	*Wilfred Grove*

Directed by John Barton

236

INDEX

(Note: Page number references in italics indicate illustrations.)